GAMES
MAGAZINE

BIG
BOOK
OF
GAMES

Edited
by
RONNIE SHUSHAN

Designed
by
DON WRIGHT

WORKMAN PUBLISHING, NEW YORK

Copyright © 1978, 1979, 1980, 1981, 1982, 1983, 1984
by Playboy Enterprises, Inc.

Library of Congress Cataloging in Publication Data

Main entry under title:
Games magazine big book of games.
  1. Indoor games. 2. Puzzles. I. Shushan, Ronnie.
GV1229.G185 1984   793   84-40344
ISBN 0-89480-806-0

Workman books are available at special discounts when purchased
in bulk for premiums and sales promotions as well as for fund-raising
or educational use. Special editions or book excerpts can also be
created to specification. For details, contact the Special Sales
Director at the address below.

Workman Publishing Company, Inc.
708 Broadway
New York, New York 10003

Manufactured in the United States of America

First Printing October 1984

20   19   18

The material in this book has previously appeared in *GAMES* and *The
Four-Star Puzzler,* which are trademarks of Playboy Enterprises, Inc.

Quality Printing by
Banta Company
Curtis Reed Plaza
Menasha, Wisc. 54952
U.S.A.

Since 1977, GAMES Magazine has provided a playing field where puzzle makers and puzzle solvers match wits. The puzzle makers continually find new ways to create chaos so that the solvers have to discover new ways to restore order. Whether with words, or numbers, or pictures, it seems that virtually everything in our culture can be twisted into a puzzle.

The puzzles selected for this first GAMES book celebrate that variety, and come from some surprising sources. As you flip through these pages, you'll find shadows and mirrors; maps and clocks; airplanes, a quilt, and Burma-Shave signs. There are challenges that come from passions as diverse as hairstyles and computers, and settings that include a city park, the Indy 500, Madison Avenue, and Tin Pan Alley.

You'll also find twists on some familiar pastimes: cartoon dominoes, solitaire hangman, mental pick-up sticks, gin rummy played with words, and 15 variations on the familiar crossword puzzle.

The goal throughout is to challenge, to amuse, and occasionally to provoke you into seeing and thinking in some unusual recreational ways. Consider, for example, the following bit of nonsense. It was created by a GAMES reader as an entry to a contest called Choplogic, and although it isn't literally a puzzle, it conveys a great deal about both the spirit of the magazine and the mental amusement park you'll find in these pages.

$$PROOF\ THAT\ E = mc^2$$

1. E is a letter of the alphabet.
2. The alphabet is used to form words.
3. Words are excluded in pantomime.
4. Pantomime is used by clowns.
5. Clowns perform at a circus.
6. A circus has a master of ceremonies.
7. A master of ceremonies who pays his debts is an emcee squared.

$$THEREFORE,\ E = mc^2$$

As we warned on the cover of one issue of the magazine, Enter at Your Own Risk.

Ronnie Shushan
Editor at Large
GAMES Magazine

4   C O N T E N T S

VARIATIONS ON A CROSSWORD THEME 113

MATH, LOGIC, AND A FEW DIRTY TRICKS 129

A QUIZ FOR ALMOST EVERY OCCASION 145

TOUGH NUTS FOR EXPERT SOLVERS 161

ALL THE ANSWERS 171

PUZZLE DIFFICULTY RATINGS

★ Smooth Sailing ★★ Uphill Climb ★★★ Rough Terrain ★★★★ Proceed at Your Own Risk

★☆ Variable Conditions

WARM-UP TWISTS AND TEASERS

★ ★

INNER PICK-UP STICKS

BY JOSEPH PARISI, JR.

We've added a new shtick to the classic game of pick-up sticks.
You must remove each stick with a *mental* flip, but only when no other sticks rest atop it.
In what order should you clear away the pile?

Answer, page 172

WHAT'S WRONG WITH OUR GAME? ★☆

BY HENRY HOOK

We've sometimes been accused of not playing with a full deck. Well, that's not strictly true. We *do* play with a full deck; it's just that our cards and some of our rules are a little crazy. Here you see the tableau of our current game of solitaire in progress. How many of the 12 errors—in the deck itself or our playing procedure—can you spot? (Red suits printed in black do not, of course, count as errors.)

Answers, page 172

COUNTERINTELLIGENCE *

BY GENE TRAUB

The answers to the 14 clues below have something in common. Can you find the pattern and fill in the blanks?

Answers, page 172

1. Last drink before driving home_____

2. Quarter, familiarly_____

3. Larry, Moe, and Curly_____

4. Lucky outdoor find_____

5. Budding beard_____

6. Wild West revolver_____

7. Snow White's friends_____

8. Familiar pool game_____

9. Cat's capacity_____

10. Moses' tablets_____

11. Last possible moment_____

12. Popular Yule song_____

13. The U.S., originally_____

14. Precious jewelry metal_____

WHOSE CLUES? ★☆

BY STEPHEN SNIDERMAN

What's in a name? Well, if you look closely at its letters, you may find that it contains a clue to its owner's life or career. Try CLARENCE DARROW, for instance: Among its letters is Darrow's profession, LAW, reading in order from left to right. And the name of decathlon champion BRUCE JENNER appropriately includes the letters that spell out RUNNER.

Below are 14 words extracted from the names of famous individuals. Using each as a clue, can you fill in the blanks to identify all 14 people? *Answers, page 172*

1. I N D I __ __ __ A __ __ __ __

2. B A __ __ __ __ T __

3. __ A R I __ __ A __ __ S

4. __ I __ __ __ __ __ __ __ __ D

5. B O __ D __ __ __ __ __

6. __ __ __ __ __ __ __ P A __ __ R

7. J __ E __ __ __ __ T __

8. __ H A __ __ __ __ __ H A __ __ __

9. __ __ __ __ __ S __ __ __ E A __

10. __ O __ __ __ __ N __ O __

11. C H I __ N __ __ A __ - __ __ __ __

12. __ __ __ L __ __ __ __ __ __ E __ __ A R __

13. M A __ __ __ P __ __ __

14. __ S __ __ __ W __ __ __ I __ M S

BORDER PATROL ★☆

BY RONALD E. NEUMAN

If these lines look like random squiggles, maybe it's time to dust off your atlas. Each group of lines is an ''aerial view'' showing segments of the borders between States of the Union. We've identified the states in the first group to get you started. Can you identify the others?

Answers, page 172

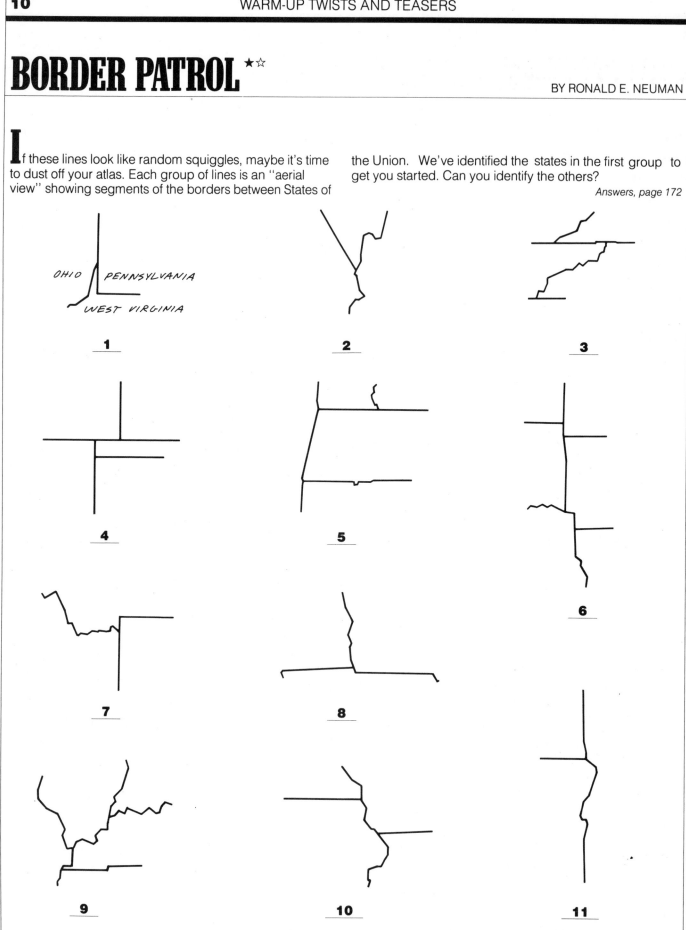

AT THE BURMA-SHAVE WAREHOUSE**

BY ANN STONE

Burma-Shave cream might be forgotten today if it hadn't been for the popular roadside advertisements that appeared across America from 1925 to 1963. Each ad consisted of several signs placed about 20 yards apart which, when read sequentially by passing motorists, formed an amusing jingle. A famous example: "He played—a sax—had no B.O.—but his whiskers scratched—so she let him go." And of course the last sign said "Burma Shave."

In the Burma-Shave warehouse below, where we imagine all good Burma-Shave signs have gone, we've mixed up eight jingles. The first signs of all the jingles appear in column A, the second signs in column B, etc. Can you put the signs in the correct order to re-create the jingles?

Answers, page 172

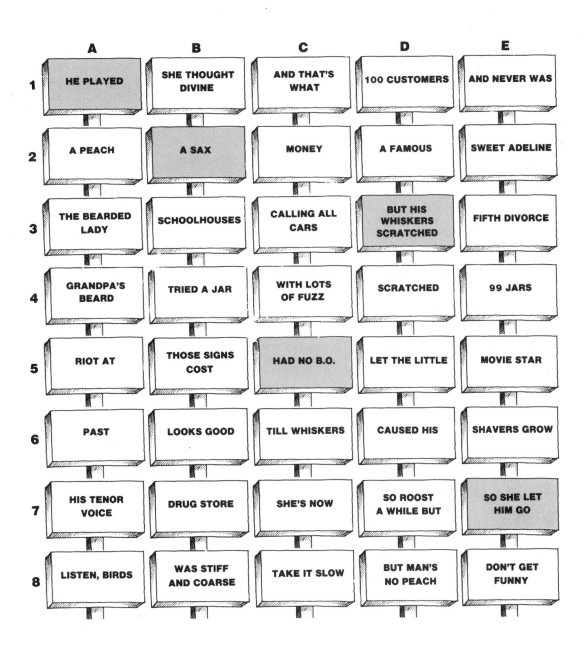

	A	B	C	D	E
1	HE PLAYED	SHE THOUGHT DIVINE	AND THAT'S WHAT	100 CUSTOMERS	AND NEVER WAS
2	A PEACH	A SAX	MONEY	A FAMOUS	SWEET ADELINE
3	THE BEARDED LADY	SCHOOLHOUSES	CALLING ALL CARS	BUT HIS WHISKERS SCRATCHED	FIFTH DIVORCE
4	GRANDPA'S BEARD	TRIED A JAR	WITH LOTS OF FUZZ	SCRATCHED	99 JARS
5	RIOT AT	THOSE SIGNS COST	HAD NO B.O.	LET THE LITTLE	MOVIE STAR
6	PAST	LOOKS GOOD	TILL WHISKERS	CAUSED HIS	SHAVERS GROW
7	HIS TENOR VOICE	DRUG STORE	SHE'S NOW	SO ROOST A WHILE BUT	SO SHE LET HIM GO
8	LISTEN, BIRDS	WAS STIFF AND COARSE	TAKE IT SLOW	BUT MAN'S NO PEACH	DON'T GET FUNNY

TOM SWIFTIES ★☆

BY GLORIA ROSENTHAL

A Tom Swifty, as you may know, is a line of dialogue that ends with a whimsically appropriate adverb. For example, "The highway pollution is terrible!" Tom said *exhaustedly*. The following Tom Swifties are lacking the all-important adverbs. We've given you the first letters to help you come up with those we have in mind. "Okay, get your pencils out," Tom said *pointedly*.   *Answers, page 172*

1. "I just bought a foreign car!"
Tom announced t_____.

2. "Nyeah, nyeah, let's have some turtle soup,"
Tom said m_____.

3. "I forgot what my wife wanted from the store,"
Tom said l_____.

4. "I'm so happy that I can float,"
Tom declared b_____.

5. "Block that kick!"
Tom shouted d_____.

6. "I've got a code in da nose,"
Tom muttered s_____.

7. "My paint canvas is blank,"
Tom said a_____.

8. "I hate quizzes,"
Tom stated t_____.

9. "This cream is bad,"
Tom said s_____.

10. "Better order 12 dozen of the blasted things,"
Tom said g_____.

11. "I always shop here,"
Tom announced p_____.

12. "Columbus, you were wrong,"
Tom stated f_____.

13. "I prefer unposed photos,"
Tom remarked c_____.

14. "All campers to their shelters,"
Tom announced i_____.

15. "Let's not cut the Valentine,"
Tom agreed w_____.

BUSMAN'S HOLIDAY ★

BY MIKE WILLIAMS

T he bus drivers of Numeropolis have a tough job. They can pick up passengers only by following the correct mathematical equations that are marked on the streets. On the route shown, for instance, the driver begins at START, with 3 passengers. If he turns to his right, he adds 2, which *doesn't* equal 6, as marked on the street; if he goes straight ahead, he adds 4, which *doesn't* equal 10; but if he turns to his left, he adds 3 passengers, which *does* equal 6, and is the only correct route he can take. From your bird's-eye view of downtown, can you plot the rest of his route?   *Answer, page 172*

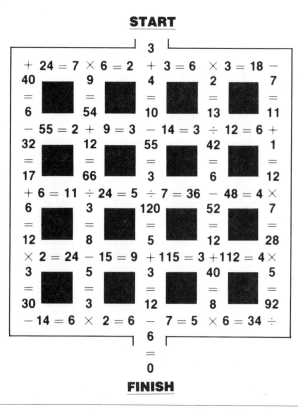

ASK A SILLY QUESTION... ★☆

BY RANDY COHEN

Fit as a fiddle...crazy as a loon...quick as a wink... They're phrases we use without a second thought. But did you ever stop to consider just how fit a fiddle is, or how crazy a loon, or how quick a wink might be? We have. As a matter of fact we've collected 12 overworked expressions to see if you can guess their literal meanings. May you be as wise as an owl—or at least have the luck of the Irish. *Answers, page 172*

1. How blind is a bat?
 a. Totally blind
 b. Partially blind
 c. Venetian blind
 d. It depends upon who's swinging it.

2. How cheap is a cheap joke?
 a. $1,239 per prime time TV sketch
 b. "Take my wife—please!"
 c. $45 per joke used on *The Tonight Show*
 d. Free if you're Milton Berle

3. How high is the moon?
 a. It's 153,758 miles from Earth during a new moon.
 b. The equivalent of 3 billion McDonald's cheeseburgers stacked end to end.
 c. The highest recorded moon is out the 20th floor of Delta Phi.
 d. On the average, it's 238,857 miles from Earth.

7. How early is the early bird?
 a. It rises about a half hour before dawn.
 b. It rises at sunrise.
 c. It gets up whenever the worm does.
 d. It always takes a 6 A.M. wake-up call.

8. How light is a feather?
 a. A duck feather weighs .013 to .063 grams.
 b. A down feather weighs upward of 3 to 4 grams.
 c. *Horsefeathers* is light entertainment.
 d. The rare feathers of the *Rara avis* weigh about .00001 to .00002 grams.

9. How deep is skin deep?
 a. $2/3$ to $3/4$ inch deep
 b. $1/16$ to $1/8$ inch deep
 c. It varies. Some people are thick-skinned, others thin-skinned.
 d. $1 3/4$ feet for an elephant

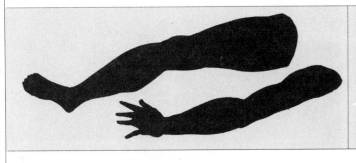

4. What is the cost of an arm and a leg?
 a. A leg of lamb costs about $8.50 a pound.
 b. The Bionic Man's arm and leg cost $3 million.
 c. *Venus de Milo*'s arms were auctioned for $4.5 million.
 d. Mannequin arms go for $18.50, legs for $100.

5. How much is a bellyful?
 a. 8 quarts for a pregnant woman
 b. 2 quarts for the average adult
 c. Howard Cosell expounding on anything
 d. 5 quarts for the average male

6. How many is as many as the hairs on your head?
 a. For brunets like Ronald Reagan, about 200,000
 b. For carrot tops like Lucille Ball, about 75,000
 c. For blondes like Goldie Hawn, about 140,000
 d. For ex-catchers like Joe Garagiola, about 55

10. How slow is a snail's pace?
 a. Brazilian tree snails move 1 foot per minute.
 b. Damn fast when Julia Child eyes them hungrily
 c. Land snails move about two inches a minute.
 d. As slow as most Amtrak express trains

11. When do the swallows come back to Capistrano?
 a. Annually on March 19
 b. Swallows have never been sighted in Capistrano.
 c. Six days before the equinox
 d. Whenever Pat Boone warbles the song

12. How long a way is it to Tipperary?
 a. 4,410 miles from Kansas City, Kansas
 b. A grenade's toss from Belfast
 c. 3,381 miles from Manhattan
 d. 358 miles from Gloccamora

HOLLYWOOD MAKES HISTORY ★☆

Film critics are always debating whether art imitates life or vice versa. To test their arguments, we've collected the 20 images seen here. The 10 on the facing page are of historical figures, while the 10 on this page are from films representing their lives. Can you match the real folks with their celluloid counterparts? And then can you name the celebrities (from both history and film) and the movies? *Answers, page 173*

BY WILLIAM O'CONNELL

CON QUEST ★☆

All the prisoners in this yard are doing time for visual punning without a license. Poetic license, that is. Each con or group of cons illustrates a word that begins with the syllable *con*. Prisoner 1, for example, illustrates CONTROL ("con troll"), while 2 is CONGESTING ("con jesting"). You are hereby sentenced to identify the others or to face 15 years of punishment. Confused? Just concentrate.   *Answers, page 173*

BY ROBERT LEIGHTON

BUBBLE TRUBBLE MAZE★

BY HAROLD ADAMS

Double, double toil and trouble . . . Can you float from IN to OUT without bursting a bubble?

Answer, page 173

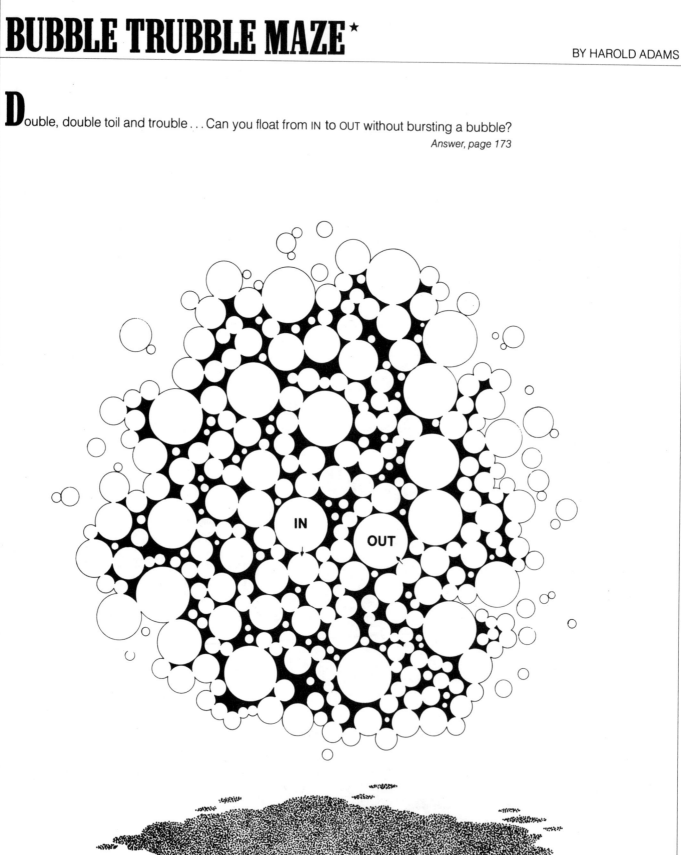

3-D CROSSWORD *

BY KEITH LEWIS

Here is—literally—a new angle on crossword puzzles. Words read in three directions around the cube, as indicated by the arrows labeled A, B, and C. Some words continue from one facet to another. Can you complete the puzzle without encountering any stumbling blocks?

Answer, page 173

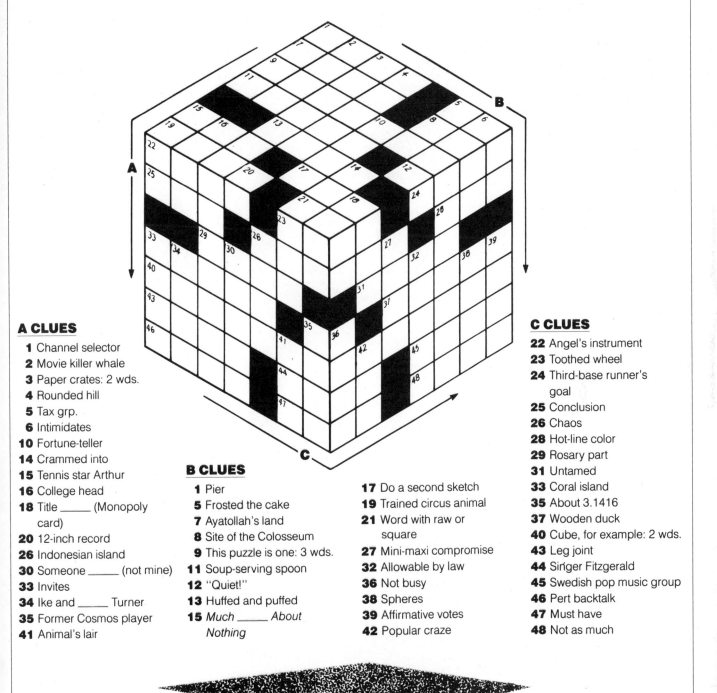

A CLUES

1 Channel selector
2 Movie killer whale
3 Paper crates: 2 wds.
4 Rounded hill
5 Tax grp.
6 Intimidates
10 Fortune-teller
14 Crammed into
15 Tennis star Arthur
16 College head
18 Title _____ (Monopoly card)
20 12-inch record
26 Indonesian island
30 Someone _____ (not mine)
33 Invites
34 Ike and _____ Turner
35 Former Cosmos player
41 Animal's lair

B CLUES

1 Pier
5 Frosted the cake
7 Ayatollah's land
8 Site of the Colosseum
9 This puzzle is one: 3 wds.
11 Soup-serving spoon
12 "Quiet!"
13 Huffed and puffed
15 Much _____ About Nothing
17 Do a second sketch
19 Trained circus animal
21 Word with raw or square
27 Mini-maxi compromise
32 Allowable by law
36 Not busy
38 Spheres
39 Affirmative votes
42 Popular craze

C CLUES

22 Angel's instrument
23 Toothed wheel
24 Third-base runner's goal
25 Conclusion
26 Chaos
28 Hot-line color
29 Rosary part
31 Untamed
33 Coral island
35 About 3.1416
37 Wooden duck
40 Cube, for example: 2 wds.
43 Leg joint
44 Singer Fitzgerald
45 Swedish pop music group
46 Pert backtalk
47 Must have
48 Not as much

DIRTY TRICKS DEPARTMENT ★☆

BY PIERRE BERLOQUIN

The puzzles on this page have two things in common: They're easy and they're not easy. What we mean is, the solutions will seem so obvious—once you've seen them—that you'll be kicking yourself for not having figured them out sooner.   *Answers, page 173*

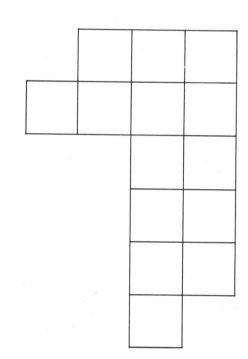

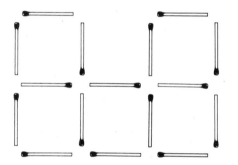

1. These 16 matches form five squares. Change the position of three matches so that only four squares are formed by the 16 matches.

2. Draw a line that divides this figure into two equal parts. (Mirror reflections don't count.)

3. What letter comes next in this series?

WLCNIT __

4. What number should go in the shaded area?

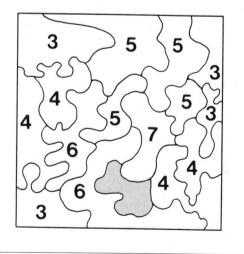

5. What four numbers complete this grid?

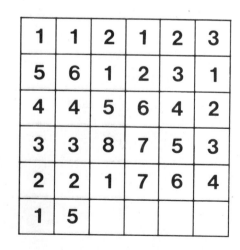

1	1	2	1	2	3
5	6	1	2	3	1
4	4	5	6	4	2
3	3	8	7	5	3
2	2	1	7	6	4
1	5				

FILM-FLAM CRYPTOGRAMS**

BY JACK LECHNER

Here are scenes from two classic films that have been dubbed into a strange foreign language—cryptogramese. Fortunately, prior knowledge of this arcane tongue is not necessary for understanding the dialogue.

The conversation in each of the movies has been translated into a simple cipher alphabet. That is, if the letter A represents an F in one word, it will represent an F in every word in the scene (for both speakers). The substitutions change for the second scene. You can break the code by using letter patterns, letter frequencies, and clues provided by the punctuation. For starters, it may help you to know that E, T, A, I, O, N, and S are the most common letters in English, and to note that there's an apostrophe in the first word of the first scene. *Answers, page 173*

Norman Bates (Anthony Perkins) gets to know motel guest Marion Crane (Janet Leigh) in "Psycho."

Rufus T. Firefly (Groucho Marx) sidles up to the wealthy Mrs. Teasdale (Margaret Dumont) in "Duck Soup."

MARION CRANE:

S'DJ YKTMJX ELT

MLQJ PHLTANJ.

NORMAN BATES:

UL. QLPRJH—QE

QLPRJH—IRKP SM

PRJ WRHKMJ?—MRJ

SMU'P FTSPJ

RJHMJNZ PLXKE.

MRS. TEASDALE:

JZ NPJQMGSOJY

SV CPR MRNRFCQSY

NSOOQCCRR,

Q GRANSOR HSW

GQCP SFRY JMOZ.

RUFUS T. FIREFLY:

QZ CPJC ZS? PSG

AJCR KS HSW ZCJH

SFRY?

CALL OUR BLUFF
PATENTLY ABSURD ★☆

Jeremy Piltdown, our in-house duke of dupery, presented us with blueprints for 11 bizarre objects. "If necessity is the mother of invention," said Jeremy, "then all these gadgets are orphans."

Nevertheless, Jeremy swears that many of the contraptions shown here were actually patented—but he confesses that he dreamed up some of them himself. Can you tell which inventions are fact and which are fiction?

Answers, page 173

1. Tipping Hat
Patented March 10, 1896. This mechanism was wound up like a clock and fastened to the inside of a hat. A number of curved-spring "fingers" secured both hat and machinery. When a gentleman bowed his head slightly, the arm and ball pendulum triggered the machinery, and to the amazement of passersby, the hat would tip itself, circle around, and gently settle back into place.

2. Bravado Rectifier
Patented April 1, 1961. Frenchman Jean Pannier designed this device for those who like to impress their friends by throwing wads of paper into a trash basket across the room. A vacuum in the bottom of the basket was connected to a hidden foot control that activated brief but intense suction—enough to attract lightweight flying objects that might otherwise have missed their mark.

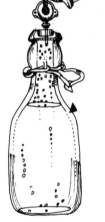

3. Carbonation Resuscitator
Patented July 10, 1913. This ingenious device resembled a bicycle pump both in form and function. Carbon dioxide was forced from a syringe through a specially designed bottle cap, thus restoring carbonation to a flat bottle of soda.

4. Dimple Maker
Patented May 19, 1896. During a time when dimples were considered especially attractive, Martin Goetze invented this dimple maker. The hard rounded knob was placed on the site of the desired dimple and the roller was rotated around and around by turning the handle. If no damage resulted, a dimple would appear and last for six to eight hours.

5. Portable Bathtub
Patented July 1, 1972. Frances Allen hoped her portable bathtub would restore the spirits of the tired traveler. The user attached one hose to a tap, another hose to a drain, and stepped in. A zipper on the inside allowed the user to close the bag. Once the bather was finished, the plastic bag was drained and rolled up.

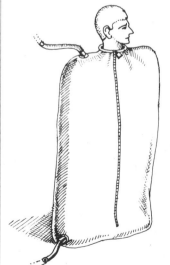

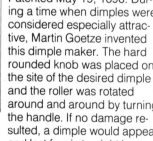

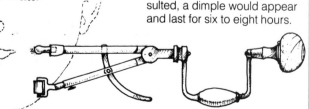

BY JEREMY PILTDOWN

6. Flyswatter Gun Patented September 18, 1923. This oversize rubber dart gun was invented to solve the fly problem once and for all. When the trigger was pulled, a coiled spring released the flat rubber head into the air or against a wall. If the user aimed carefully, the fly census would be down by one.

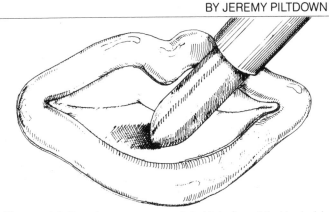

7. Lipstick Template Patented May 1, 1922. A pioneer in the cosmetic industry, Willis Mehr tried several times to come up with an easy way for women to apply lipstick. Mehr found that by holding a wax template against the lips, women could apply lipstick accurately. Ten different templates were available for a personal fit.

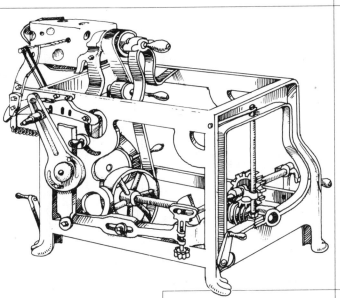

8. Sunbather's Toe-Rings Patented January 23, 1973. Russell Greathouse was worried that people were getting uneven tans, so he devised these sunbather's toe-rings. They were placed over each big toe to prevent the feet from spreading apart when the user was stretched out on the beach, thus ensuring an even tan.

9. Swiss Cheese Simulator Patented August 29, 1942. Various size drill bits were arranged to meet a block of cheese from many angles. The Simulator enjoyed a good market for several years, but sales declined after World War II, when Swiss cheese became available again.

10. Jumping Shoes Patented January 3, 1922. George and May Southgate designed these shoe attachments to be worn over ordinary footwear. The six steel legs were very strong and springy and encouraged children to jump by enabling them to reach new heights. Rubber pads on the bottom softened the landing.

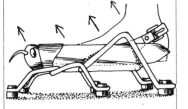

11. Hair-Cutting Machine Patented December 11, 1951. John Boax's hair-cutting machine used an air exhaust system to suck hair into tiny holes where electric coils would burn the hair to the desired length. Unfortunately for Mr. Boax, this damaged the hair (and smelled vile), so scissors are still used to cut hair today.

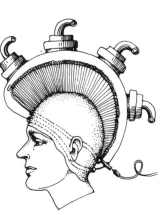

PICTURE DOMINOES ★★

BY ROBERT LEIGHTON

The dominoes below, like their spotted counterparts, can be linked to form a chain. The difference here is that these dominoes are to be linked according to story lines suggested by the pictures: The bottom half of each domino begins a story that continues in the top half of another domino. For example, the bottom half of domino A (man frightened by shark) leads to the top of domino I (laughing kid with shark fin on back). The bottom of domino I, beginning a new story, leads to the top of . . . ? Eventually, the chain ends up at the top of domino A. *Answers, page 173*

ROLL CALL DICE GAME*

BY PIERRE BERLOQUIN

Gather five dice, a friend, and all your luck to play this sophisticated version of tic-tac-toe. The object is to capture either four consecutive squares in a line or a total of any 13 squares, by rolling the dice combinations shown.

Players compete on the same game grid, marking squares with two different colored pencils or, for repeated play, two different colored sets of tokens (13 each).

PLAY

After rolling a die to determine who goes first, players alternate turns. On each turn a player rolls all five dice. If he rolls a combination shown in the grid, he captures that square and crosses it out (or covers it) with his color. That combination is then no longer available. If a player fails to capture a square on his first roll, he may throw any or all of the dice a second time and, if necessary, a third time, trying to get an available square. If he hasn't matched an open combination after three rolls, he must pass.

COMBINATIONS

For squares that show four dice, four of the five dice must match those shown in order to capture the square; the fifth die is disregarded. In the other squares, all five dice are taken into account: A straight requires five consecutive numbers (either 1-2-3-4-5 or 2-3-4-5-6); a full house requires three of a kind and two of a kind (as 2-2-2-5-5); and a five-of-a-kind requires all five dice to match (as 3-3-3-3-3).

WINNING

When a player captures four squares in a row (horizontally, vertically, or diagonally), or any 13 squares, he wins the round. If more than one round is played, the loser should start the next.

FROM OUR CAST OF CHARACTERS

Have you made the acquaintance of these three GAMES irregulars? You'd be hard-pressed to find a more puzzling trio of conversationalists than the observant Elizabeth Ferret-Frowning, the picky Aunt Hildegarde, and the ever-circumlocutory Harry Hardway.

ELIZABETH FERRET-FROWNING ★
BY PEG KEHRET

The tiny sidewalk café had fresh flowers on each table. Ace detective Elizabeth Ferret-Frowning could not resist sitting for a few moments among the blue-and-white checkered tablecloths and the bouquets of yellow daisies.

She ordered a lemonade and sipped it contentedly while she viewed the passersby. The early afternoon traffic, both automobile and pedestrian, was heavier than usual. She watched as two boys on bicycles pedaled up the road, across the railroad tracks, and through the intersection. Behind them came a bread truck, a school bus, and two passenger cars. All speeded up slightly in order to make it through the intersection before the light changed from amber to red.

Lizzie heard a siren, jumped to her feet, and flagged down a police car.

"Has there been a crime in this area?" she asked.

"A bank robbery," replied the policeman. "Just five minutes ago in the next block."

"Your suspects," said Lizzie, "are traveling south on Windon Street in a yellow school bus."

What made Lizzie suspicious?

AUNT HILDEGARDE ★★
BY DAVID DIEFENDORF

The last time we saw Aunt Hildegarde, she'd been to visit Aunt Abigail, and had come home liking stores but not shops, ghosts but not goblins, and operas but not arias.

That's because Aunt Hildegarde likes things that have the same word structure as the name of the relative she has seen most recently. And Abigail, stores, ghosts, and operas all begin with two consecutive letters of the alphabet. Shops, goblins, and arias do not.

Recently, Aunt Hildegarde went to visit Uncle Toby, and this is what she came home liking:

She loves CASHMERE, but not ANGORA.
She prefers TRIPLETS to TWINS.
She'd rather live in a PALACE than a CASTLE.
She loves PAGEANTS, but doesn't like SPECTACLES.
She'd rather eat MEAT than VEGETABLES.
She's bought a pet PARROT, and has given away her PARAKEET.
When she goes to Spain, she's going to see MADRID, but not GRANADA.
She prefers TAPESTRIES to MURALS.

Next Aunt Hildegarde went to visit Aunt Louella, and came home with a brand new set of preferences.

She loves the taste of CINNAMON, but dislikes CURRY.
When it comes to composers, she prefers BEETHOVEN to BRAHMS.
She'd much rather be caught in an AVALANCHE than a ROCKSLIDE.
She has a TERRARIUM, but not an AQUARIUM.
She prefers to put things in a STOREROOM, not an ATTIC.
She'd rather watch a LIFTOFF than a SPLASHDOWN.
She thinks she looks better in a BIKINI than a WETSUIT.
She GIGGLES, but never LAUGHS.

Can you figure out what guided Aunt Hildegarde's tastes on her two recent visits?

HARRY HARDWAY ★★★
BY BURT HOCHBERG

The questions we're asked on a typical day are simple: "What time is it?"; "Which way is Fifth Avenue?"; "Daddy, why does your face turn red when Mommy beats you at chess?" And they require simple answers: "Three o'clock"; "Straight ahead one block"; "Go to your room."

Not for Harry Hardway. Harry's a lovable fellow—got a wife, kids, lots of friends, a good job—but he can never bring himself to answer a simple question simply, to the exasperation of said wife, kids, and friends.

For instance, if you had just walked from Third Avenue and now stood on Fourth Avenue, and if you happened to ask Harry which way Fifth Avenue was, he'd tell you to go back to Third, turn right for two blocks, make three more rights and two consecutive lefts, then go straight ahead one block.

Not everybody loves Harry. Waiters do not love Harry. Take the other night.

Harry went out to dinner with his friends Larry, Barry, and Gary. Harry sat across from Gary. At Gary's right, opposite Barry, sat Larry.

When the waiter came to take their orders, Larry and Barry ordered steak, Gary chose fish, and Harry ordered like this:

"Unless the man at the left of the man opposite the man who ordered fish is not having what the man across from the man at the right of the man at my left is having, then I'll have what the man across from the man at the right of the man opposite me ordered. Otherwise, bring me duck à l'orange."

Assuming "right" and "left" from the viewpoint of the diners, what did Harry order?

OBSERVATION PUZZLES TO TEST YOUR EYE-Q

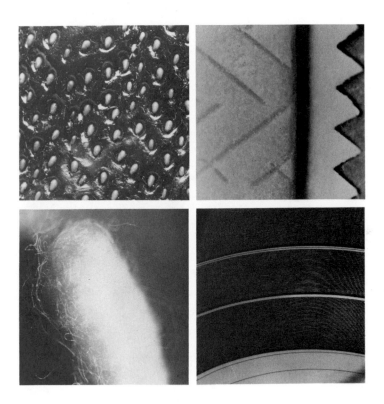

★☆

EYEBALL BENDERS
BY SUELY SINTO

Can you identify these objects? The clues below may or may not help.

1. Darryl, e.g.   2. Choo-choo!
3. Ears to you!   4. Turn, turn, turn

Answers, page 173

ILLUSIONS & DELUSIONS ★☆

A

B

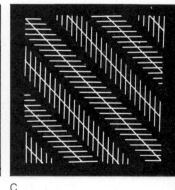

C

Many of us remember being fooled the first time we saw these figures and tried to determine which horizontal line was longer:

Even though a ruler proves they're exactly the same length, and even though we know it's the direction and angle of the arrows that confuse us, we still *see* the lines as unequal.

Geometric patterns that deceive the eye date back to prehistoric art. Only in the last century, however, have psychologists and physicists begun to study them systematically. They still don't understand them fully, but they now know that these illusions fool not our eyes, but our brain, which misinterprets certain combinations of images.

Forewarned, can you see through the trickery on these pages? No fair using a ruler.   *Answers, page 173*

1. PARALLEL BARS
Top: In which figure are all the long diagonal lines parallel?

2. RISING SUN
Middle: In which figure are the two horizontal lines parallel?

3. ROUND AND ROUND
Right: In which figure do the black and white rings form a set of discrete circles, rather than a continuous spiral?

A

B

C

A

B

C

BY DAVID POPE

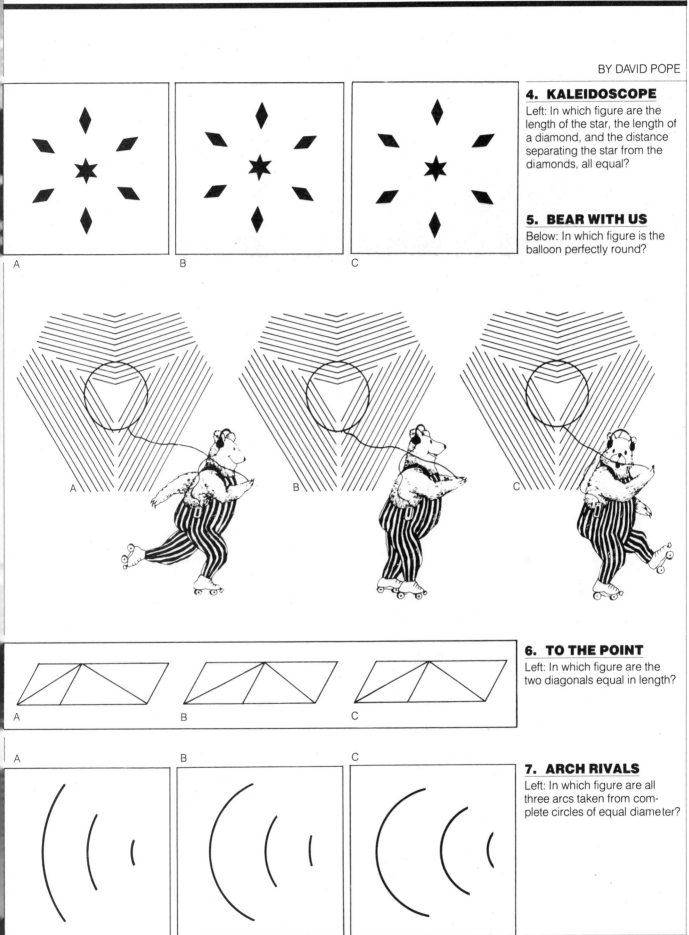

4. KALEIDOSCOPE
Left: In which figure are the length of the star, the length of a diamond, and the distance separating the star from the diamonds, all equal?

5. BEAR WITH US
Below: In which figure is the balloon perfectly round?

6. TO THE POINT
Left: In which figure are the two diagonals equal in length?

7. ARCH RIVALS
Left: In which figure are all three arcs taken from complete circles of equal diameter?

KEYS TO THE DUNGEON**

BY R. WAYNE SCHMITTBERGER

This is the 13th-century dungeon maze of the infamous Balmanian Inquisition, in which, according to legend, thousands of men and women perished. Balmanian prisoners faced a cruel obstacle in trying to negotiate the maze, as they had to grope their way in the dark while pursued by a pack of wild dogs. By contrast, the puzzle as presented here should be almost child's play. The plan for the dungeon shows the prisoner's cell in the middle (marked START), a network of hallways, six locked rooms, and six key rooms located on the periphery. To enter or leave a locked room, you must first secure the appropriate key: Key TC unlocks the Torture Chamber, Key A unlocks the Archives, and so on. Once a room has been unlocked, it remains unlocked, and you may carry as many keys as you wish. Retracing your steps is allowed. To escape, in what order must you visit the rooms?

Answer, page 174

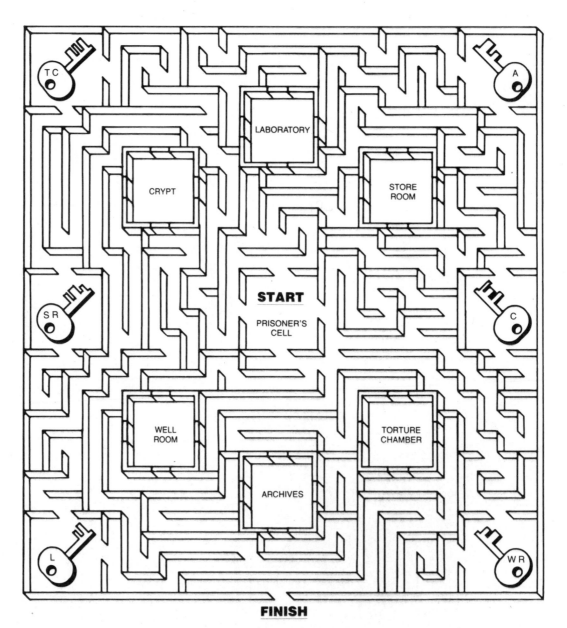

WHAT'S WRONG WITH
THE HAUNTED HOUSE *

BY GREG SCOTT

There are 34 grave errors in this haunted setting. How many can you find before something finds *you*?   *Answers, page 174*

KITSCH AND TELL SEQUENCE PUZZLE *

Customizing old automobiles is a popular pastime these days. In fact, thousands of enthusiasts have formed car clubs in Los Angeles, Phoenix, and elsewhere in the West and Southwest.

Unfortunately, the person who souped up the car shown on these pages overdid it on the chrome and accessories. Each step in the remodeling is shown, starting with the original automobile in picture E. Can you put the 14 other pictures in correct sequence?   *Answer, page 173*

A B
14

B 3

C 12

D 10

E 1

F 6

G 8

H 7

I 9

J 5

K 14
15

L 2

M 11

N 4

O 12
13

EYEBALL BENDERS ENCORE ★☆

What are these objects?
Answers, page 174

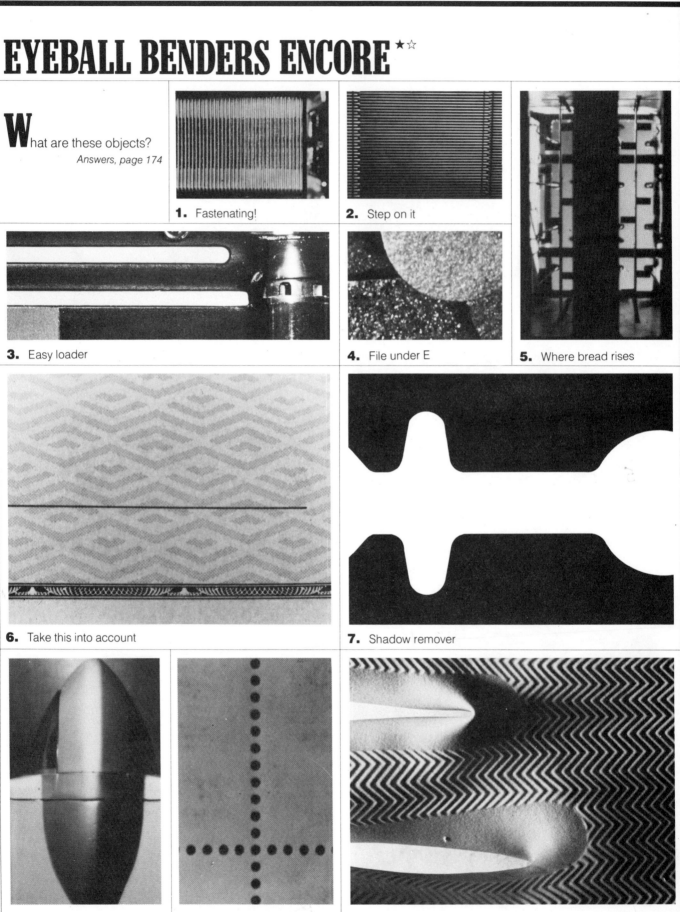

1. Fastenating!

2. Step on it

3. Easy loader

4. File under E

5. Where bread rises

6. Take this into account

7. Shadow remover

8. Lovely Rita's beat

9. May be canceled any time

10. Hand holder

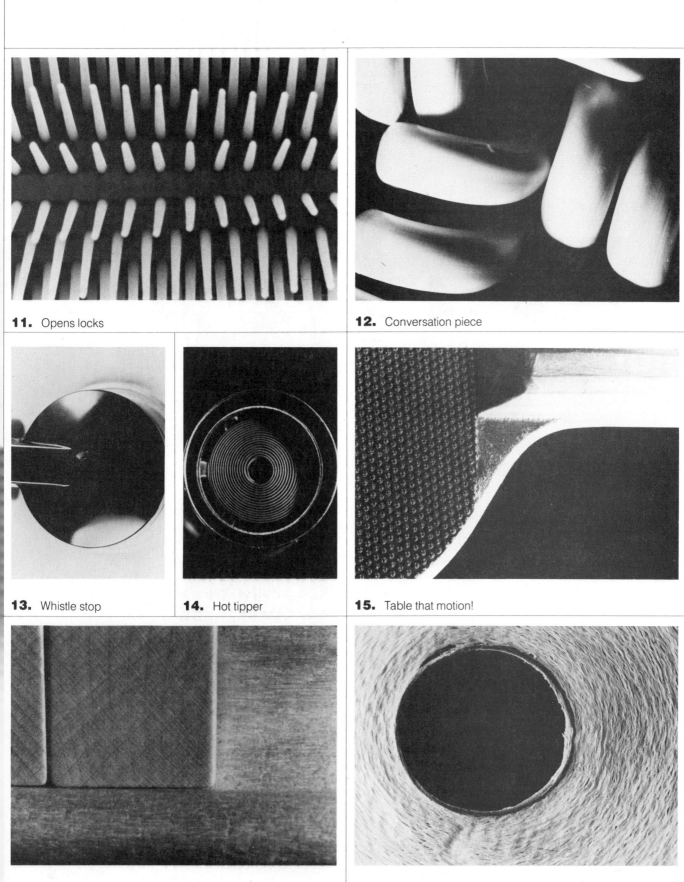

11. Opens locks

12. Conversation piece

13. Whistle stop

14. Hot tipper

15. Table that motion!

16. Draw a blank?

17. An absorbing subject

EYE EXAM ★☆

Can't see the forest for the trees? Always looking over a four-leaf clover? The 13-minute test on these two pages will help you find out how observant you really are. Watch ready? Go!

Answers, page 173

1. LOST AND FOUND
Which silhouette matches the picture on the left?

A   B   C   D   E   F

2. ODD ONE OUT
Which of the four pieces *cannot* be found in the jigsaw design? (Do not flip over any of the pieces.)

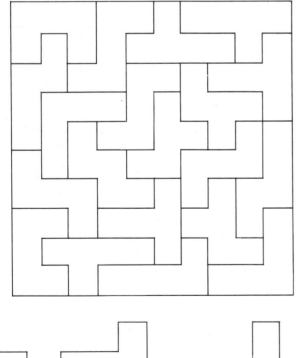

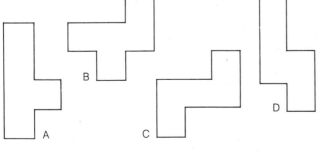

A   B   C   D

3. JIGSAW
Which two pieces below fit together to form the figure at right?

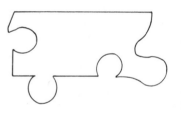

A

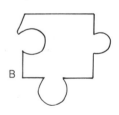

B

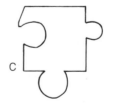

C

D

E

F

BY DR. SEYMOUR D. TAYLE

4. TWINS

How can you cut this figure along the printed lines to produce two identical shapes?

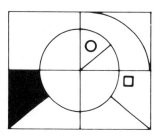

5. MIRROR, MIRROR

Which of the designs at right is a perfect mirror image of the one above?

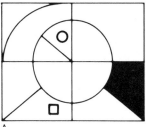
A

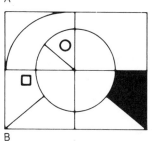
B

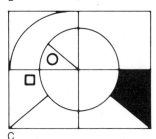
C

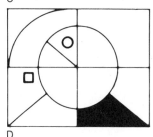
D

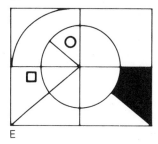
E

6. MISSING PIECE

Which of the following pieces fits the empty circle in the picture?

A

B

C

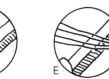
D

E

"Oh, come on—it's not that windy out."

7. DON'T GO

Somewhere on these two pages (other than in this question) the letters S-T-O-P appear consecutively. Where?

ARCHITECT'S NIGHTMARE **

BY ULRICH KOCH

Can you find the seven errors in this architectural drawing? *Answers, page 174*

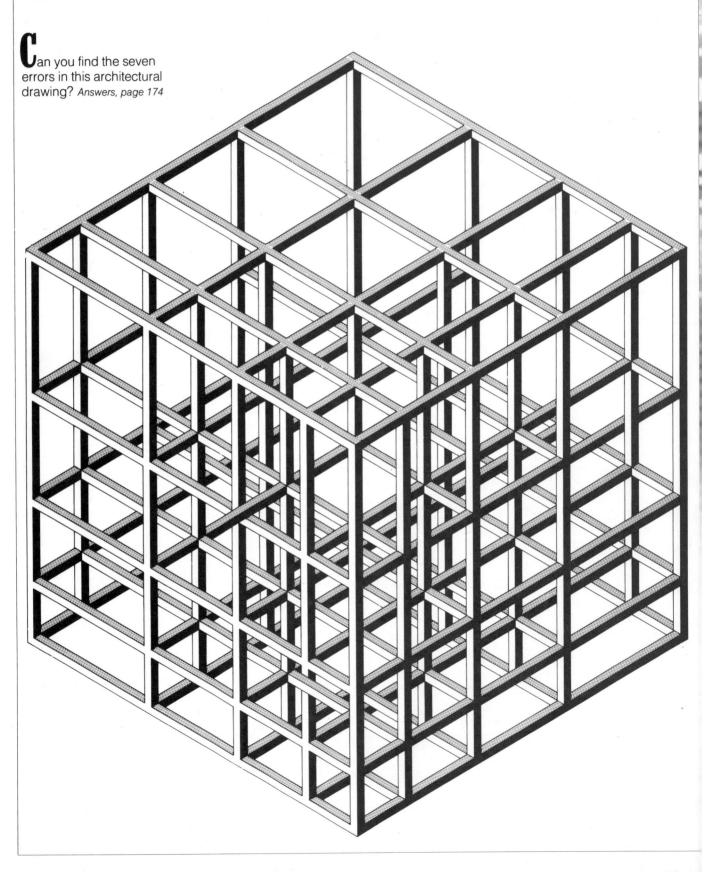

THE BONE ZONE *☆

BY KATHY KESTING

Pictured on this page are the skeletons of 13 modern-day animals for you to identify. They may be tough to recognize, but if you use clues such as number of feet, size of head, characteristic standing position, and so on, you should soon feel the answers in your bones.

Answers, page 174

THE PAPER-AND-PENCIL DECATHLON ★☆

If you've stuck with our observation tests this far, you've obviously been seeing things, and you deserve a rest. That's why we'd like you to perform 10 Olympic feats of dexterity—*with your eyes closed.*

To pass the qualifying heat, just gather two pencils and a penny. Warm up for each event by practicing with your eyes open, using the eraser end of a pencil. (Gray lines on some events indicate sample paths.)

Instructions and scoring procedures accompany each event. Every competition is worth 10 points; the maximum decathlon score is 100. Record the individual scores in the boxes at right, then tally them and turn to page 174 to find out if you've won a medal.

SCORING

1	2	3	4	5	6	7	8	9	10	TOTAL

EVENT 1: 100-METER RUN (1 TRY)

Place pencil on START. Close eyes. Make 10 dots, trying to put one in each of the 10 boxes. *Score:* 1 point for each box that contains one and only one dot.

START ●

EVENT 2: LONG JUMP (BEST OF 3 TRIES)

Place pencil on START. Close eyes. Draw a straight line to the striped jumping box. Without lifting the pencil, draw an arc ending in the long sand pit. *Score:* Number of the farthest scoreline passed. No score if the arc does not start in the striped box and end in the sand.

START ●

EVENT 3: HURDLES (1 TRY)

Place pencil on START. Close eyes. Draw 10 continuous arches while leaping over each of the 10 hurdles. *Score:* 1 point for each hurdle cleared. No score for any jump that does not end between the top and bottom of the hurdles.

START ●

EVENT 4: JAVELIN (BEST OF 3 TRIES)

Place pencil on START. Close eyes. Staying within the delineated area, draw as long a line as possible. *Score:* Number of the farthest scoreline passed. No score if any part of your line leaves the javelin area.

START
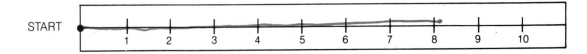

BY CHARLES BANASKY

EVENT 5: TRAPSHOOTING (TOTAL OF 5 TRIES)

This is a two-pencil event. Place the tip of one pencil on TARGET, the tip of the other on SHOOTER. Close eyes. Simultaneously draw lines with both pencils toward the shaded box. *Score:* 2 points each time the lines intersect within the shaded box, 1 point if lines cross on the edge of the box.

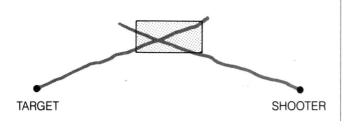

TARGET   SHOOTER

EVENT 6: ARCHERY
(TOTAL OF 3 TRIES)

Hold pencil about one foot over target. Close eyes. Lower pencil to target and make a dot. *Score:* Number indicated on target. Add 1 bonus point if you make three bull's-eyes.

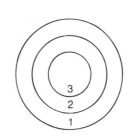

EVENT 7: SHOT PUT
(BEST OF 3 TRIES)

Place penny on circle at bottom right. Place pencil on START. Close eyes. Push or shoot penny upward with tip of pencil. *Score:* Number of the farthest scoreline the penny passes. No score if penny leaves shot put area.

10 —
9 —
8 —
7 —
6 —
5 —
4 —
3 —
2 —
1 —

EVENT 8: HIGH DIVE

Place pencil on platform 1. Close eyes. Draw a line into the pool below. Open eyes. If dive successfully lands in pool, climb to platform 2, close eyes, and repeat. Continue until a dive is unsuccessful. *Score:* Number of the highest platform from which you successfully dive.

EVENT 9: UNEVEN BARS (TOTAL OF 2 TRIES)

Place pencil in START. Close eyes. In one continuous line, draw a loop around the center dot on the first bar, then a loop around the center dot on the second bar. *Score:* 2 points each time one dot is successfully circled, 5 points each time both are successfully circled. No score for a loop that goes above or below the edge of the bar.

START

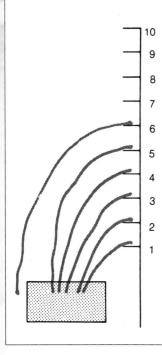

10
9
8
7
6
5
4
3
2
1

EVENT 10: BASKETBALL (TOTAL OF 5 TRIES)

Place penny on lower circle. Place pencil point on START. Close eyes. Push penny toward basket. *Score:* 2 points each time penny lands completely within basket.

START

START

GOOD KNIGHT, SUITE PRINTS ★☆

BY MARY ELLEN SLATE

We offer this "homophone story" with apologies to Walter Mitty. Homophones are words that sound alike but differ in spelling and meaning, like knight/night, suite/sweet, and prints/prince. How many of the 141 pairs can you find in this tale?   *Answers, page 174*

Russell Wood, a nearly bald man of modest mien, wore clothes of worn serge and a tie with just the merest flecks of color. Unless you focused on his tie, he almost disappeared: His hair matched his face, which matched his suit—all grays.

Alone at his teller's cage, idle and bored, Russell took a peek at the frieze along the bank's ceiling. There was a knight, a minstrel with a lute, an urn, a lyre. Russell swayed on his feet and the room began to reel as he daydreamed.

Sir Claude de Bois reined his horse and rode at a slower gait. As the castle bell tolled, he saw the lord of the manor wave his sword at an empty metal coffer. "You vile villein, to steal my gold!" The weak serf cowered as the baron sent the steel weapon toward his heart. Sir Claude bawled, "Stop, by the Holy Rood! I am de Bois! I mete out justice and bring aid and succor to all men, howe'er base. Don't try my mettle or, rude coward, you'll be sealing your fate."

Suddenly through the grille of the cage came the hoarse bass voice of a constant cougher: "Freeze, sucker! Now, raise your hands. High."

Russell looked but saw no one.

"Didn't you hear me?" There was an edge of real pique verging on choler in the rough voice. "Do as I told you."

"Do you mind, sir? I heard you but I can't see you," sighed Russell.

"Never mind the sighs, liar. Look down here. Damn! I'm losing patience."

The teller ducked his head and saw a vain, wee man only four feet high who paced up and down, stopping at intervals to flex his impressive arm muscles. He wore a tee shirt, a suede jacket, and blue jeans. Over his seamed forehead and apelike brows perched a wig, apparently tacked on with flour paste. His nose went straight for a bit, then took a sharp turn to the side. Yet Harry "Peewee" Farplotz, the world's smallest and most inept bank robber, had style. As he paced, a veil seemed to fall over Peewee's eyes.

Doctor Malcolm Farquahar stepped out of the hansom cab and paid his fare. "Another wholly daring feat accomplished for The Cause," he said as he flicked his ruff. None of his patients, indeed few in London, knew that the foppish medico was in fact a one-man-war-against-injustice in the guise of the Purple Pimpernel, master spy, who mined the terrorists of the French Revolution of their cache of francs.

During the instants that the pint-size hood mused, thoughts chased through Russell's mind. He was considering gambling on an act of derring-do when he saw Peewee's aide, a very broad broad, pointing a big black gun at him.

Rose "Mean Queen" Farplotz was as outsize as her husband was undersame. Her beet-red hair was tied in a messy knot. She wore a wrap of mangy furs masquerading as minks and a four-carat rhinestone ring. "Not well-bred," thought Russell, "but oddly handsome." And then she too fell into a daze.

Chaste Rosalind, the shepherdess, rowed on the incoming sea tide. She began to wade in with her pail of mussels, as behind her on the strait, the surge of the surf moved to the barren shore. The rays of the morning sun glinted from a vein of silver ore in a boulder. A lone tern wheeled. As Rosalind headed for her secret vale, she could sense its peace. The dew had disappeared and the mist had vanished, quiet as a nun. She heard the caws of crows as the flocks soared over the copse of yews; a sole hare started to browse. Near the fields of hay and rows of rye, a deer family—hart, doe, and half-grown fawn—stopped to graze. A bee buzzed over the furze.

Rosalind hugged her slim waist in delight as she inhaled the scent of phlox. She picked a flower and heard a rustle in the bushy brake as a herd of sheep appeared, a woolly lamb gamboling beside each ewe. She passed by the stile, went through the gate, and bathed her feet in the crystal water of the tiny duct that led from the dam. She hummed a hymn for this balm to her soul.

Rose's return to reality was abrupt. "This doll could waste you," Peewee snarled. "She knows how to use that gun. Last week she blew away four guys. And," he held up a vial of pale liquid, "this is a bomb. So let's have the bread, the loot, the dough."

Russell stopped and weighed the situation as an uneasy silence reigned. Then he got out the cash box and threw it on the counter. "Take it. Be my guest, but the sum total is only eight hundred dollars and some cents."

Russell's eyes were drawn, as though by a magnet, to Rose's big gun, which was now held loosely at her side. He knew that the tough facade had cracked and he felt bolder. With a wry smile, he said, "I'm only a simple teller."

"Gimme a break," Peewee whined. "We didn't figure you for a real big-shot magnate like chairman of the board, for instance—not even a pipsqueak loan officer. You're nothing but—" There was an astonished pause. "But you're de Bois. I've seen you in my dreams."

By now Russell had also guessed Peewee's alter ego. "Hey! I know you too. Well, hi! You're my idol, the gallant Pimpernel, the prince of spies. And," he made a bow to Rose, "this minx, this belle, this fair maid would be Rosalind."

Russell stopped with a groan. "Oh, dear, I owe you an apology. I pushed the alarm, and the police will be here soon."

"No need to fret, son, we'll beat the rap," said Peewee. "Not a penny has changed hands. Close the cash box and wipe off my prints. Then, just watch as Rosy eats her piece of hardware." Rose ate the gun, a creation made of a carrot dyed black.

"And now," said Peewee, "I'll just drink the liquid bomb and that ought to sew it up." He knocked back the tea that had posed as TNT.

When the cops got there, they found a disappointing paucity of perpetrators; no villain to collar, no one to grill. "It was a false alarm, in a manner of speaking," Russell told them with tact.

The police made out their report while Rose started to coo at their fierce attack dogs, who wagged their tails, put their paws in her lap, gently clawed her furs, and licked her nose.

For the three new-found friends, the nonheist had been a coup. One night a week they would meet for a "Days of Yore" fête when they ate well and wined well, and told tales of the past.

WORDPLAY AND OTHER VERBAL ACROBATICS

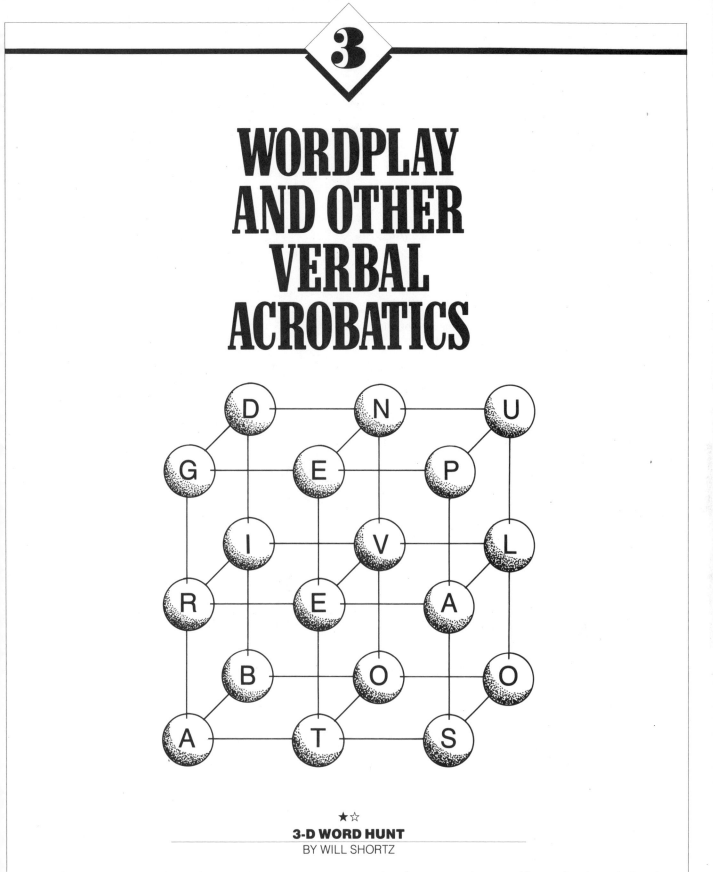

★☆
3-D WORD HUNT
BY WILL SHORTZ

In the three-dimensional block of letters above, how many five-letter words can you find? A word may start at any letter, but must proceed along straight lines connecting consecutive balls. For example, the word STOVE starts at the S in the lower-right front corner, moves left to the T, backward to the O, up to the V, and forward to the E. In forming a word you may return to a letter (like the S in LASTS), but you may not stand on a letter and use it twice (like the B in RABBI). Proper names are not counted, but plurals are fine. We found 44 common five-letter words.

Answers, page 175

WACKY WORDIES ★☆

In 1979, GAMES readers started sending in Wacky Wordies, clever typographic word pictures that were circulating everywhere.

So we made some up and ran a page of them. When readers sent more, we ran another page. And another. "No more!" we cried—to no avail.

The Wacky Wordies still roll in, and despite our protests, we always print them—one more time.

The object is to discern a familiar word, phrase, or proper name from each pictorial letter arrangement. Number 1, for instance, depicts the phrase "life of ease," and 2 is "rule of thumb." And please, if you think of any others, don't tell us!

Answers, page 175

1 eeee LIFE eee eee

2 THUMB

3 pruorhd

4 ME

5 WRITER'S

6 FEVER

7 Joes

8

9 TEST

10 Chief

11 GAME

12 Sheepdog

BY CHARLES ADKINS

13

14

15

16

17

18

19

20

21

22

23

24

25

MENTAL BLOCKS ★☆

BY FREDERIC H. KOCK

Tennis, anyone? In each stack of blocks served up below, use the three-letter tennis word at the top to complete the words in the seven rows below it. Each letter in the top row must be used at least once in each of the other rows in the stack, and no additional letters may be used. As a start, the letters S E T in stack 1 can complete the word STEWS in the next row down. Are you game for the others? All answers are common words. *Answers, page 175*

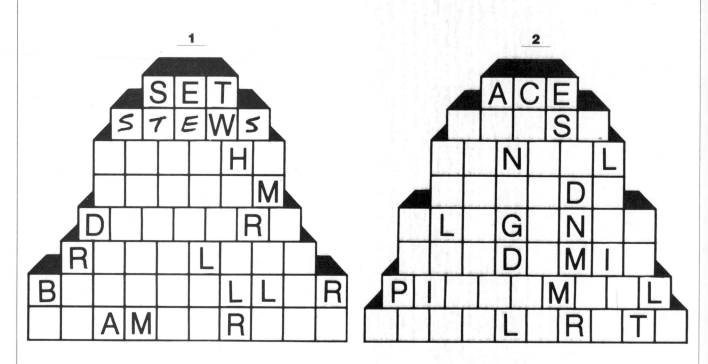

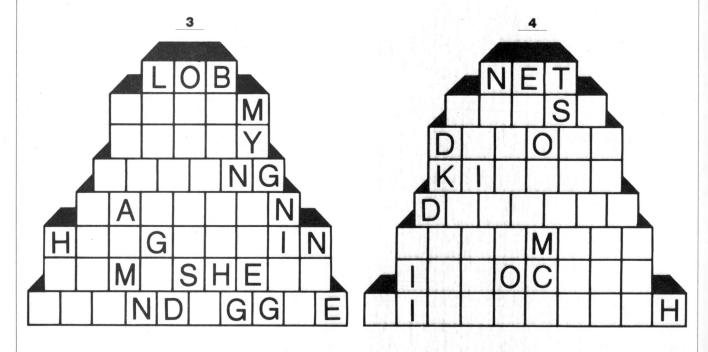

RHYME AND REASON *☆

BY STEPHEN SNIDERMAN

The sentences below may look a bit strange, but they should sound vaguely familiar. That's because each one is merely a familiar proverb in which every word has been replaced by a rhyme. (In some cases, punctuation has been altered, too.) For example, the sentence "Brittle folks tell weight jokes" is rhyming language for "Little strokes fell great oaks." Can you restore reason to the following 12 rhymes?   *Dancers, page 175*

1. Letter rate can sever. _____
2. Slime wasn't gray. _____
3. Factions seek chowder, ban birds. _____
4. Leggers pant, see losers. _____
5. True Feds mar wetter van run. _____
6. Cootie whiz—lonely in sleep. _____
7. Penny brands break night clerk. _____
8. Go choose his wood shoes. _____
9. Small loads seed new home. _____
10. I'm banned—I'd hate war foe plan. _____
11. Fall wood brings trust from you, tan friend. _____
12. Walls bear din of band store. _____

RARE PAIRS *

BY DON MATHEWS

If "hay and oats" are STEED FEED, and a "magician's group" is a TRICK CLIQUE, what must the following be? (The missing word in each answer rhymes with its mate.)

Answers, page 175

1.	Electrocardiogram	_____ CHART	7. Helsinki hotel	_____ INN
2.	*Moby Dick*	_____ TALE	8. Headache	BRAIN _____
3.	Oleo	BREAD _____	9. Realtor's job	_____ SELLING
4.	A joust	KNIGHT _____	10. Band-aid	SCRATCH _____
5.	Gardening	SOIL _____	11. Acrophobia	_____ FRIGHT
6.	Eighty	FOUR _____	12. Trade union	_____ GUILD

NOAH'S ARK *

While the world's more serious animals were making their way to Noah's Ark to weather the Great Flood, a group of more fanciful beasts found shelter aboard another ark, shown here. The names of these 12 creatures are common English words that playfully describe these very special animals. For example, the large, dapper cat (# 11) is a *dandelion*. Can you match the other animals with their names?   *Answers, page 175*

Bumble   _____

Caftan   _____

Cardiac   _____

Conceal   _____

Dandelion   *11*

Melancholy   _____

Euphonious   _____

Hypocritic   _____

Investigator   _____

Nightmare   _____

Rampage   _____

Tycoon   _____

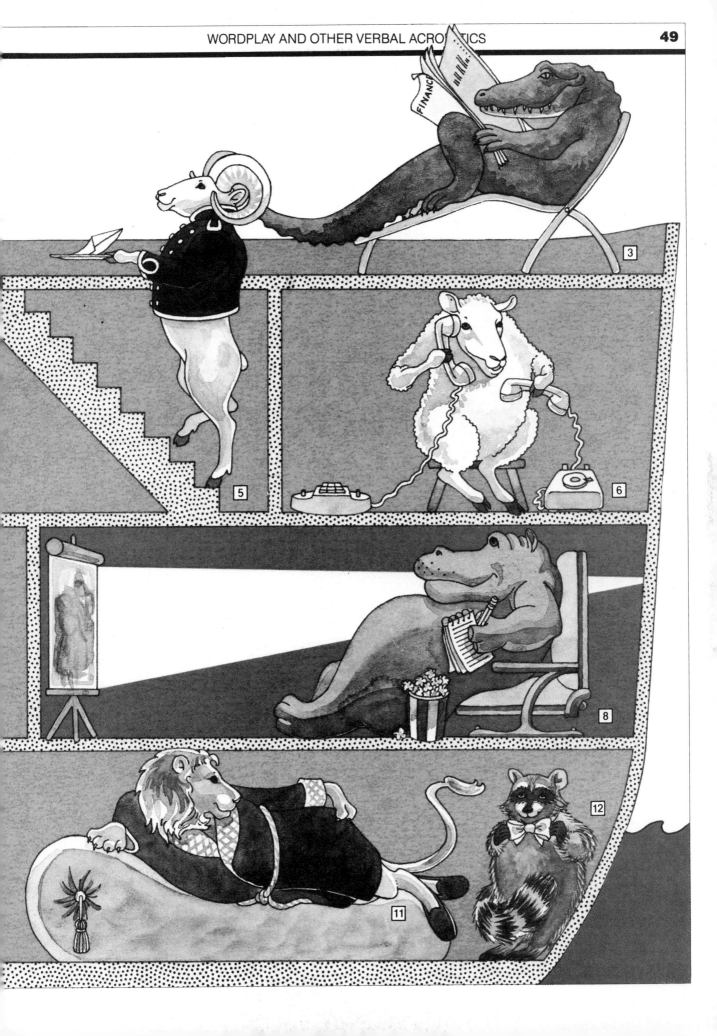

HEART TRANSPLANTS ★☆

BY M. HOREJS

Each of the following sentences includes three incomplete five-letter words, which are identical except for their middle letters. The first sets of dashes have been filled in. Can you fill in the others to complete the sentences?

Answers, page 175

1. The **L O N E R**—a great **L O V E R** of solitude—would seldom travel from his mountain home into the **L O W E R**, more populated valleys.

2. One of the __ __ J __ __ reasons the __ __ Y __ __ failed to get reelected was that he lived in a stately old __ __ N __ __ outside the city!

3. The most __ __ E __ __ of film-score composers can __ __ A __ __ the music of others and even __ __ O __ __ the style of a past composer to write original songs.

4. Angus had just finished off a __ __ F __ __ of Scotch when he stumbled from the bank into the briny __ __ R __ __, but the __ __ L __ __ and floating debris didn't bother him—he was just as polluted as the water!

5. The __ __ E __ __ of my cheeks will always __ __ U __ __ red with embarrassment when I'm caught unawares by the __ __ A __ __ of a camera.

6. The beam from the __ __ S __ __ quickly burned through the thin sheet of aluminum, but it wasn't until much __ __ T __ __ that it made a hole in the thick __ __ Y __ __ of steel.

7. How can you support a regime that, after a number of riots and attempted __ __ U __ __ __, __ __ __ O __ __ up members of the Peace __ __ R __ __ in the local jails?

8. Some gauchos carelessly __ __ I __ __ a few ashes from their cigars while herding the __ __ O __ __, which occasionally will result in a burnt __ __ E __ __ of wool.

9. The swimming __ __ A __ __, while giving lessons on the beach, found a beautiful __ __ N __ __ shell, which she decided would look good in the display case next to her comfortable __ __ U __ __ at home.

10. The usually long-winded English teacher grew uncharacteristically __ __ R __ __ every time we would __ __ A __ __ him by deliberately using the wrong __ __ N __ __ or grammatical case.

11. The way many __ __ B __ __ soldiers would carouse and __ __ V __ __ in the overtaken cities was enough to __ __ P __ __ even the most faithful supporters of the Confederacy.

ODD COUPLES ★

BY BILL LEONARD

Galloping and Eydie Gorme, Corn and Ty Cobb—those are our idea of "odd couples." Below are 16 more twosomes with their last names deleted. Can you complete them?

Answers, page 175

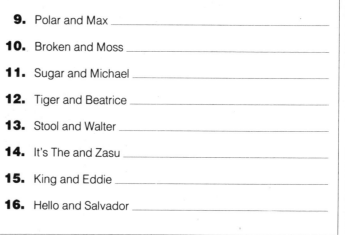

1. Ballpoint and William _____

2. Book and Groucho _____

3. Big Bad and Virginia _____

4. Stock and Ernie _____

5. Oil and Orson _____

6. Deuces and Oscar _____

7. Foot and Clare Booth _____

8. Alaskan King and Buster _____

9. Polar and Max _____

10. Broken and Moss _____

11. Sugar and Michael _____

12. Tiger and Beatrice _____

13. Stool and Walter _____

14. It's The and Zasu _____

15. King and Eddie _____

16. Hello and Salvador _____

MATCHMAKER**

BY LAURENCE URDANG

Here's your chance to play matchmaker. The clues below suggest 14 common two-word phrases that can be formed by pairing the 28 words in the list. But be forewarned: The clues are not straightforward definitions of the answers, but plays on unexpected meanings. Number 1, for instance—"Film clips about Atlantic resort"—is answered by BERMUDA SHORTS. Each word in the list is used only once.   *Answers, page 175*

CLUES

1. Film clips about Atlantic resort *BERMUDA SHORTS*

2. English heat wave _____

3. Fire dancers suffer from it _____

4. Pan bad actor _____

5. "The swim club is now open" _____

6. Mild punishment _____

7. Undersized goat _____

8. Spanking _____

9. Examination for amnesia _____

10. December 21, officially _____

11. Attorney's apartment _____

12. Irritating beauty _____

13. Belgian children _____

14. ". . . lived happily ever after," "finis," etc. _____

WORD LIST

BELT	CHAFING	HAM	ROAST
~~BERMUDA~~	CHECK	LEGAL	SEAT
BLANK	CUE	LIGHT	~~SHORTS~~
BOOK	DISH	LONDON	SOLE
BROIL	ENDS	PAD	SPROUTS
BRUSSELS	FALL	PEANUT	SWITCH
BUTTER	GRILLED	POOL	THROUGH

HOW TO HUG*

BY DANNY LOZER

There's an old story about a boy who borrowed a library book titled *How to Hug,* thinking it would tell him everything he wanted to know about lovemaking. You can imagine his disappointment when he got home and discovered that the book was just one volume in a set of encyclopedias. Recently there's been a rash of such misunderstandings at our local library. A seamstress mistakenly checked out *Eye of the Needle,* and *Fahrenheit 451* was borrowed by an oven manufacturer. Additionally, each of the books listed below (A–L) was borrowed by one of the people listed at the bottom (1–12). Can you match the books to the misguided borrowers?   *Answers, page 175*

A. *All the King's Men*

B. *The Complete Book of Running*

C. *The Day of the Locust*

D. *Deliverance*

E. *For Whom the Bell Tolls*

F. *From Here to Eternity*

G. *The Happy Hooker*

H. *Of Mice and Men*

I. *Ragtime*

J. *Roots*

K. *A Study in Scarlet*

L. *Watership Down*

1. Cleaning woman _____

2. Chess master _____

3. Crop duster _____

4. Fisherman _____

5. Gardener _____

6. Interior decorator _____

7. Lab worker _____

8. Midwife _____

9. Politician _____

10. Submarine officer _____

11. Telephone operator _____

12. Undertaker _____

CHINESE MENU PUZZLE★★

BY WAYNE WILLIAMS

Doing this puzzle is a little like ordering a Chinese dinner for 15 people. Choose one word from column A, one from column B, and one from column C—15 times—to form a set of single long words composed of the three smaller words, reading left to right. For example, CAR at the top of column A can join PEN in column B and TRY in column C to create the word CARPENTRY. Every short word in the three columns should be used exactly once. *Answers, page 175*

COLUMN A	COLUMN B	COLUMN C	
~~CAR~~	AT	ABLE	CARPENTRY
COMB	CUT	AGING	
CON	EACH	ANTS	
DISC	FOR	ASTERN	
END	HE	CEMENT	
FEAT	HERB	CENT	
FLU	OR	GALE	
IMP	ORES	IONS	
NEW	OUR	PER	
NOR	~~PEN~~	RAIN	
NIGH	RAN	RATE	
PARENT	SIDE	SING	
PROSE	SPA	SIS	
REIN	THE	TIES	
WAR	TIN	~~TRY~~	

EXPAND YOUR VOCABULARY★★

BY RALPH MAUS

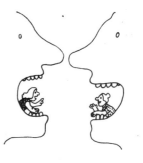

Each of the words in the middle of the lines below can be expanded into a longer word by adding letters before and after, one letter per blank. How many can you expand? The first example shows how OPENS expands to PROPENSITY. *Answers, page 175*

1. _P_ _R_ OPENS _I_ _T_ _Y_
2. __ __ FELON __
3. __ HOLES __ __ __ __
4. __ __ GAME __ __
5. __ __ MEOW __ __ __
6. __ __ __ DEVIL __ __
7. __ __ __ TURBAN __ __
8. __ NORTH __ __

9. __ __ __ PAGAN __ __
10. __ __ THROB __ __
11. __ __ __ HOPED __ __
12. __ __ __ RARE __ __
13. __ __ ORBIT __ __
14. __ THERE __ __
15. __ __ __ BLEST __
16. __ __ __ __ AURA __

PICTURE PALINDROMES ★☆

BY EMILY LIME

Each of the pictures below represents a palindromic phrase—a phrase spelled the same forward and backward. The answer to each picture can be written on the corresponding dashes, one letter per space. For example, the first picture shows RACE CAR. We'll leave the other nine for you to reflect on.   *Answers, page 175*

1. _R A C E_ _C A R_

2. _ _ _ _ _ _ _ _

3. _ _ _ _ _ _ _ _

4. _ _ _ _ _ _ _ _

5. _ _ _ _ _ _ _ _

6. _ _ _ _ _ _ _ _ _ _ , _ _ _

7. _ _ _ _ _ _ _ _ '_ _ _ _ _ _ _ _

8. _ _ _ _ _ _ _ _ _ _

9. _ _ _ _ _ _ — _ _ _ _ _ _ _

10. _ _ _ _ _ _ _ _ _ _

REBUS CARTOONS ★☆

Back in the 1930s and the late 1950s, rebus cartoon contests swept the country, with newspapers offering tens of thousands of dollars to readers who solved the difficult puzzles correctly. To the contestants, though, the lure of the money was probably secondary to the delight of solving, which is why we revived these amusing puzzles.

For each cartoon, the category of the answer and the number of letters in the answer are given. Thus, in the first one, "Athlete: 5,7" indicates that the answer is the name of an athlete whose first name has five letters and whose last name has seven letters. All the parts of each answer are found phonetically in the cartoon. These may appear in one or more of the following five ways:

1. Words or hyphenated syllables actually spoken by the cartoon characters;
2. Synonyms of words spoken by the characters;
3. Names of prominent objects in the picture;
4. Letters in the picture;
5. Words implied by the action or subject of the scene.

In the cartoon below, for example, the answer is "Jimmy Connors." It is sounded out by the picture of the GYM, the word EEK spoken by the girl, and HONORS, a synonym for "award": GYM–EEK–HONORS. Can you figure out the others?   *Answers, page 175*

FILM ACTRESS: 6, 7

SPORTS EVENT: 5, 4

ATHLETE: 5, 7

COMEDIENNE: 7, 4

FOREIGN CITY: 9

FILM CLASSIC: 7, 4

TV PERSONALITY: 5, 5

WORLD CAPITAL: 8

NEWSCASTER: 3, 6

TRANS4MATION WORD SEARCH *

BY WILL SHORTZ

Hidden in this letter grid are the 50 words listed below. They may appear in any direction—horizontally, vertically, or diagonally, forward or backward—but always in a straight line. You will not find the words, however, exactly as they are printed. Each word contains the *sound* of one or more numbers, and we have substituted these numbers for their corresponding letters in the grid. AFFORD, for example, will appear in the grid as AF4D, and ASININE will appear AS9. One word has been looped for you as a start.

Complete word list, page 175   Answers, page 176

AFFORD	FORENSICS	ONCE	TENNIS
ASININE	✔ FORMULATE	PETUNIA	THREESOME
BEHALF	FORTITUDE	PITCHFORK	TOODLE-OO
BENIGN	GATEWAY	PRENATAL	TUESDAY
CANINE	GEODESICS	PRETEND	TUTU
CARTOON	GRATEFUL	QUININE	UNWON
CELEBRATE	GUTHRIE	SEVEN-UP	UP-TO-DATE
CLASSICS	HERETOFORE	SIXPENCE	VERMILION
CONFORM	HOLE-IN-ONE	SOMEONE	WAITER
CONTENT	HUNDREDWEIGHT	STENCIL	WEIGHTY
ENFORCE	LEAN-TO	STRAIGHTFORWARD	WONDROUS
EXTENUATE	OBTUSE	STUPID	ZETA
FIVEFOLD		TENDERLOIN	

```
1 E Y P R E 1 O D L O F 5 O G 1 N U K L L 7
K C U M I 2 A E 5 J E B A F 4 D P L A Z I N
D 4 E 4 D T C Y P D S H S U G 2 T 8 2 W C 2
I N Q L M N C ½ E 2 2 V I O D C N N S V O S
S E E U E U E H L U B R 9 8 M E A 4 E 9 1 D
U O N P 2 B L M 4 N O C 8 H R E O R X I S A
O J 6 D A M R 8 S K P F G P L A 1 W 1 U G Y
R H I R S T R 8 4 W A R D C A O N X O Q A 4
D C S T 1 U C H Y I 8 N U 8 O G I A U W 2 E
1 O D E R L O I N F F 1 Z O W T E V 8 E P N
E N 8 N A 7 D 2 U 2 O L O Z R O L G R M W 6
W 1 H S Q U E L T N R O 9 6 E D O E G O 8 Z
7 O 6 D I P 2 S I U O A A P 8 1 H 1 R S O E
4 T I 2 D E M S 9 E B N C S W L 5 G U 3 H T
```

FOLLOW THE CLUES ★★

BY JULES ROTH

The missing letters in each word below form a synonym for the word that follows. The object of the puzzle is to follow the trail of clues down the first column, and back up the second, returning to the point at which you started.

For example, the first word (at the top of the puzzle) should be INTELLIGENCE. The letters that go in the empty boxes—TELL—are a synonym of the next answer, EXPLAIN.

Its missing letters—PLAIN—spell a synonym of the next answer, and so on. The missing letters in the last answer (a synonym of your native INTELLIGENCE) complete the circuit.

If you get stuck, jump ahead and try working backward. For example, the fifth answer, PET _ _ _ _ UM, is a synonym of the missing letters in the previous word. A slippery one, at that.

Answers, page 175

SKELETON CRISSCROSS★★

BY WILL SHORTZ

This skeleton is two puzzles in one—a word game and a crisscross puzzle. In the word game, which you solve first, pairs of words are given: One of them (you determine which) has a synonym that rhymes with the other. The answers are grouped by length. For example, the three-letter answer to the first pair is HIT. When you have solved all the clues you are ready to begin the crisscross. Fit the answer words into their proper spaces in the skeleton grid to complete an interlocking pattern of words.

Complete word list, page 175   Answers, page 176

3-LETTER WORDS

Strike, Mitt ___ *HIT*

Peon, Age ___

Couple, You ___

Point, Blot ___

4-LETTER WORDS

Happy, Sad ___

Waive, Hoard ___

Chicken, Prowl ___

Expert, His ___

Best, Leisure ___

Summit, Seek ___

Orient, Leased ___

Yearn, Whirl ___

Boat, Carry ___

Crave, Bead ___

Stockings, Goes ___

Virgo, Therefore ___

Kelp, Aid ___

Stop, Go ___

5-LETTER WORDS

Tang, Vice ___

While, Grin ___

Districted, Moaned ___

Dresses, Towns ___

6-LETTER WORDS

Estimate, Beckon ___

Girl, Laden ___

Crystal, Gun ___

Quarrels, Ethics ___

Bar, Cavern ___

Station, Land ___

Usual, Formal ___

Puzzle, Drink ___

7-LETTER WORDS

People, Spire ___

Here, Pheasant ___

8-LETTER WORDS

Whiten, Scare ___

Stalemate, Wedlock ___

SOLITAIRE HANGMAN ★☆

BY R. WAYNE SCHMITTBERGER

As in the two-player version of Hangman, the object of this solitaire challenge is to guess the identity of a word before being "hanged."

To begin, choose any letter of the alphabet you think might be in word I. Suppose you pick E. Go to the Letter Chart on the right and find the number listed in row E of column I (because you are working on word I). The number is 19; you now look in box 19 in the Position Chart below and find the number 5. This means the letter E occurs in the fifth position (and nowhere else) in word I. If a letter occurs more than once in a word, the Position Chart will show all its locations.

If you find from the Position Chart that a letter appears in position 0, then that letter does not appear in the word. As a penalty for an incorrect guess, you must draw part of a stick figure below the scaffold beside the word blanks. On your first incorrect guess, draw the head; on the second, the body; and on the next four, the arms and legs. If you complete the figure before identifying the word, you are "hanged."

Answers, page 176

POSITION CHART

1	2	3	4	5	6	7	8	9	10	11	12	13	14
6,8	3	5	3,6	0	7	3	5,6	4	2,4	0	3,4	1	0
15	**16**	**17**	**18**	**19**	**20**	**21**	**22**	**23**	**24**	**25**	**26**	**27**	**28**
8	2	0	1	5	6,7	0	2,3,6	6	0	2	0	5	0
29	**30**	**31**	**32**	**33**	**34**	**35**	**36**	**37**	**38**	**39**	**40**	**41**	**42**
2	3,7	5	0	7	0	1	2	0	1	0	2	3	0
43	**44**	**45**	**46**	**47**	**48**	**49**	**50**	**51**	**52**	**53**	**54**	**55**	
7	1	6	0	1,5,7	4	0	8	5	0	7	6	6	
56	**57**	**58**	**59**	**60**	**61**	**62**	**63**	**64**	**65**	**66**	**67**	**68**	
2,3,7	0	1	3	0	1	2,7	0	8	6	0	7	0	
69	**70**	**71**	**72**	**73**	**74**	**75**	**76**	**77**	**78**	**79**	**80**	**81**	
2	5	0	4,7	4	0	6	5,8	0	6	4	0	3	

LETTER CHART

	I	II	III	IV	V	VI	VII	VIII	IX	X
A	66	14	49	63	79	46	70	39	67	5
B	52	39	11	28	68	16	5	46	24	14
C	28	74	65	34	52	11	18	26	13	71
D	46	3	37	74	28	63	42	66	39	11
E	19	30	52	80	71	43	39	14	57	25
F	26	46	39	57	21	77	17	52	32	68
G	60	17	68	11	46	39	57	3	63	37
H	49	63	36	21	2	17	40	75	34	61
I	11	24	51	10	74	54	7	77	49	41
J	24	57	46	37	17	14	74	42	68	52
K	63	37	71	42	32	68	46	34	60	74
L	74	32	14	21	57	41	78	37	50	3
M	44	26	66	47	14	34	49	28	12	64
N	5	42	77	59	36	26	63	74	45	34
O	57	13	34	71	17	35	32	41	69	20
P	14	66	18	52	8	74	37	5	26	57
Q	32	5	60	37	80	31	14	71	77	24
R	78	48	24	66	42	60	53	29	17	48
S	41	28	72	32	63	52	77	21	14	66
T	9	77	17	60	26	71	52	6	37	49
U	34	55	63	23	58	45	68	48	27	80
V	17	69	21	26	60	42	73	32	52	39
W	39	52	42	5	37	66	34	38	21	26
X	71	11	26	77	5	49	21	57	74	32
Y	62	34	81	14	33	57	15	60	71	77
Z	68	21	71	49	66	28	80	24	46	63

I. ___ ___ ___ ___ *E* ___ ___
   1 2 3 4 5 6 7

II. ___ ___ ___ ___ ___ ___ ___
   1 2 3 4 5 6 7

III. ___ ___ ___ ___ ___ ___ ___
   1 2 3 4 5 6 7

IV. ___ ___ ___ ___ ___ ___ ___
   1 2 3 4 5 6 7

V. ___ ___ ___ ___ ___ ___ ___
   1 2 3 4 5 6 7

VI. ___ ___ ___ ___ ___ ___ ___
   1 2 3 4 5 6 7

VII. ___ ___ ___ ___ ___ ___ ___ ___
   1 2 3 4 5 6 7 8

VIII. ___ ___ ___ ___ ___ ___ ___
   1 2 3 4 5 6 7

IX. ___ ___ ___ ___ ___ ___ ___ ___
   1 2 3 4 5 6 7 8

X. ___ ___ ___ ___ ___ ___ ___ ___
   1 2 3 4 5 6 7 8

CRYPTOQUIPS ★☆

The jester is playing with his baubles, preparing tonight's show for the royal couple. To find out what everyone's saying, solve these simple substitution ciphers. Letter substitutions remain constant throughout each quote (if L represents E in one word, it represents E in every word), but change from one quote to the next.

Hints: One-letter words are almost always A or I; frequent two-letter words are IT, IS, IN, and TO. An asterisk (*) indicates a proper noun. If you've never tried puzzles like these before, the clues at the bottom of the page will be helpful. No fooling.   *Answers, page 176*

1.   O FPM'Y ESMY YP SVJORBR OQQPTYSZOYU YJTPIHJ QU EPTL. O ESMY YP SVJORBR OY YJTPIHJ MPY FUOMH.

2.   F QFP CUUXIGME YGVL IXZSGU CW CVLMW GQICWVFPV ZXJGPMJJ UFPPCV, FPE PMME PCV, FVVMPE VC JIMSSGPH.

3.   VDJ BADO VDJ'ZG SGFUPGW NHWWEG FRG OPGA VDJS OGHRPYEHCYHAR UDAKHKYK NGSGEV DC KYFAWHAR JQ.

BY NORMA GLEASON

4. AJK NTTV
OTAJ AJQYH JK QZ
RQZK, LSA AJK RQZK GMY
HYTRZ JQGZKVN AT
LK M NTTV.

5. O'D Q
DQKCTSGXL
IGXLTATTHTK. TCTKN
ZODT O STQCT Q
DQF, O ATTH
IOL IGXLT.

6. OSG KGQO
UAYHQ LWG YTO AY
DTNGWYUGYO. AB LYC
FGWG, KIQAYGQQ
FTIMH SAWG
OSGU LFLC.

7. KPDOB DRO
PSQRD SC YFOB
KXN *PBKJSOB NYX'D
KXCHOB DRO LOVV, S'W QYXXK
TEWZ YFOB DRO BYZOC KXN
S'W QYXXK HREZ
*RYHKBN *MYCOVV.

BULL'S-EYE 20 QUESTIONS ★★

BY WILL SHORTZ

Here's a test of your word marksmanship. The answer to each of the 20 questions in the puzzle is one of the 25 words in the bull's-eye target. As you hit each answer, you may cross it off, since no word in the target is used more than once. When all the questions have been answered, the five unused words can be rearranged to form a fashionable quotation.   *Answers, page 176*

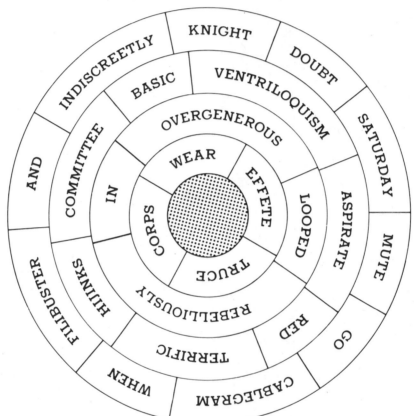

WHICH WORD...

1. contains all the letters of the word BULL'S-EYE?
2. would become opposite in meaning if you changed the last three letters to BLE?
3. contains all the letters of the alphabet from L to V except one?
4. would have the same pattern as DOODAD in a cryptogram?
5. becomes a new word if you delete every A in it?
6. contains a word meaning "border" inside another word meaning "burdensome"?
7. would sound like a medical facility if you pronounced the first two letters last?
8. would spell a new word no matter what other vowel you substituted for its second letter?
9. is a present-tense verb that has no letters in common with its past tense form?
10. would have three dotted letters if written in script?
11. contains a word, formed by every second letter, meaning "elegant detail"?
12. would become a word meaning "deliberate" if you removed its fourth letter and read the rest backward?
13. completes this pun: "During rush hour it's often necessary to _____ capacity"?
14. can be broken into three common words of equal length?
15. is an anagram of a common breed of dog?
16. has three pairs of double letters?
17. ends in two silent letters?
18. would sound like a word meaning "gospel" if pronounced with a lisp?
19. would spell new words if you successively removed its first, first two, first three, first four, and first five letters?
20. has exactly one letter in common with each of the other five remaining words?

WORD RUMMY ★★★

BY JULES ROTH

Can you score 500 or more points in Word Rummy hands from the card spread at right?

Answers, page 176

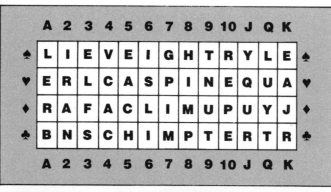

♠ HOW TO PLAY

Find as many common seven-letter words as you can whose cards form Word Rummy hands. A Word Rummy hand is a seven-letter word whose cards make up one *set* (three or four cards of a kind, like 7 7 7 or K K K K) and one *sequence* (three or four cards of the same suit in numerical order, such as ♠ A 2 3 or ♣ 9 10 J Q). Either the *set* or the *sequence* may come first. The letters of a *set* may be used in any order; the letters of a *sequence* must be used in the left-to-right order given in the grid. The same card cannot be used twice in one hand. Sets and sequences may be used over and over in different words to form other words. Proper names and foreign words are not allowed, but plurals are fine.

♥ SCORING

Each card in a Word Rummy hand scores its face value. A 6 scores 6 points, for example. Aces are low and count 1 point each. Jacks, queens, and kings count 10 points each.

♦ EXAMPLE

The word BELIEVE forms a Word Rummy hand. The ♣A ♡A ♠A are a set with the letters B-E-L; ♠ 2 3 4 5 are a sequence with the letters I-E-V-E. The cards used have values 1 1 1 2 3 4 5, for a total of 17 points.

CARDS & WORDS							POINTS
B	E	L	I	E	V	E	
A	A	A	2	3	4	5	17

CARDS & WORDS	POINTS

♣ RATINGS

Knock: 350 points (good game)
Gin: 500 points (winning game)
Gin-off: 704 points (our best score)

TOTAL SCORE

EQUATION ANALYSIS TESTS ★☆

When GAMES published the first Equation Analysis Test in 1981 (below, left), it sparked lots of response—not only did readers send us their own examples (see ''In the Last Analysis,'' at right), they sent us *our* own examples. It seems the original puzzle was reproduced and reprinted, passed around at parties, broadcast on the radio, even passed out at a Maryland shopping mall by an enterprising character who sold the answers for $1. Several readers, who'd missed the puzzle in GAMES, thought we'd be interested in the craze we had in fact started.

These equations don't test your IQ, and certainly not your math ability, but they will give your creativity a workout. It may be helpful to know that few people solve more than half a set at a sitting, but that many find they can finish them all over a few days.

Each equation contains the initials of words that will make it correct. To solve, just supply the missing words. For example, *26 = L. of the A.* would be *26 = Letters of the Alphabet*.

Answers, page 176

THE ORIGINAL TEST
BY WILL SHORTZ

a. 26 = L. of the A. *LETTERS OF THE ALPHABET*

b. 7 = W. of the A.W. _____

c. 1,001 = A.N. _____

d. 12 = S. of the Z. _____

e. 54 = C. in a D. (with the J.) _____

f. 9 = P. in the S.S. _____

g. 88 = P.K. _____

h. 13 = S. on the A.F. _____

i. 32 = D.F. at which W.F. _____

j. 18 = H. on a G.C. _____

k. 90 = D. in a R.A. _____

l. 200 = D. for P.G. in M. _____

m. 8 = S. on a S.S. _____

n. 3 = B.M. (S.H.T.R.!) _____

o. 4 = Q. in a G. _____

p. 24 = H. in a D. _____

q. 1 = W. on a U. _____

r. 5 = D. in a Z.C. _____

s. 57 = H.V. _____

t. 11 = P. on a F.T. _____

u. 1,000 = W. that a P. is W. _____

v. 29 = D. in F. in a L.Y. _____

w. 64 = S. in a C. _____

x. 40 = D. and N. of the G.F. _____

IN THE LAST ANALYSIS
BY GAMES READERS

a. 20 = Q. (A., V., or M.) _____

b. 10 = L.I. _____

c. 7 = Y. of B.L. for B. a M. _____

d. 3 = P. into which A.G. was D. _____

e. 2,000 = P. in a T. _____

f. 4 = S. on a V. _____

g. 76 = T. that L. the B.P. _____

h. 2 = G. of V. _____

i. 3 = L.K. that L.T.M. _____

j. 18½ = M.E. from the W.T. _____

k. 1 = R.A. in E.B. _____

l. 20 = C. in a P. _____

m. 6 = P. on a P.T. _____

n. 66 = B. of the B. (in the K.J.V.) _____

o. 9 = J. of the S.C. _____

p. 10 = D. in a T.N. (including the A.C.) _____

q. 7 = D. with S.W. _____

r. 30 = S. over T. _____

s. 8 = D. a W. (in the B.S.) _____

t. 15 = M. on a D.M.C. _____

u. 4 + 20 = B.B. in a P. _____

v. 9 = S. in T.-T.-T. _____

w. 3 = S.Y.O. at the O.B.G. _____

x. 5 = T. on a C. (including the S. in the T.) _____

A COLORFUL JOURNEY THROUGH THE PAGES OF GAMES

★ ★ ★

STAR STRUCK

BY WAYNE McLOUGHLIN

A how-many-sided star?

Answer, page 177

A SHORT HISTORY OF AMERICA

SEQUENCE PUZZLE BY R. CRUMB

★☆

R. Crumb is best known as the underground cartoonist who brought us Fritz the Cat, Mr. Natural, and *Zap Comix* in the 1960s. But he's decidedly gone aboveground with these 11 views of America's changing scenery. Can you place them in sad-but-true sequence, from bucolic grassland to urban wasteland? Be careful where you're standing; there's a turnpike due in about a hundred years.

Answer, page 177

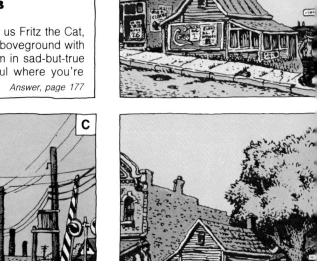

WELCOME TO TRUMP'S GENERAL STORE

Created by Joan Steiner

WHERE THINGS ARE NEVER WHAT THEY SEEM. ★☆

Can you find a comb-back chair, an edible lamp, and some 150 other common objects that deceive the eye?

Answers, page 177

Wall Paper Paint Glass

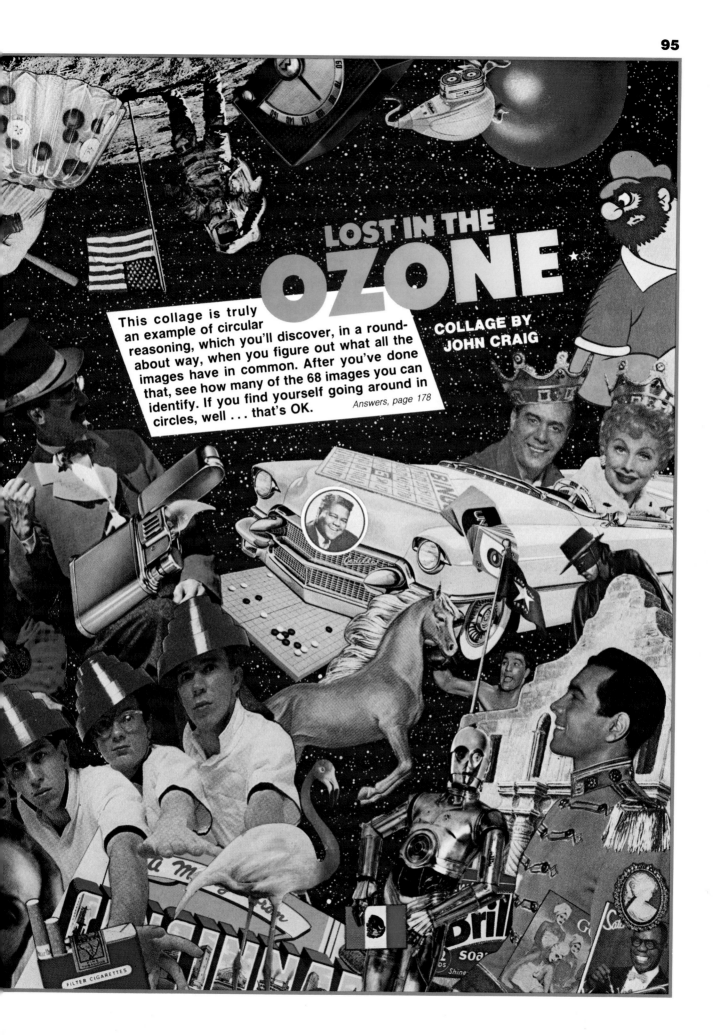

LOST IN THE OZONE

COLLAGE BY JOHN CRAIG

This collage is truly an example of circular reasoning, which you'll discover, in a round-about way, when you figure out what all the images have in common. After you've done that, see how many of the 68 images you can identify. If you find yourself going around in circles, well . . . that's OK.

Answers, page 178

EYEBALL BENDERS
IN ORBIT

★☆

What part of the United States do you see in each photo?

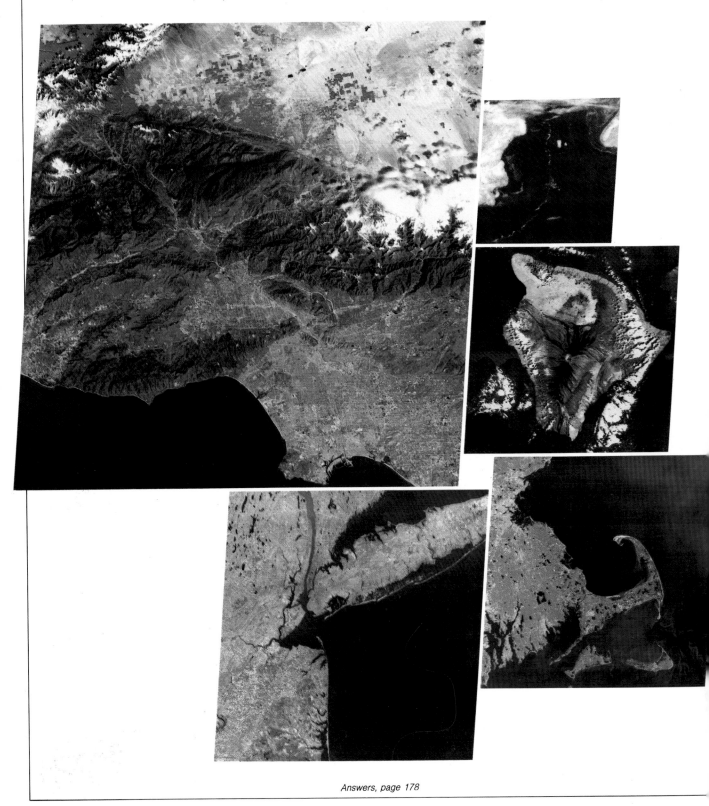

Answers, page 178

5

THE FAMOUS, THE INFAMOUS, AND OTHER TRIVIA

★★

HOLLYWOOD BAD GUYS

BY BILLY MERNIT

Can you name the actor behind each of these disguises, as well as the movie in which each character appeared?

Answers, page 180

WHOSE ZOO IN ADVERTISING*

Unless you're just returning from a long safari in Kenya, most of these advertising animals will look familiar to you. But can you name the company or product that each one represents? *Answers, page 180*

11

12

13

14

15

16

17

18

19

20

21

THE SOUND OF MUSIC ★☆

Everyone's brain is littered with bits and pieces of lyrics. "Amber waves of grain" nestles beside "ticket to ride." "Don't cry for me, Argentina" is squashing "mairzy doats" (and probably a good thing, too).

Here's a quiz that asks you to sort through your musical storage bin. It covers an eclectic mix of pop songs and performers from the past four decades. Can you sing along?

Answers, page 181

LADIES AID

Help! We have 15 damsels in distress. They're stranded in Tin Pan Alley and can't find their way back to the hit songs in which they belong. Can you help? And for extra credit, who made each song famous?

1. "Second Hand _____"
2. "_____ Eyes"
3. "_____ on My Mind"
4. "Long Tall _____"
5. "_____ May"
6. "Runaround _____"
7. "Honeysuckle _____"
8. "Good Golly Miss _____"
9. "_____ Rigby"
10. "Proud _____"
11. "_____'s Restaurant"
12. "_____ Tuesday"
13. "_____'s Turn to Cry"
14. "Help Me, _____"
15. "Wake Up Little _____"

HOORAY FOR HOLLYWOOD

Sometimes the music of a movie is as memorable as the movie itself. Can you name the films that featured these songs?

1. "Everybody's Talkin'"
2. "Mrs. Robinson"
3. "Duelling Banjos"
4. "Raindrops Keep Fallin' on My Head"
5. "Evergreen"
6. "Stayin' Alive"
7. "Nobody Does It Better"
8. "I'm Easy"
9. "As Time Goes By"
10. "Eye of the Tiger"

WHERE OR WHEN?

You know that "76 trombones led the big parade," but how many whats were "close at hand?" If you answered "110 cornets," you're ready to try this who-what-when-where-why-and-how lyric quiz.

1. "When you're alone and life is making you lonely," where can you go?
2. "In Penny Lane there is a barber with a photograph . . . ." Name two other inhabitants of Penny Lane.
3. "Tie me kangaroo down, sport." What other pets are you asked to mind in this song from Down Under?
4. "I'll be down to get you in a taxi, honey." What time should you be ready, and where are we going?
5. There must be "50 ways to leave your lover." Name three of them.
6. "You're the cream in my coffee." What else are you?
7. "When this old world starts getting me down," where do I go?
8. "You're the top, you're the Colosseum . . . ." Name three other superlatives that describe you.
9. "Someone's in the kitchen with Dinah"—doing what?

WHERE CREDIT IS DUE

1. Who wrote the words to the theme from *Exodus*?
2. Who sings backup for Carly Simon on "You're So Vain"?
3. Who sings backup for James Taylor on "You've Got a Friend"?
4. Aretha Franklin made the song famous, but who wrote—and later recorded her own version of—"A Natural Woman"?
5. A then-unknown singer sang on The Crystals' classic "Da Doo Ron Ron." Who was she?

SPLICED TAPES

In the mixing room of our recording studio, lyrics from two different songs somehow got spliced together as one. Can you name the song to which each fragment belongs?

1. "I give to you and you give to me/Warm face, warm hands, warm feet."

2. "Please allow me to introduce myself/I'm as helpless as a kitten up a tree."

3. "The big baboon by the light of the moon/May not be the man some girls think of as handsome."

4. "I met my old lover on the street last night/Because a good man nowadays is hard to find."

5. "JoJo was a man who thought he was a loner/Meaner than a junkyard dog."

6. "Each night before you go to bed, my baby/Put it in the pantry with your cupcakes."

7. "I have often walked/Right out of my hair."

8. "When will they ever learn?/Well, maybe next year."

9. "I went out for a ride and I never went back/What a long, strange trip it's been."

THE PARTY'S __ __ __ __

In every relationship, there are times of harmony and times of dischord, and then there are situations—like the conversation below—when there's just something missing between two people. Using your lyric sensibilities, can you fill in the gaps in this dialogue?

"Well, hello (**1**) __ __ __ __ __! Why sit outside in this stormy (**2**) __ __ __ __ __ __ __ __? (**3**) __ __ __ __ __ __ __ __ __ keep falling on my head. At least you should button up your (**4**) __ __ __ __ __ __ __ __. Baby, it's (**5**) __ __ __ outside."

"I really hadn't noticed. I feel like we're having a heat (**6**) __ __ __ __. I'm walking on the (**7**) __ __ __ __ __ side of the street; everything's coming up (**8**) __ __ __ __ __.
(**9**) __ __ __ __ __ __ __, (**10**) __ __ __ __ __ __ __ won't be just any night. I'm writing an ode to (**11**) __ __ __ __ __
(**12**) __ __ __. You know, happiness *is* a thing called (**13**) __ __ __."

"But what about me? You go to my (**14**) __ __ __ __. I want to hold your (**15**) __ __ __ __. I long to dance with you (**16**) __ __ __ __ __ to (**17**) __ __ __ __ __. I've got you under my (**18**) __ __ __ __."

"Oh, for heaven's sake. Hang down your head (**19**) __ __ __ (**20**) __ __ __ __ __ __ __. Just because we spent a lovely (**21**) __ __ __ __ __ in Paris and (**22**) __ __ __ __ __ __ in New York doesn't mean I'm yours till the end of (**23**) __ __ __ __. Won't you please go home, (**24**) __ __ __ __ __ Bailey; besides, your (**25**) __ __ __ __ __ too big."

"Bill? My name's Tom. But good night (**26**) __ __ __ __ __, and remember, I'll always love you come (**27**) __ __ __ __ or come (**28**) __ __ __ __ __."

"Irene? My name's Dolly."

FAMOUS LAST WORDS

We've excerpted the last word from each line in the first stanza of six well-known songs. Can you supply the titles?

1. down
    down
    down
    down
    lady

2. money
    show
    ready
    go!

3. house
    Mars
    planets
    stars

4. morning
    chime
    stopper
    whopper
    time

5. palaces
    roam
    humble
    home

6. ocean
    sea
    ocean
    me

I GOT RHYTHM

The music goes round and round, as the song says. Can you complete these song titles with musical terms?

1. "The Birth of the _____"
2. "Mr. _____ Man"
3. "_____ _____ Bugle Boy"
4. "_____ on the Run"
5. "Jailhouse _____"
6. "Alexander's _____ Band"
7. "It's Only _____"
8. "The _____ Goes On"
9. "American _____"
10. "Boogie On _____ Woman"

ON BROADWAY ★☆

These 13 renowned Broadway shows
Have posters that everyone knows.
Can you tell them apart
From the clues in the art
And disclose with which show each one goes?

Answers, page 180

BY M. GILL

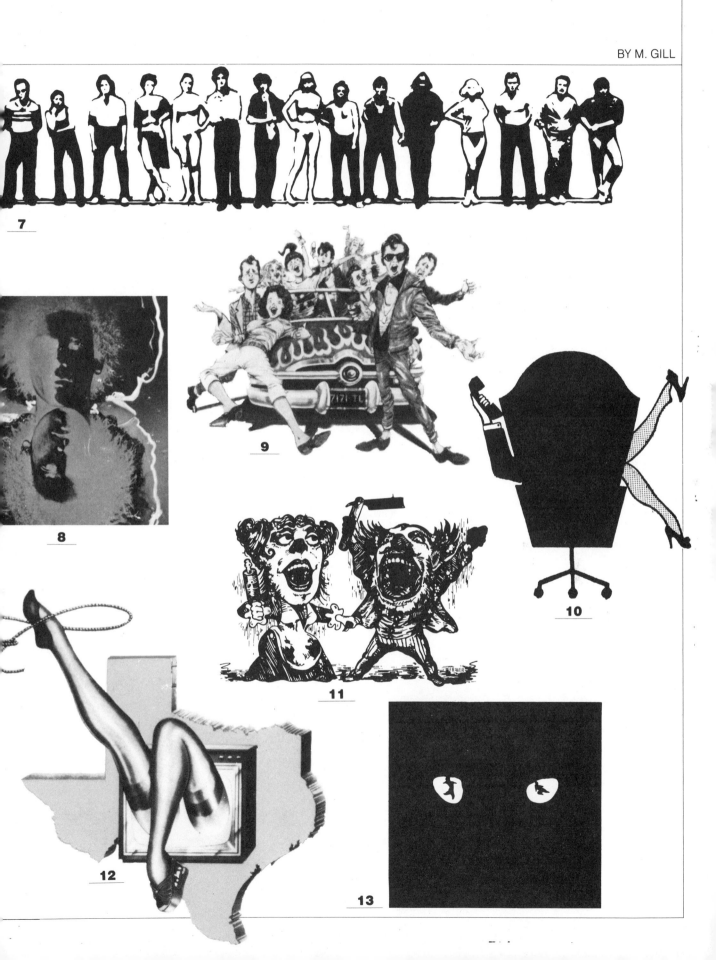

7

8

9

10

11

12

13

PENCIL IN-TERTAINMENT

MOVIE SHORTS ★☆
BY DOUG AND JANIS HELLER

A roster of big movies is scheduled to play at a small theater—but the titles are too long to fit on the marquee. The theater manager solved the problem by instructing the sign boy to leave out all the vowels—every A, E, I, O, U, and Y—and to run all the consonants together, eliminating spaces between words. Following the manager's rules, the boy posted *Gone With the Wind* as GNWTHTHWND.

Below are the theater marquees as they will appear during the next 20 weeks. Can you tell what's playing?

Answers, page 180

1. CSBLNC
2. RTHQK
3. CBRT
4. THPPNDNNGHT
5. NMLHS
6. NNHLL
7. THDDCPL
8. LSTTNGNPRS
9. SPRMN
10. LWRNCFRB
11. NTRS
12. NTRRS
13. DLMFRMRDR
14. LLBTV
15. BNNNDCLD
16. DPTHRT
17. JWS
18. RPRT
19. DNR
20. DRN
21. LF
22. BDHT

THE IDIOT BOX ★★
BY N. M. MEYER

Each row and column in this 6 x 6 grid contains the six-letter name of a well-known TV show, past or present. The names read in order from left to right and top to bottom, one letter per square. Each letter is used only once, so cross off the letters as you find the names. When you're done, the 36 uncanceled letters—reading in order from left to right—will spell out a quote related to television.

Answers, page 180

	1	2	3	4	5	6
1	K TQ	B UE	M NL	E LG	T VF	I FU
2	B US	I EA	T OA	A MN	I AO	N ST
3	I LH	A NI	N RK	E SR	Y PC	H OR
4	N FE	W AS	M IN	N IS	G PL	Y OG
5	U CD	O MA	F LI	L OI	E AR	T OS
6	C HY	E NA	X MN	N EI	N OR	P DN

ON A FIRST-NAME BASIS ★☆
BY DOUG AND JANIS HELLER

Each group of first names below belongs to four famous people with something in common. You needn't give all four last names; just find the common bond. For example, the names Andrew, Michael, Kate, and Jesse all belong to famous Jacksons.

Answers, page 180

1. Johnny, Hank, Kenny, Dolly
2. Arthur, John, Jimmy, Virginia
3. Alfred, Mel, Otto, Roman
4. Charles, Walt, Garry, Chic
5. Alan, Loretta, Jamie, Mike
6. Alan, John, Frank, Neil
7. Bob, Bill, Gene, Richard
8. Roger, Terry, Joe, Fran
9. Peggy, Linda, Dorothy, Scott
10. Bobby, Larry, José, Boris

STAR CROSSED ★☆

To solve this case of split personalities, you'll need to consult Rona Barrett, not Sigmund Freud. During Oscar frenzy one year, we created this identity crisis by cutting up and splicing together the faces of eight former Oscar winners. Can you guess which three stars make up each composite face? *Name list, page 180 Answers, page 182*

HERE'S JOHNNY ! ★☆

BY BARRY SIMON AND CURTIS SLEPIAN

Wow. Thank you for the applause. But will you still respect us in the morning? Yes, this is *The Tonight Show* Quiz. These pages contain the sum total of trivia about America's perennial night-light . . . here's everything you'd ever want to know about Johnny Carson and *The Tonight Show.* How much do you know?   *Answers, page 181*

MONOLOGUE

Before we start Johnny's monologue, we want to apologize for the NBC censors. They went a little haywire, so you'll have to fill in the blanks.

"It's great to be back here in beautiful (**1**) _____. I want to thank (**2**) _____ for filling in for me last week. We used to have so many guest hosts that our executive producer, (**3**) _____, would go out on Santa Monica Boulevard interviewing winos. Filling in for Doc tonight is Mr. Personality himself, (**4**) _____. Well, what's going on? I went today for my annual physical to the NBC doctor, (**5**) _____. I tell you, when you leave his office you feel healthy and happy, but your wallet suffers from anorexia.

"If you folks want to eat, I don't recommend the NBC (**6**) _____. It's not exactly clean. A roach motel over there will not do the job. They use a roach high-rise.

"The other day I took my car over to the service station. You know my attendant, Mr. (**7**) _____. He has no manners. I said check my tires for air. He stuck a nail in and said, 'Yeah, you have air in there.'

"We have a good show for you tonight, including some of our favorite guests. We have a couple of our resident animal experts: from *Wild Kingdom,* (**8**) _____, and from the San Diego Zoo, the lovely (**9**) _____. Also, the man whose wife is so ugly that when you look up the word *ugly* in the dictionary, you see her picture . . . yes, he's the man who gets no respect, (**10**) _____. And just back from entertaining our troops in New York City, (**11**) _____. We've also got a man who's traveled billions and billions of light-years to be here, (**12**) _____. And we'll be out in the audience to play (**13**) _____. So stay where you are and we'll be right back."

*Now watch this great segue (they don't call Johnny the Prince of (**14**) _____ for nothing) . . .*

What does Johnny do just after the monologue?
a. Imitates Porky Pig saying, "That's all, folks!"
b. Throws an imaginary discus
c. Blows kisses to the crowd
d. Swings an imaginary golf club

THE KING OF COMEDY

1. What show did Johnny host before *The Tonight Show?*
a. *The Today Show*
b. *Who Do You Trust?*
c. *The Johnny Carson Hour*
d. *Hollywood Palace*

2. What is Johnny's favorite Burbank restaurant?
a. Pick-A-Pig
b. Chasen's
c. Vinnie Abruzzi's Little Touch of Newark
d. Montezuma's House of Pancakes

3. What is special about Johnny's pencils?
a. They have erasers on both ends.
b. He throws them at boring guests.
c. They're edible.
d. They have lead at both ends.

4. Which two of the following hosted *The Tonight Show* B.C. ("Before Carson")?
a. Steve Allen
b. Joey Bishop
c. Regis Philbin
d. Jack Paar
e. Merv Griffin
f. Dave Garroway

5. According to Johnny, where did he spend his youth?
a. On the plains of Nebraska
b. In the casinos of Las Vegas
c. In the Catskills
d. In the San Fernando Valley

6. Johnny admits to suffering from nictophobia. What is this ailment?
a. The fear of bumping one's forehead into a boom mike
b. The fear of meeting Nick the Greek in a dark alley
c. The fear of the applause sign breaking down during the show
d. The fear of walking backward into a cold doorknob

7. On the average, how many people watch *The Tonight Show* nightly?
a. 5 million
b. 15.5 million
c. 25.5 million
d. 40 million

8. Which of the following is *not* one of Johnny's on-air mannerisms?
a. Shaking his pencil
b. Rubbing his nose
c. Touching his cuff link
d. Clipping his fingernails

TIME FLIES

Johnny's tenure on *The Tonight Show* has been long. (How long has it been, anyway?) Through the years he's seen some changes—including wives, salary, and hair color. Can you put the four photos below in the correct chronological order?

SECOND BANANAS

1. What is Doc Severinsen's real first name, and what instrument does he play?
   a. Sven/harmonica   c. Carl/trumpet
   b. Buddy/piano   d. Vladimir/violin
2. Which one of the following does Ed wear to bed?
   a. Socks with the toes cut off   c. Skivvies
   b. A clip-on bow tie   d. A Marine hat
3. Ed and Johnny have a running debate over the relative intelligence of what two animals?
   a. A bear and a dog   c. A cow and a bull
   b. A pig and a horse   d. A llama and a wildebeest
4. With which two products is Ed McMahon associated?
   a. Wheaties and Kool-Aid
   b. Ex-Lax and Dexatrim
   c. Black & Decker and Jockey shorts
   d. Alpo and Budweiser

JOHNNY'S JESTS

Match the joke to the jokee:
1. He's one of the few people who can walk into a forest and be the oldest living thing there.
2. He got his start as a heckler at the Special Olympics.
3. He could be a good president—he's had a lot of practice going around in circles.
4. He fell off a horse again this week. One more time and he breaks Gerald Ford's record.
5. His library and museum should be a fascinating place to visit. There's no charge—you just break in.
6. The paramedics had to apply jumper cables to his liver.
7. He's so vicious that Bing Crosby once hired him as a baby-sitter.
8. He should donate his golf clubs to the Pentagon—Reagan needs all the lethal weapons he can get.
   a. Ed McMahon
   b. Prince Charles
   c. Billy Martin
   d. Richard Nixon
   e. Ronald Reagan
   f. Gerald Ford
   g. Don Rickles
   h. John Glenn

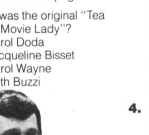

IN CHARACTER

1. Can you identify the five familiar Carson characters pictured on this page?

2. Who was the original "Tea Time Movie Lady"?
   a. Carol Doda
   b. Jacqueline Bisset
   c. Carol Wayne
   d. Ruth Buzzi

3. According to Art Fern, what should you do on the L.A. freeway at the Slauson cutoff?
   a. Turn left for Oxnard
   b. Stop at the nearest Denny's
   c. Avoid the fork in the road
   d. Cut off your slauson

4. Carnac the Magnificent, the all-knowing, all-seeing, all-omniscient famous seer, sage, soothsayer, and former massage parlor trainee, can divine the answers without seeing the questions. Can you guess the setups to these Carnac punchlines?
   a. "Jaws 3-D"
   b. "St. Elsewhere"
   c. "The pages are numbered."

We hold in our hand the last question. (If you applauded, may a yak in heat become your sister's French tutor.)

5. Where are Carnac the Magnificent's questions kept?
   a. In a safe deposit vault under the careful guard of Price Waterhouse
   b. Sealed in a pickle jar in the glove compartment of Ed McMahon's dashboard
   c. In the tamper-proof desk of Bombastic Bushkin, Johnny's lawyer, guarded by the A-Team
   d. Hermetically sealed in a mayonnaise jar on Funk & Wagnalls' porch since noon

THE COMIC STRIP STRIP*

Good grief! Our favorite comic strip characters all took their costumes to the dry cleaner, but when they went to pick them up, no one had a claim check. Can you help the characters (1–14) find their outfits (A–N) in time for the Sunday paper? And can you name each character and his or her strip?

Answers, page 182

BY VANESSA DE LISTY

HAIR APPARENT ★☆

BY RUTH PODEMS

Pictured below are the distinctive heads of hair (including, in some instances, beards, mustaches, and eyebrows) of 11 famous individuals, past and present. Can you provide the keys to identify these locks?

Answers, page 180

NUMBER PLEASE!★★

BY JOHN B. KLEIN

Get ready for a double play. First you'll need to determine the numbers for each of the 25 "trivial" calculations labeled A through Y. Then you'll need to perform each calculation and enter the answer in the correspondingly lettered box in the grid. (Each number from 1 to 25 will be used once.) When all the boxes are correctly filled in, every row, column, and corner-to-corner diagonal will total the same key number. Once you've determined what that number is, you'll have a clue to filling in the other boxes—in much the same way that interlocking words provide clues in solving crossword puzzles.   *Answers, page 182*

A	B	C	D	E
F	G	H	I	J
K	L	M	N	O
P	Q	R	S	T
U	V	W	X	Y

CLUES

A. Baseball team + Steps in a major musical scale

B. Apostles × Gentlemen of Verona

C. Dave Clark _____ – Horsemen of the Apocalypse

D. Octopus's arms + Generals in a squad

E. Baker's dozen + Faces of Janus

F. Jack Benny's "age" – Tennessee Ernie's "_____ Tons"

G. Legs of a bovine + Eyes of a Cyclops

H. Ounces in an avoirdupois pound – The Muses

I. Snow White's dwarfs + "The _____ seas"

J. Television "Route" – Golden anniversary

K. Degrees in a circle ÷ Degrees in a right angle

L. Dozen and a half – Signs of the zodiac

M. Amendments in the Bill of Rights + Triangle's sides

N. Octogenarian ÷ Pecks in a bushel

O. Adult human's teeth – One decade

P. The senses + The Great Lakes

Q. Labors of Hercules + Attack hour in war

R. Original colonies + Sides of a hexagon

S. Lowest "natural" in craps × The Fates

T Known planets ÷ Feet in a yard

U. "Dinner at _____" + The R's

V. Wilson's points + Bits in a half dollar

W. Pentagon's sides × The Little Peppers

X. Booth Tarkington book – Men on a dead man's chest

Y. The Commandments – Dots in a semicolon

CAN YOU ANSWER THIS? ★☆

BY HENRY HOOK

Despite the currently inflated supply of trivia questions, these 30 are guaranteed to significantly increase your knowledge of the extraordinary, the arcane, and the just plain useless.

Answers, page 182

1. In 1978, what book achieved the dubious distinction of being most frequently stolen from public libraries in England?

2. Whose teeth number more—the average human's or the average mosquito's?

3. The largest arena of its kind is in Tokyo, and accommodates 504 games simultaneously. What is played there?

4. Where will you find the letters C, D, E, F, L, O, P, T, and Z, and no others?

5. What fruit has its seeds on the outside?

6. In the early 1930s, what person was single-handedly responsible for a drastic drop in undershirt sales?

7. Oddly, all three of the following blanks will take the same number: For every _____ individual children born, one set of twins is born; for every _____ sets of twins, one set of triplets is born; and for every _____ sets of triplets, one set of quadruplets is born.

8. Rome's Italians, Dublin's Irish, Tel Aviv's Jews—which of these groups are outnumbered by their compatriot populations in New York City?

9. Why did Orville, and not Wilbur, make that first flight at Kitty Hawk?

10. Within 10 percent, what percentage of Monaco's residents regularly gamble at Monte Carlo?

11. The can opener, the carpet sweeper, the ice cream freezer, the typewriter—in what order were these four items invented?

12. What unusual thing do singers Enrico Caruso, Tony Martin, and Elvis Presley have in common?

13. Besides being state names, what do the words *Colorado, Oklahoma,* and *Rhode Island* have in common?

14. The Scots call it shinny. What do both Americans and Canadians call it?

15. What are Mizaru, Mikazaru, and Mazaru famous for *not* doing?

16. The first pay phone was installed in Hartford, Connecticut, in 1889. How much did a call cost?

17. In 1926, Charlie Chaplin, Rudolph Valentino, and Douglas Fairbanks, Sr., were all defeated in Warner Bros. popularity polls. By what superstar were they outshined?

18. The models for this famous painting were the artist's sister and dentist. Name the painting.

19. How many inches of snowfall equal the volume of water in one inch of rainfall?

20. The first modern one appeared on a corner on Euclid Avenue in Cleveland, Ohio, in 1914. What was it?

21. Which national anthem would take the longest to sing—Greece's, Japan's, or Qatar's?

22. Statues of heroes on horseback sometimes show the horses rearing. What is the significance of the horse's position?

23. We've all heard the phrase "a pig in a poke." What's a poke?

24. We use rice. The ancient Romans used wheat. For what nonculinary purpose?

25. A classic novel was written by a neighbor of Nathaniel Hawthorne, and was dedicated to him. Name the novel and the neighbor.

26. Why was it necessary for Admiral Byrd to take along a refrigerator on his Antarctic expedition?

27. Everyone's heard of Colonel Sanders and his Kentucky Fried Chicken franchises. Where did Sanders get the money to start his multimillion-dollar business?

28. In cost per acre, which was a better bargain—Alaska or the Louisiana Purchase?

29. You're on the beach. You pick up a seashell, and you think you hear the ocean. What do you really hear?

30. In number of sales per year, what company is the world's largest manufacturer of feminine apparel?

VARIATIONS ON A CROSSWORD THEME

1. Airplane trip
2. Kind of puzzle
3. Complain loudly
4. Native of Alaska
5. Mindless person
6. Prohibit

7. Win through strategy
8. Pure "air"
9. Get retribution
10. Observe
11. Choice
12. Infield out (2 wds.)

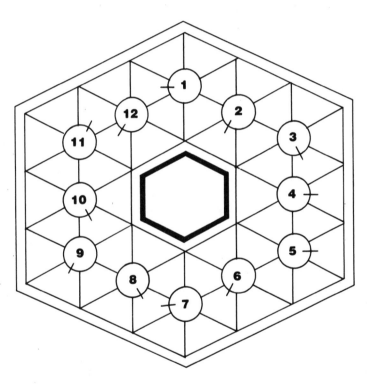

★★
BEEHIVE
BY WILL SHORTZ

The answer to each clue above is a six-letter word to be entered around the appropriate number in the beehive, beginning at the triangle indicated by the short line and proceeding one letter per space. An answer may read clockwise or counterclockwise—the direction in each case is for you to determine. As a small solving aid, we'll tell you that all 26 letters of the alphabet are used at least once in the completed hive.

Answer, page 182

RIGHT ANGLES *

BY E. R. GALLI

The special twist of Right Angles is that each entry in the puzzle grid makes one 90-degree turn somewhere along its length. It's up to you to determine where each word or phrase makes this turn and in which direction.

The starting direction of each answer (before it makes a turn) is indicated by a letter following the clue number—N for north, etc. As in a regular crossword, each square in the grid is part of exactly two answer words.

For Puzzle 1, the words to be entered in the grid are listed. The first answer has been filled in to start you off.

For Puzzle 2, only clues to the answer words are given, with the number of letters in each answer in parentheses. A little help has been provided here, too. (Remember, each letter in HELP is also part of a second word.) *Answers, page 182*

1E	NEST EGG
2S	SEMICOLON
3E	CHEFS
4W	EGOS
5W	FINGERBOWL
6W	MASON
7N	RETE
8S	MORELLO
9W	IMAGE
10E	BIMINI
11S	INLAY
12S	NOEL COWARD
13W	COED
14S	ALLOW
15N	COMANCHE
16W	ENDED
17S	YAM
18E	ALE
19W	CLOWN
19E	CHAMELEON
20N	HOOLIGANS

1W	Carroll's adventuress (5)
2S	Diner's music source (7)
3W	Toronto baseballers (4,4)
3S	Hand drum (5)
4E	Cowpoke's horse (6)
5S	Dreaded exile site (4,4)
6S	Abnormal thing (5)
7S	Man of steel? (5)
8S	African nation (5)
9S	Sink one's teeth into (4)
10S	Orange or Sugar (4)
11S	Magazine copy (5)
12N	Tenochtitlán residents (6)
13N	Four-time adjective for Koufax (2-3)
14S	Minnie, in the song (7)
15N	Expectant (7)
15E	Indian greeting, in old movies (3)
16N	Stop transmitting (4,3)
17N	"_____ Rose" (song oldie) (8)
18E	Bridge cost (4)
19N	Prefix with sphere (4)
20E	Houseplant with colorful leaves (6)

PUZZLE 1 ★

N	E	S	T	E			
				G			5
		6	7	G			
8	9	10			11	12	
		13					
		14		15			
16				17	18		
		19	20				

PUZZLE 2 ★★

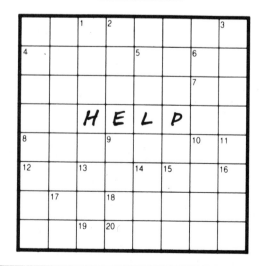

MISSING IN ACTION ***

BY MIKE SHENK

The answer to each clue in this crossword has been removed from the clue itself, letter by letter. For example, if the answer were COCOA and the corresponding clue were "Chocolate," the letters C-O-C-O-A would be removed in *proper order* and replaced by asterisks to leave the clue "*h***l*te."

Answer, page 182

ACROSS

1 Ca** le*de*
5 Mis***e sp*t
9 ***dy shap*
13 So* *n So**ra
14 ****id* facts about
16 C*nve*sation**
17 F**set**
18 **s****ry
19 Simo* th* f**m writer
20 ***nt, a* in *h* su*
22 **p****lion*
24 **nke* hand*
25 S*r*ng*r
26 *ket** of mov***nts
29 *n*er and *rri****
33 Fa*s*ty cre*to**
34 *apr* *l*ha
35 *ie f*rtively in the da**
37 F*med pugi**st
38 ***i*active eleme*t
39 **w*y
40 I**s o* *aw
42 Is**yre or gir*so*
43 *annet or T*ul*u**
45 * **om*n's **se*
47 ***la** a rul*
48 Ba*e's dr**ble catcher
49 Of**ci*l edic*
50 E***u****
54 **ti*ely *n**re*
58 Went from s*dd*e to d*r*
59 Vibr*nt*y act***
61 *r*nted; deli**red
62 ***ic*
63 Moder* crus****
64 B*de***t
65 **same yi*l*
66 I*p*i**
67 Robi* r**or*

DOWN

1 *aili*g d*n*er
2 *o** in the soi*
3 "*gai*s*" s*de
4 B***d'* fa*h**
5 *ha*e of t** g*ap*
6 "St**" b**d*
7 *arge am*un*
8 Ab***; mo*e
9 Ens**** tot**ly
10 *c***ge
11 **b the sw*nd*er
12 **bow *ink*
15 *xhi**ra****
21 *ops in the Gr**pian*
23 _____ with (*u**)
26 *te*a of m*r*le
27 Bron*h*al **ning h*ir
28 **v*ng a fur** look
29 **m of some *iv**
30 *u*rdh*use, in *ondon
31 Ins*r*c***
32 Cl*a* * *lat*
34 *orrid* tem*t*r
36 *i*d of br**ches
38 **le pla*ed *y N*wm**
41 **li*er****
43 *iv* g**b to
44 It's c*nne**ed *t ei*ht p*i*ts
46 L*ke *sle*
47 *el* lu*ch***
49 **r*ent d*si*e
50 Mo*ing w*go**
51 He**thful fl*w*r
52 *all *n*o att*ntion
53 **ug; h*m*er
55 ***bl*
56 ***nt preceder*
57 Fen**r *o*ch
60 Nancy Walker, *n *Rho***

SPELL WEAVING ★★

BY MIKE SHENK

If you weave the right spells, this puzzle will fill in like magic. When the answers to the clues are entered in the grid, they form two continuous threads, marked A and B, that interweave like a tapestry.

Enter one letter per space, beginning in the upper left corner for Thread A, lower left for Thread B, and continue diagonally. Whenever you hit the outer border, make a 90-

degree turn in the direction of the arrow, and continue in the new diagonal direction until you hit the border again and make another turn.

The clues appear in order, and the number of letters in each answer is given in parentheses after the clue. Heavy lines inside the grid indicate divisions between words.

Answer, page 182

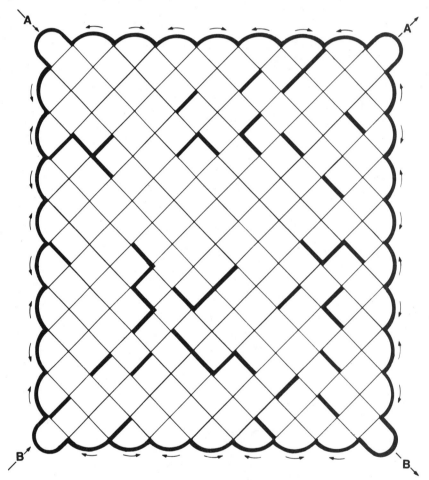

THREAD A

1 Weaving (12)
2 Attacked physically (9)
3 Loafer (4)
4 Makes a hole in (7)
5 Making wagers (7)
6 Springy and stretchy (7)
7 "Boxcars" (5)
8 Fuss (3)
9 Hard, shiny stone (6)
10 Put back in previous condition (7)
11 Navy diver (7)
12 Economize (8)
13 Break into pieces (5)
14 Kneecap (7)
15 Bottle openers (10)
16 Weave drunkenly (5)
17 Save (6)
18 Fools (7)
19 Ohio city (6)
20 Set design (5)
21 Spa goer's goal (7)
22 Abounds (5)

THREAD B

1 Old TV western (7)
2 Renoir and Matisse, e.g. (8)
3 Author W. ___ Maugham (8)
4 Stand up (5)
5 Lantern fuel (8)
6 Smudge (4)
7 Two-wheeled cart of India (5)
8 Befuddles (8)
9 Eastern state (11)
10 Another Ohio city (5)
11 Sudden, violent declarations (9)
12 Mendacious (9)
13 Like some early space shots (8)
14 Sounded the hour (6)
15 Swift (4)
16 In-depth look (5)
17 Tied sneakers (5)
18 Emily Post concern (7)
19 Satisfied (9)
20 Carnival (6)
21 Puts in place (8)

PETAL PUSHERS **

BY WILL SHORTZ

This flower blooms only when you recite the mystical incantation of 32 six-letter words. You can discover these special words with the help of the flower petals and the two sets of clues. Answer the clues and enter the words inward from the tips of the petals to the heart of the blossom, one letter in each space. Half the words proceed clockwise from the numbers, the other half proceed counterclockwise.

Answer, page 183

CLOCKWISE

1 Barnum's circus partner
2 California beach resort
3 Australian relative of the opossum
4 Most loyal
5 Central hall of an ancient Roman house
6 Rushed forward
7 Household servant
8 Heroine of *The Merchant of Venice*
9 Infant's toy
10 Spraying
11 Repudiation
12 Folk song
13 Tangled, as hair
14 Perceived
15 Comedian in the king's court
16 Washington's ___ International Airport

COUNTERCLOCKWISE

1 Cleared the table, as a waiter
2 Ice cream drink
3 Cried loudly
4 Bell ringer
5 Military forces
6 Short and squat
7 Governmental unit
8 Stickler for tradition
9 Cheap and inferior liquor
10 Home of the Globetrotters
11 "Sign on the ___ line"
12 Rouse
13 Kind of envelope
14 Salty
15 Traveler's woe
16 Kind of floss

SIAMESE TWINS**

BY MIKE SHENK

What with inflation, we thought we'd give you a break—two identical grids for the price of one. And two sets of clues to go with them, of course, so you can work both crosswords at the same time. What's the catch? Each clue number is followed by two different clues, which require two different answers—but the two clues in each pair are in random order. That means you'll have to figure out which answer to put in which grid. We've filled in the answers to 1-Across to get you started.   *Answers, page 183*

ACROSS

1 Converted a check into money
Soda sippers
7 Give ___ (frighten): 2 wds.
Have ___ in (take part): 2 wds.
13 Actor Peter
Adjusted ahead of time
14 Grabs
Grew close to
15 Ethical concern: 3 wds.
Not informed: 4 wds.
17 Grain
Roof ornament
18 Boat's rear
"Cold" or "saddle" hurts
19 Me, to Miss Piggy
Oahu garland
20 "Thanks ___!": 2 wds.
Previously owned
22 She sheep
Sunbather's goal
23 Light ray
Destiny

24 Actor Robert et al.
Took back a card
26 Stair part
Madrid museum
27 Cleared a path: 2 wds.
Thumbed through
29 "___ Bill," of tall tales
Challenged
32 Conservative's opposite
Desert illusions
36 Chemical suffixes
___ Bator, Mongolia
37 ___ Vegas
Stadium cheerer
38 Number of Muses
Run gently
39 Past
Used a stool
40 Gives the boot
Hospital sections
42 Monk's title
Feathery scarf
43 Successful one's place: 4 wds.
Reach the lowest point: 3 wds.

46 Different from
End of some threats: 2 wds.
47 French girl's name
Microscopic organism
48 Some Impressionist paintings
Made a noise
49 Vegetable plot
Remain for a while: 2 wds.

DOWN

1 Hue, in Britain
Distribute
2 Army "relax!": 2 wds.
Almost a home run
3 Area
Make spongier
4 Fiery
Fire remnant
5 Moistens
Yale students
6 ___ the Union: 2 wds.
Signified
7 Grayish
Conductor Previn
8 Pictures
Stitched
9 Detroit product
Stashed
10 Fragrances
Funnel-shaped flower
11 Discern again
Study over
12 More nervous
Yukon native

16 Bulletin: 2 wds.
Company logo, e.g.
21 Little imp
Grows weary
23 Orator William Jennings ___
Cuba's Castro
25 Disencumber
Cooking with ___
26 Course goal
Confederate man, for short
28 Lends an ear
Talkative one
29 Bit of algae
Arm-strengthening exercise
30 Wool-yielding goat
Graduate girl
31 Look into again,
as a police case
Ranch stock
33 Walter Scott novel: 2 wds.
Endowed with talents
34 Dress like a judge
NASA moon project
35 Dull gray
Mariner
37 Stringed instruments
Confronted
40 "Spirit ___ Louis": 2 wds.
Came to
41 Loretta, of *M*A*S*H*
Body: Greek
44 Shred
Bullfight yell
45 Craggy hill
Woodland sorrel

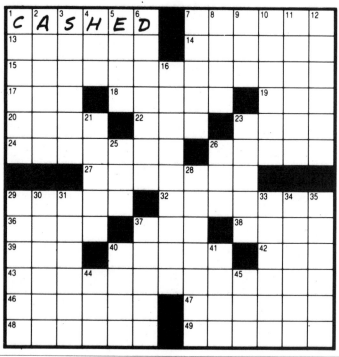

BLOCKOUT ★★

BY EMILY COX AND HENRY RATHVON

Each clue below has two parts. The answer to Part A is a six-letter word; the answer to Part B is a shorter word whose letters are all contained within the A word, in order but not necessarily consecutively.

For each pair of clues, first fill in the six-letter A word in the appropriately numbered row of the grid. Then, in that same row, shade in the letters of the B answer. When you are done, the unshaded letters in the diagram will spell out a phrase appropriate to the shape that they form.

Answer, page 183

1						
2						
3						
4						
5						
6						
7						
8						
9						
10						
11						
12						

CLUES

1A Farther down
B Bucks and does

2A Czechoslovakia's capital
B Book leaf

3A Scruples
B Spoken

4A Assented
B Avarice

5A Munchies
B Bags

6A Mollycoddle
B Thesis

7A Search for food
B Smithy

8A Climb, as a pole
B Lustrous

9A Actor Marlon
B Cattle mark

10A *The ___ the Mohicans:* 2 wds.
B Concerning: 2 wds.

11A Cortege car
B Rabbit's relative

12A Counted calories
B Conked out

GIVE IT A WHIRL ★☆

BY JORDAN LASHER

The puzzle on this and the next two pages is from our series **The World's Most Ornery Crossword**. It has two independent sets of clues: Hard and Easy. First, fold this page back on the dashed line so the clues below face the solving grid on page 121. If you use only the Hard Clues (appearing below, and continuing under the grid), you'll find the puzzle uncommonly challenging. If you want help, or prefer a less severe challenge, open to the Easy Clues (tucked in beneath your fold on page 120). *Answer, page 183*

HARD CLUES

ACROSS

1 Gym gear
5 School-calendar highlight
12 9-mm pistol
17 Moslem judges
22 Hankering
23 Wail
24 Novelist Wylie
26 Much woe
27 Shortest distances, on a sphere
29 Song adapted from the Book of Ecclesiastes
31 Olav's kingdom
32 Western Indians
34 Dors and Lynn
35 Pass the plate
36 At right angles to a ship's keel
37 Maul
40 Capital of Western Australia
42 Mouth: Prefix
43 Like "Merrie Englande"
44 Fleet
45 Entertainer from Kakaako, Hawaii
47 ___ never (ultimatum)
49 Land west of the Urals
51 Honshu city
52 Aswirl
54 Est Est Est, e.g.
55 Massachusetts town
58 Cheerful ditty
60 Singular
62 Word with cracker or jerk
64 Lettuce or kale
65 Alluring woman
67 Prepared
69 Ocean-floor feature
72 Casualty of Tiny Tim's tiptoeing?
73 Ambracian Gulf
74 Slips by
75 Vinegary
77 Clay mixture
78 Nonecclesiastic
79 Geometrical surface
80 Electra's father
82 Deleted
83 One of three baseball brothers
84 Greek city-state
85 Coast Guard women
86 Witching hour
88 Cassia plant extract
90 Nearest star to Earth
91 Trenchant
92 One-time English teenager
95 Journalist Milton ___ (1858–1930)
99 Fuchsin or eosin
101 Mermaid, reputedly
102 Moslem leader
104 Bay at the moon
105 Chemist's measures: Abbr.
108 Winter wheels
112 Pigeonhole
113 Geminated
114 DC regulars
116 "Supply is always matched by demand"
117 Lollobrigida or Loren, e.g.
118 Ancient Peruvian: Var.
119 "He was a scholar, and ___ a good one . . ." (Shakespeare)
121 "___ me God"
122 Amahs
123 Relinquishes
124 Units
126 Turnov's river
127 Mother of purl?
128 Hebrides island
129 Child's toy
132 Element No. 26
134 Transportation to Oz
137 Pro Bowl side: Abbr.
140 Baseball umpire's call
141 One way to evaluate stocks
143 Sycophant
144 German river
145 Achromat
147 Applicator
149 Kin of mister
151 Pre-___
152 Razor-billed auk
153 Part of NATO, for short
154 Photog's chemical
156 Memorable boxer

(continued)

GIVE IT A WHIRL

DON'T PEEK AT THE EASY CLUES UNTIL YOU READ PAGE 119

EASY CLUES

ACROSS

1 Small rugs
5 December 31, in the year: 2 wds.
12 Olympic sledder
17 Islam law-givers (ACIDS anag.)
22 Hurt
23 Lament (LULU TEA, anag.)
24 Actress Donohue
26 Great grief
27 Global circumferences: 2 wds.
29 Hit song by The Byrds: 3 wds.
31 Land of fjords
32 Arizona Indians
34 Ross and Rigg
35 Panhandle
36 Shipboard orientation (AMEBA anag.)
37 Handle clumsily
40 ___ Amboy, NJ
42 Opening: Prefix (MOST anag.)
43 Ye ___ Shoppe
44 Dark blue
45 Honolulu singer: 2 wds.
47 "It's ___ Never" (Presley hit): 2 wds.
49 France's continent
51 Japanese statesman
52 Swirling (like crooner Nelson?)
54 Chablis, e.g.
55 Boston suburb
58 Graceful song
60 Unusual
62 Drink mixer
64 Money: Sl. (IRONED anag.)
65 Mythical beauty (60 minutes + I)
67 Ready: 2 wds.
69 Foxhole
72 Amsterdam flower
73 Mediterranean gulf (A RAT anag.)
74 Passes by
75 Sour (TO CAUSE anag.)
77 Beaten down: Fr. (PIES anag.)
78 Secular
79 Donut surface (DORITO anag.)
80 Greek chieftain
82 Crossed out
83 Matty or Felipe, of baseball
84 Namesakes of Jason's ship
85 Shadowboxes
86 Roman 12

88 Medicinal herb (ANNES anag.)
90 Mr. Hurok
91 Very bitter
92 British youth of the '60s
95 Outfielder Hal (CREAM anag.)
99 Artificial coloring
101 Ambulance sound
102 Neighbor of Nev.
104 Laugh riotously
105 Metric measures: Abbr.
108 Winter treads: 2 wds.
112 Put a book away
113 Twofold
114 Congressmen, for short
116 Economic principle: 2 wds. (SAL'S WAY anag.)
117 Sicilian, e.g.
118 "___ Dinka Doo"
119 Live to ___ old age: 2 wds.
121 "___ me God": 2 wds.
122 RNs and LPNs
123 Gives up
124 Single-celled organisms (DAMSON anag.)
126 Elbe feeder (RISE anag.)
127 Make a cardigan
128 New Rochelle college
129 Hand-held windmill
132 Steel ingredient
134 Twister
137 Packers' conference: Abbr.
140 Off the streets
141 Breaking even, in golf: 2 wds.
143 Lackey
144 German river (RODE anag.)
145 Camera part
147 Sailor's mop
149 Mister: Sp.
151 Average: Abbr.
152 Arctic bird (sounds like MYRRH)
153 Assn.
154 Crystalline powder (OL' MAID anag.)
156 Nye or Armstrong
158 Escaped: 2 wds.
159 Hot water pipe: 2 wds.
162 Coil-like stellar system: 2 wds.
166 Bulgarian capital (I will get in the couch?)
167 Very mysterious
168 African republic
169 ___ instant (quickly): 2 wds
170 African grasses (FALA'S anag.)
171 Partisan (DRIES anag.)
172 ___ of the House
173 Dental degrees: Abbr.

DOWN

1 Actress Anna
2 Circus performer
3 Ours began in 1775: 2 wds.
4 St. Lawrence ___
5 *Peanuts* girl
6 Fighter Muhammad
7 Big ___, CA
8 Very gentle treatment: Abbr.
9 Newscaster John
10 Devoured: 2 wds.
11 Agreeing ones
12 Chubby Checker hit: 3 wds.
13 Eskimo knife (found in NEBULUS)
14 Encircle
15 County Clare's capital (NINES anag.)
16 Spins on an axis
17 Tuna containers
18 Secret Service man: Abbr.
19 DNA molecule: 2 wds.
20 Dressed like Riding Hood: 2 wds.
21 Irish dramatist, a contemporary of Yeats
25 Expire, as a subscription: 2 wds.
28 ___-o'-shanter
30 Strict disciplinarian
33 ". . . maids all in ___": 2 wds.
37 Pea's place
38 Some
39 Swirling water
41 Ace, e.g.: 2 wds.
43 Let me in!: 2 wds.
45 Insecticide: Abbr.
46 Jackie or Ari
48 Cashes in
50 "Step ___!": 2 wds.
52 Mr. Wallach
53 Avarice
56 Get up
57 Sulked
59 Prone to anger (ACID RUN anag.)
61 Little ones: Suffix
63 Poker payment
65 Football's "Papa Bear"
66 Papal cape (A ROLE anag.)
67 Then: Fr. (SOLAR anag.)
68 *Key ___* (Bogart film)
70 Ending for "sit" in TV talk
71 Attila the ___
74 Greek letter
76 Red or White team

80 "___ moi le déluge"
81 Pilfer (MIN anag.)
85 Airplane "prop": 2 wds.
87 I serve: Ger., 2 wds. (CHIN DIE anag.)
89 Yes votes
91 Bomb warnings: 2 wds.
92 Powerful whirlpool
93 Kukla's friend
94 Met performers
96 Like a carousel ride: 3 wds.
97 Wide-eyed
98 Fitzgerald et al.
100 After ems
101 Region of Europe
102 *Ben Hur* vehicle
103 Marsh
105 Charley horse, e.g.
106 "Vive ___!": 2 wds.
107 Starting a new TV series from an old one: 2 wds.
109 Alliance of the Americas: Abbr.
110 Cheyenne's state: Abbr.
111 African language (THIS anag.)
112 Spectacular feat
115 Breeds, as salmon
117 Pen filler
120 Old English letters (SHED anag.)
123 Bill and ___
125 Earthquake: Prefix
128 Mt. ___, Charley Weaver's home
130 Actress Booth
131 Directors
133 One billionth: Prefix (ANNO anag.)
135 No: Scot.
136 Do math
138 Giant fennel plants (SURF ALE anag.)
139 Greek islanders
142 Wakes: Sl.
144 Succeed at an auction
145 "___ luck, sucker!"
146 Actor Flynn
148 Italian bowling game
150 Shred: 2 wds.
152 One of the Three Stooges
154 Down with: Fr.; 2 wds.
155 Burden
157 Trigonometric ratio
158 Growl
160 Actress Farrow
161 Suffix with Joseph or Paul
163 Inlet
164 Inquire
165 Fib

HARD CLUES (continued)

158 Withdrew
159 Steam duct
162 Heavenly helix
166 Balkan capital
167 Sphinxlike
168 Where beys ruled
169 ___ unenviable position
170 First code words
171 "East" or "West" city resident
172 Stereo part
173 Dental degs.

DOWN

1 The Rose Tattoo star
2 The man on the flying trapeze
3 It ended at Yorktown
4 Canal
5 Ethel's cohort
6 Baba, of fable
7 Lebanese seaport
8 Short term for mothering
9 ___ City, San Francisco suburb
10 Enjoyed: Sl.
11 Gnathonic ones
12 Hit song of 1961
13 Indian grass
14 Prepare for action
15 Texas city
16 Circumvolves
17 Gives the axe
18 Ten-percenter: Abbr.
19 Genetic shape
20 "The Lady ___"
21 Dramatist John
25 Equestrian feat
28 Burns hero
30 Muzzle-loader
33 Lined up
37 Small herd of whales
38 ___ Wednesday
39 Charybdis
41 Likely trick taker
43 Tell all
45 Rachel Carson subject
46 An Aristotle
48 Turns from sin
50 "Don't count ___!"
52 Biblical judge
53 Rapaciousness
56 Insurrect
57 Had the blues
59 Short-tempered
61 French connections
63 Pot sweetener
65 NFL pioneer
66 Fanon
67 Zut ___! (French exclamation)
68 Slow, in music
70 Matthew Perry's rank: Abbr.
71 Follower of Atli
74 Flight-board initials
76 Hose: Var.
80 After, in Arles
81 Take-away game
85 Boat mover
87 Motto of the Prince of Wales
89 Nautical assents
91 Sounds heard in London during WWII
92 Turbulence
93 Stan's friend
94 Prima donnas, literally
96 Perry Como hit
97 Vigilant
98 Greece, to Greeks
100 Metaphysical being
101 Wroclaw's region
102 Vehicle for the sun, in myth
103 Chinese coin
105 Inhibit, as one's style
106 Dramatist Jones
107 Ejecting centrifugally
109 W. Hemisphere alliance
110 Colo. neighbor
111 Akwapim language
112 Trick
115 Engenders
117 Cuttlefish fluid
120 Icelandic letters
123 Whisper sweet nothings
125 Prefix for Richter's "graph"
128 Mt. ___, home of Grandpa Ogg
130 Girl's name meaning "valuable friend"
131 Fishing lines
133 Dwarf: Prefix
135 No, in Ayr
136 Say further
138 Asafetida-yielding plants
139 Subjects of King Minos
142 Separates sleeper from sack
144 Offer more than
145 ___ Luck, Dom DeLuise show
146 First name in swashbuckling
148 Pastime in Sicily
150 Make confetti
152 Athlete-author Berg
154 King of Argolis
155 Stow cargo
157 ___ die
158 Act like an angry dog
160 Ex-Mrs. Sinatra
161 Chemical suffix
163 Estuary
164 Petition
165 Emulate Munchhausen

HELTER-SKELTER★★

BY E. R. GALLI

Helter-Skelter puzzles have answers running in eight directions, but don't worry—the numbers tell you which way to go. To solve, begin each answer in the square corresponding to its clue number and proceed toward the next consecutive number. That square will contain the first letter of the next word but will not necessarily mark the end of the preceding word. The first two answers have been entered in Puzzle 1 as examples. When a puzzle is completed, every square will be filled in.

Answers, page 183

PUZZLE 1

21	15			16		
	1 C				11	10
7	18 L		19			6
	O		22	4		
	2 W	A F	3 F	F	L	E
20	N				14	
23				17		5
12	9			8	13	

PUZZLE 2

25	21	22					6
			23	13	19		7
9	2		15	14		18	
						12	
24	16				20	17	
		8					
10						11	
5	3			4		1	

1 Bozo the ___
2 Breakfast dish
3 Slapstick play
4 Seaweed, e.g.
5 Embarrass
6 Alternative to sandwich bread: 2 wds.
7 Penny ___ (shoe)
8 Payment, with thanks
9 Palm fibers
10 Plan
11 Made by hand
12 Underwear
13 Wiser
14 Stared icily
15 Loyal enthusiast
16 Tale of suspense
17 Envelop
18 God
19 Tiers
20 Burns with hot liquid
21 One who flouts rules
22 Hand-held coolers
23 WWII Navy worker

1 Notwithstanding
2 Walk very quietly
3 Have being
4 Highest dice roll
5 Small amounts
6 Malicious
7 Canoe hollowed from a tree
8 Horse's pace
9 Gin and ___
10 Noted deep-sea diver
11 Capital of Texas
12 Land hopper
13 Boldly confronts
14 Converse
15 Pelvic projection
16 Indian, early on
17 Task
18 Chill
19 Formal headwear
20 Earth color
21 Rats and mice
22 Small whale
23 Precipitate
24 Famous
25 Like this answer!

CONNECT-A-WORD**

BY LORI PHILIPSON

When the grid below is correctly completed, each pair of adjacent boxes will contain a compound word or a familiar two-word phrase. Clues are identified by the numbers in the boxes, and the answers are to be entered left to right and top to bottom. The answer to 1-2 Across, HIGH-FLYING ("Giddily happy"), has been filled in as an example. Now you know that the first part of 1-6 Down is HIGH and that the first part of both 2-3 Across and 2-7 Down is FLYING. Every box is part of two or more answers, so if the clue in one direction stumps you, you can try another connection.

Answer, page 183

ACROSS

1-2	Giddily happy
2-3	Marine sighting, perhaps
3-4	Seafood diner's bane
4-5	Idiot
6-7	Register
7-8	Queued up
8-9	Hang out laundry
9-10	Castaway's destination
11-12	Soon to appear
14-15	Voter attendance
15-16	Defeat in a game
16-17	Conduct oneself according to Hoyle
17-18	Even exchange
19-20	Fail to notice
20-21	Reminisce
21-22	Setting
22-23	Polished, as a diamond
25-26	Very informal seating
27-28	1962 dog film
28-29	Blitz, in football
29-30	Pooch competition
30-31	Display prominently
32-33	Stage illumination
33-34	Mariner's warning
34-35	Floating residence
35-36	Shipful

1 HIGH	2 FLYING	3	4	5
6	7	8	9	10
11	12	■	13	■
14	15	16	17	18
19	20	21	22	23
■	24	■	25	26
27	28	29	30	31
32	33	34	35	36

DOWN

1-6	Secret gesture
2-7	Arriving by plane
3-8	Rod and reel attachment
4-9	Moistureless
5-10	Promontory
6-11	Enlist
7-12	About to take office
9-13	Teetotaling district
11-14	Improving trend
12-15	Social debut
13-17	Local agricultural exhibit
14-19	Pastry treat
15-20	Future view
16-21	Videotape feature
17-22	Exposition site
18-23	Make a bad bargain
20-24	Quick investigation
22-25	Entry level
23-26	Item for a bed fight
24-28	Become enraged
25-30	Cabaret offering
26-31	Cushion cover
27-32	Cousin of the Abominable Snowman
28-33	Stop signal
29-34	Place of disgrace, in metaphor
30-35	1927 Hammerstein-Kern musical
31-36	Court quota

HOW TO SOLVE CRYPTIC CROSSWORDS

BY EMILY COX AND HENRY RATHVON

The two warm-up cryptic crosswords on this page illustrate all the basic types of cryptic clues. Each clue contains two parts: a direct or indirect definition of the answer and a second description of the answer through wordplay. (The number in parentheses indicates the number of letters in the answer.) The first step in solving a clue, and a great part of the fun, is to find the dividing point between the parts. Here are examples of the eight main clue types.

Anagram "Rule breaker ruined the race (7)." The word "ruined" cryptically suggests that the letters of the adjacent words, THE RACE, are to be rearranged to get the answer, CHEATER (defined as "rule breaker"). An anagram clue always contains a word or phrase (like "crazy," "reorganized," "drunkenly," or "in a heap") that suggests mixing or poor condition. The signal is always adjacent to the word or words to be rearranged.

Charade "To put it another way, others had dinner (7)." Here the answer word combines two or more shorter words: REST ("others") and ATE ("had dinner") are combined to form RESTATE ("to put it another way"). Sometimes a charade has more than two parts (e.g., TO + GET + HER = TOGETHER), but they are always defined in order unless a signal suggests otherwise.

Container "Forest's edge divided city, in time (10)." The answer, TIMBERLINE ("forest's edge"), is BERLIN ("divided city") inside TIME (given directly). The word "in" indicates the container. Other container clue signals are "inside," "within," and "held by"; or, from the other perspective, "surrounds," "has," and "swallows."

Deletion "Votes for President after Grant is beheaded (4)." If you delete the first letter of HAYES ("President after Grant"), you get the answer AYES ("votes for"). Deletion of the first letter is called a beheadment. A letter may also be deleted from the end ("curtailment") or the middle; the place is always specified by a signal, like "topless" for a

beheadment, "heartless" for the center letter, or "endless" for curtailment.

Hidden Word "Overthrow in coups, etc. (5)." The answer here is literally spelled out in the clue: UPSET ("overthrow") is found in "coUPS ETc." The word "in" indicates where the answer is hidden. Other hidden word signals are "features," "holds," and "contains" when following the hidden answer, or "part of" and "found in" when preceding it.

Homophone "Reduces homework assignments, we hear (7)." The answer, LESSENS ("reduces"), sounds like LESSONS ("homework assignments"). The phrase "we hear" signals the homophone. Other homophone indicators are "they say," "orally," and "by the sound."

Second Definition "Wax from Warsaw (6)." Structurally this is the simplest type of cryptic clue, merely defining the answer twice. POLISH means both "wax" and "from Warsaw," depending on pronunciation. This type of clue is often short.

Reversal "Encounter swarm returning (4)." The answer, MEET ("encounter"), is a reversal of TEEM ("swarm"). The word "returning" tells you to reverse the adjacent word to get the answer. Other reversal signals are "retreating," "retrospectively," and "turned"; for a Down entry, "up," "rising," and "northward."

The byword in solving cryptics is simply this: Follow the literal instructions in the clues. They'll tell you what to do. Also, keep your mind flexible—the words in the clues do not always mean what they seem to say, but they always say what they mean! If you're new to cryptic crosswords, warm up with the small puzzles on this page, build your endurance with the Crackerjack Cryptics, opposite, and then—for a real workout—turn to the Musical Chairs Variety Cryptic, page 169.

Answers and explanations, page 184

WARM UP 1 ★

ACROSS

1 Preacher is beheaded for setting fire to a building (5) *beheadment*
4 Nest among kangaroos temporarily (5) *hidden word*
5 Coiling adder inspires fear (5) *anagram*

DOWN

1 Anger in commercial is televised (5) *container*
2 Twenty songs in a musical (5) *second definition*
3 No member of the Kennedy family is famous (5) *charade*

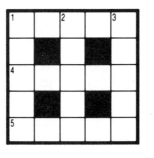

WARM UP 2 ★

ACROSS

1 Seat for you and me and the woman over there (5) *charade*
4 Look into exotic ingredients for cake topping (5) *hidden word*
5 Fish around while getting art equipment (5) *container*

DOWN

1 Join Ute in dancing (5) *anagram*
2 Say, rabbit's fur? (5) *homophone*
3 Served up beer fit for a king (5) *reversal*

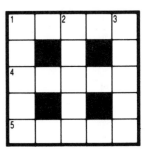

CRACKERJACK CRYPTICS★★★

PUZZLE 1
BY EMILY COX AND HENRY RATHVON

Answer, page 184

ACROSS

1 Get right out of tropical current (7)
5 Protective wall in part caging monkey (7)
9 Exist in brand-new spire (7)
10 Sorrow about codemaker (7)
11 Free in Waterloo's environs (5)
12 Check choo-choo during vacation (9)
13 Begin to jump (5)
14 Scandinavian person on a lurching bus? (9)
17 Picture of sunbeam coming through door (9)
19 Dance found in America perhaps (5)
22 Food tossed at the pigs (9)
25 Tries bizarre ceremonies (5)
26 Mr. Carson's sheltering ten cats (7)
27 Unimportant court case involving six in Rome (7)
28 To tell a story is awfully near art (7)
29 Get zany bends in Chinese river (7)

DOWN

1 Stories about Mom's Mexican food (7)
2 Mythical girl's father penning some choice words? (7)
3 President Jimmy holds pen—for cabinet maker? (9)
4 Last-minute surge from the side (9)
5 Divides belt up (5)
6 Heard lodger's gossip (5)
7 I depart drunk, having caroused (7)
8 Movie house showing first half of this: *Diner* (7)
15 Man initially is captivated by mere kind of fortune-telling (9)
16 A "C" string—one on musical instrument (9)
17 Russian author has to promote relatives (7)
18 Nuclear device has mad creator (7)
20 Countryman and Irish fellow brawl (7)
21 Promise to crack clues again (7)
23 Laugh about urge in animal (5)
24 Doctored a test sample (5)

PUZZLE 2
BY MERL REAGLE

ACROSS

1 Kitchen appliance for 1001 Blackbird Avenue (9)
6 Genius: Britain lacks it (5)
9 Not quite enough for container in street (5)
10 *That Girl*'s broadcast in a twinkling? (9)
11 Choice potion mixed (6)
12 They're generous to soldier with unfinished poetry (6)
15 Point to one sick Democratic leader (3,6)
17 Charo arranged "La Cucaracha" in English (5)
18 Scandinavian right in front of airplane (5)
20 Cassettes rewound for experiments (4,5)
22 Hop madly with endless prejudice and fear (6)
23 Grab a customer concealing a calculator (6)
27 Snakes cried—that's bleak (9)
28 Teacher shows tailless bunny (5)
29 Run-down witness with Dick York's initials (5)
30 *I Spy* agent converted Tut's followers (9)

DOWN

1 *M is for Melody* is a disaster (10)
2 Fixed tacos and roll (5)
3 *Our Town* reviewed as trite (7)
4 Radical socialist advertises, too (4)
5 Preacher gets an evil reformed (10)
6 South American hero, 54, trapped by pig (7)
7 Grain sale upset certain Africans (9)
8 Stagger up to lunatics (4)
13 Asian navies meet secretly (10)
14 High spots marred by South Sea derelicts (5,5)
16 Sit on broken cane, maybe (9)
19 Polluted mess by a diplomat's home (7)
21 Nude appearing in Kitty's nightclub (7)
24 Cora holds head of black snake (5)
25 Sheep exercise, we hear (4)
26 James Taylor has to wait (4)

Answer, page 184

DOUBLE PARKING

BY WILL SHORTZ

Solve these two puzzles like regular crosswords, but put two letters in each square—one in each triangle.

Answers, page 183

PUZZLE 1 ★

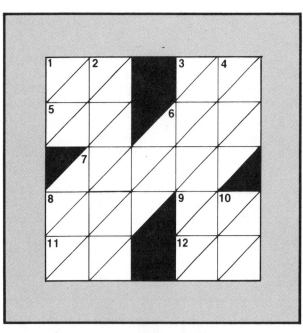

PUZZLE 2 ★★

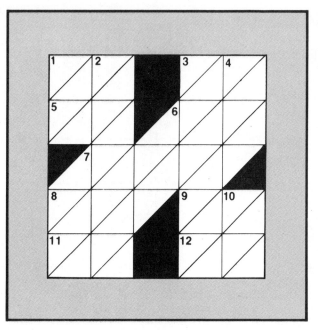

ACROSS

1	Halloween cover-up
3	Stallion or bull, e.g.
5	Lock openers
6	Snowbank
7	Harsh feeling
8	Beats, as wings
9	Draw permanently
11	One in debt
12	Eye-dropper?

DOWN

1	Brand of car
2	Chicago's Sears Tower, e.g.
3	It has strings pulled
4	Southpaw
6	Turns down (the lights)
7	Moving, like lava
10	Scorch

ACROSS

1	Big party
3	Fictional detective
5	Nimble
6	Buffalo's home
7	Give rise to
8	South American capital
9	Storyteller
11	Some Islamic names
12	Thus

DOWN

1	Sound of astonishment
2	Why one might be at a loss for words?
3	Ballroom fixture
4	Rile
6	Gambling haven
7	A twin
10	Jason's ship

MARCHING BANDS ★★

BY MIKE SHENK

The words in this puzzle march around the grid in two ways. In one formation ("Rows"), words march across—two words for each numbered line, reading consecutively from left to right. The dividing point between these answers is for you to determine, except in Row 7, where the words are separated by a black square. In the second formation ("Bands"), words march around each of the six shaded and unshaded bands, starting at the lettered squares (A–F) and proceeding clockwise, one word after another. For example, when Band A is filled in, it will contain six consecutive words starting in Square A and reading around the perimeter of the grid. Band B will contain a series of five words (a–e) starting in Square B. The dividing point between these answers, as before, is for you to determine. All clues are given in order. When the puzzle is completed, each square will have been used once in a Row word and once in a Band word. March!

Answer, page 183

ROWS

1 a *Saturday Night Fever* dance style
 b Aperitif wine

2 a Heavy hammer
 b Dirty, deteriorating building

3 a Summer drink
 b Gallic "thanks"

4 a The Gem State
 b Orthodontic problem

5 a Zeppelin
 b Rhythmical, as writing

6 a Not in the sun
 b Territory within a foreign region

7 a Peaceful
 b Indian groups

8 a Houston player
 b Short musical work

9 a Gains with difficulty
 b Colonizes

10 a Peace Prize benefactor
 b Unfounded

11 a Breaking wave
 b Sight or smell

12 a Black Sea port
 b Crazy fellows

13 a Mondale or Kennedy
 b Stores cargo

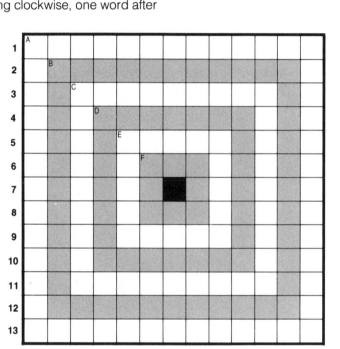

BANDS

A a Find
 b Phone parts
 c Evaluated
 d Site of wedding vows
 e Humiliating setback
 f English Christmas drinks

B a Accounts book
 b Eye appeal
 c Abel's brother
 d Accumulated
 e Baseball, in slang

C a ___ Lisa
 b Point off for bad behavior
 c Texas city
 d "The final frontier"
 e Lama's land
 f ___ *avis* (eccentric one)

D a Famed FBI director
 b Disparage
 c Fine furs
 d Beatty-Keaton film

E a "Father of Medicine"
 b Pebble

F a Auto injury
 b Prow

THE SPIRAL ★★

BY A. BRAINE

This is a double-dealing puzzle. The spiral's Inward clues yield a sequence of words to be entered counter-clockwise in the spaces from 1 to 100. The Outward clues yield a different set of words to be entered clockwise from 100 back to 1. Write the answers in, one letter per space, according to the numbers beside the clues. Keep track of which way you're proceeding, and have many happy returns.

Answer, page 183

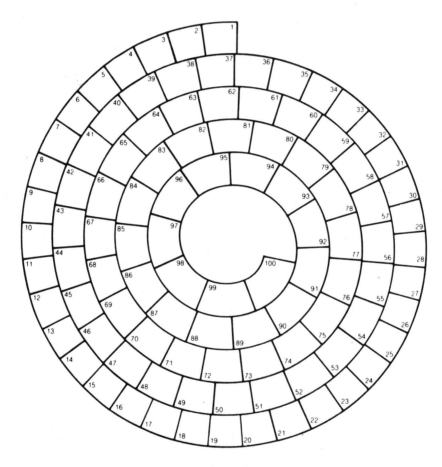

INWARD

1-6	Outer tooth layer
7-10	Naked
11-18	Put off until later
19-21	Unit of work
22-28	Held in high esteem
29-34	Polar covering
35-38	Painful
39-43	Up and about
44-48	Pull out, as feathers
49-53	Dinner à la ___
54-63	Auto combustion device
64-70	Electrical power, as measured by the meter
71-78	Money taken in
79-85	Honeymoon falls
86-90	"Filthy" money
91-100	Propped up

OUTWARD

100-94	Supper finale
93-84	Relating to a lung disease
83-77	Opposed to
76-72	Fragment
71-65	Yacht race
64-60	Composed
59-57	Chafe
56-48	Churchill Downs, e.g.
47-40	Guilty ones
39-31	The earth's atmosphere and beyond
30-26	Apple drink
25-17	Landscape shrub
16-13	Chooses
12-5	Working; in effect
4-1	Lion's or horse's tresses

MATH, LOGIC, AND A FEW DIRTY TRICKS

A = 2	G = 2
B = 0	H = 4
C = 2	I = 2
D = 0	J = 2
E = 3	K = 4
F = 3	L = 2

★★

BREAKING THE CODE

BY EMILY COX AND HENRY RATHVON

There's something about these letters that determines their numerical values,
as shown here. Can you break the code and find the only
remaining letter of the alphabet that would, according to this system, have the value of 1?

Answer, page 184

MY TEN FAVORITE BRAINTEASERS ★☆

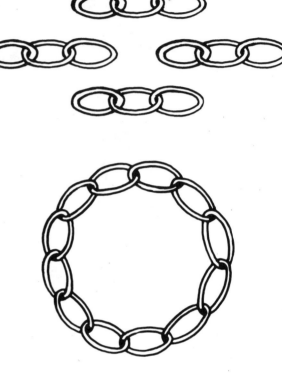

For almost 30 years I have been writing about puzzles in books for children and adults and, until 1981, in a regular *Scientific American* column, ''Mathematical Games.'' Here are my 10 all-time favorites. None requires a knowledge of math, and all are ridiculously easy if you think about them the right way. But beware of booby traps! *Answers, page 185*

1. ONION ROLL

Arrange four matches, as shown, to represent a martini glass, with a fifth match head placed inside to represent an onion. The puzzle is to move just two matches so that the glass is re-formed, but so that the onion—which may not be moved—winds up outside the glass. At the finish, the glass may be turned to the left or right, or even be upside down, but it must be exactly the same shape as before.

2. CUTTING DOWN

You would like to join four pieces of a silver chain, shown at top, to form the circular bracelet above. Since it takes a bit of doing to cut open a link and weld it together again, you naturally want to cut as few links as possible. What is the minimum number of links you must cut to do the job?

3. DISSECTION DILEMMA

Each of the two shaded figures is divided into four identical parts. Can you divide the blank square into *five* identical parts?

4. DEALER'S CHOICE

After you have dealt about half the 52 cards for a bridge game, the telephone rings. You put down the undealt cards to answer the phone. When you return, none of the cards has been touched, and no one can remember where the last card was dealt. Without counting the cards in any hand, or the number of cards yet to be dealt, how can you finish dealing rapidly and accurately, giving each player exactly the same cards he would have received if you hadn't been interrupted?

5. DASH IT ALL!

Saul and Sal race each other for 100 yards. Sal wins by 10 yards. They decide to race again, but this time, to even things up, Sal begins 10 yards behind the start line. Assuming that both run at the same constant speed as before, who wins?

BY MARTIN GARDNER

6. HIEROGLYPHICS?

The seven symbols shown below look like some kind of ancient writing. But there is a meaning for each symbol, and if you can puzzle it out, you should have no trouble drawing the next symbol of this curious sequence.

7. FIVE-AND-TEN

Three nickels and three dimes are distributed in three boxes so that each box holds two coins. The total number of cents in each box is written on the top of the box. However, someone has switched the tops around so that no box is labeled correctly. You may not open any box, but you are allowed to shake a box until just one coin slides out of the slot at the bottom. What is the minimum number of coins you must remove until you know for certain the exact contents of each box?

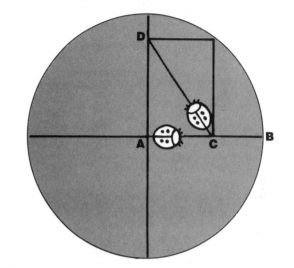

8. CRAWL SPACE

On the geometrical pattern shown above, one ladybug starts at A and crawls toward B. At the same instant another ladybug starts at C and crawls toward D. If both bugs move at the same constant speed, which will finish first?

9. A MOVING STORY

Place a chess queen on a square next to a corner square of a chessboard as shown at top. The problem is to move the queen four times, making standard queen moves, so that she passes through all nine of the lightly shaded squares. (A queen may move any number of squares in any direction: horizontally, vertically, or diagonally.) The figure above shows a way to do it in six moves, but that's two too many.

10. SHADY LADIES

Miss White, Miss Black, and Miss Gray are out for a stroll together. One is dressed in white, one in black, and one in gray.

"Isn't it odd," says Miss Gray, "that our dresses match our last names, but no one of us is wearing a dress that matches her own name?"

"So what?" said the lady in black.

Give the color of each lady's dress.

TRAVEL FEVER LOGIC PUZZLES

THREE VACATIONS ★
BY PHIL WISWELL

Miss English, Mrs. French, and Ms. Lapp all went on vacation recently, one to England, one to France, and one to Lapland. If only one of the following four statements is true, who went where?

1. Ms. Lapp went to England.

2. Ms. Lapp did not go to France.

3. Miss English did not go to France.

4. Miss English did not go to Lapland.

Answer, page 184

JULY 4 HOMECOMING ★★
BY R. H. DRAKE

The Clarks were looking forward to July 4, when their six sons, and their sons' wives and children, were coming to their Utah home for a holiday celebration organized by their son Ron. Everyone was due to arrive July 3. Each couple had one, two, or three children. From the following clues, can you match the sons with their wives, determine how many children each couple had, deduce their time of arrival, and figure out where each family lived?

1. One couple crossed no state or national borders in getting to the homecoming.

2. The couples arrived July 3 at 8 A.M., 10 A.M., noon, 2 P.M., 3 P.M., and 5 P.M.

3. The couples from Germany and Japan have the same number of children.

4. George has only one child, a boy; Eileen has only two girls; and Carol has only one girl.

5. The son from Texas arrived at 10 A.M.

6. Pat, who hails from Wyoming, has three children and did not arrive either first or last.

7. Frank flew in from Germany and arrived after noon, two hours after his brother from Japan.

8. Bert and Bob don't have the same number of children. The son from Texas has one less child than the son from Wyoming. The son from Arizona has one more child than Frank.

9. Wendy arrived after Jill, who arrived after Linda. But Linda arrived before Eileen, who arrived before noon.

10. Keith drove all night and arrived before 10 A.M. with his three hungry children.

11. Bert packed his wife and two children into the car that morning and arrived three hours after Frank.

Answer, page 184

WILL THE REAL JOHN SMITH STAND UP? ★★
BY EILEEN KENT

My old friend John Smith, in his continuing saga of the hazards and hassles of being blessed with that particular name, told me this story of confused identities.

While waiting in Chicago's O'Hare Airport for a plane to Washington, he responded to a page for John Smith. To his surprise, four other men named John Smith also showed up at the ticket counter, each headed for a different city. Each of the five men had a different middle initial (one was John H.), a different occupation (one was an editor), and a different purpose for traveling (one was going to a chess tournament). From the clues below, can you match each John Smith with his occupation, his destination, and the purpose of his trip, and also tell the order of their departures?

1. The five men arrived at the ticket counter in the following order: the actor, John S., the conventioneer, the man bound for Paris, and the man going to a wedding.

2. John M.'s flight, which was not the one to Los Angeles, was scheduled to leave after both the surgeon's plane and the flight to New York, but before both the flight of the man going to the wedding and John A.'s plane.

3. The man headed for a job interview, the conventioneer, and John F. were all at the ticket counter when the steelworker arrived; the accountant had already left.

4. The last flight was to Houston; the first flight was to New York, which was not the destination of the vacationer.

5. The third man to arrive at the ticket counter caught the third flight out. None of the other arrivals at the counter coincided with flight departures in this manner.

Answer, page 184

ON THE ROAD TO CANTERBURY ★★
BY J. MARK THOMPSON

Five pilgrims met by chance at an inn on their way to the cathedral at Canterbury. They were a franklin, a knight, a miller, a clerk, and a summoner, and their names were Thomas, Derek, Lewis, Piers, and Hugh (not necessarily in that order). They agreed to travel together and decided that each of them would tell a story along the way. The five drew straws to determine the order in which they would speak, and one by one they related the tales of Orlando, Narcissus, Robin Hood, Esther, and St. George (although not necessarily in that order).

Using the information below, can you deduce the profession of each pilgrim, which story each one told, and in what order they spoke?

1. Thomas and the summoner agreed privately that the clerk's tale was silly, and each resolved to do better when his turn came.

2. While one pilgrim was telling the tale of Orlando, Hugh began to quarrel with the second storyteller (who had just finished). Lewis and the knight separated the two men while the teller of the tale of Orlando waited impatiently to finish.

3. Lewis and Piers found the summoner's tale lacking in interest.

4. The franklin laughed so hard at the tale of Robin Hood that he fell into a roadside ditch. Thomas helped him up as the storyteller continued. The knight, who was usually helpful in such emergencies, was preoccupied with the story he was planning to tell.

5. The tale of Esther, which immediately followed the tale of Narcissus, was very long; lulled by the steady plodding of his horse, Derek dozed off during the telling. The knight woke him, since Derek's tale came next. Fortunately, the storyteller noticed none of this. *Answer, page 184*

NUMBER STRATEGY SOLITAIRE ★★

BY SID SACKSON

In this unusual version of solitaire, you're allowed to look at all your cards—but even so, it's tough to plan a good strategy.

To begin, remove the face cards from a standard deck, shuffle the remaining cards, and deal out 16 cards in a 4 x 4 tableau such as the one shown. The undealt cards form your "hand," and the object is to play them onto any of the 16 tableau piles. Suit is irrelevant; only the number values of the cards determine where you may play them. An ace always has a value of 1.

There are two simple rules:

1. You may play a hand card horizontally or vertically adjacent to any pair of tableau cards that add up to its value or to its value plus 10.

2. You may not play a hand card onto a tableau card of equal value.

Let's say the first card in your hand is a 7, and you are playing on the tableau shown. You may play your 7 on top of any card adjacent to a pair that totals 7 or 17, but not on top of another 7. In the second horizontal row, there's a 3 and a 4, flanked by a 7 and a 5. Thus you may play your 7 on the 5 (but not on the 7). But there's another 3 and 4 combination in the second vertical column, this one flanked by a 7 and a 9. So you have the additional option of playing your card on the 9. Finally, in the first horizontal row, there's a 10 and 7 combination (totaling 17), flanked by an 8 and a 6. So you may also play your 7 on either the 8 or the 6.

This is where the strategy comes in. Although you must play the cards in the order in which you've shuffled them, you are free to study all the cards in your hand to make the most efficient combinations possible. The game ends when you reach a card that you cannot play, or when you win by playing out your hand.

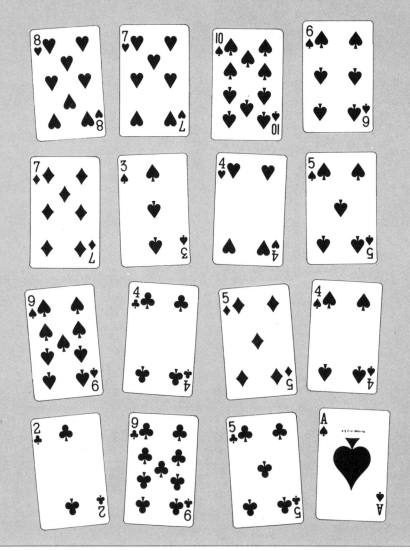

FAMILY PICTURES **

BY MIKE SHENK

The 18 jumbled pictures below can be grouped into six families of three members, each family related by some common element. Can you pick out the six triplets and de-termine what ties each of them together? (It will help to think about the word each picture represents.)

Answers, page 184

STAR: A TWO-PLAYER BOARD GAME★★

BY CRAIGE SCHENSTED

EQUIPMENT Two contrasting sets of approximately 30 pieces each (such as pennies and nickels), and the board shown.

PLAY Each player in turn places a piece on any vacant light-gray hexagonal space. Once placed, a piece is never moved or captured. Play continues in this manner until both players choose to pass (that is, when further moves cannot influence the outcome).

SCORING A player receives points for each of his connected groups of pieces that touch at least 3 of the 33 dark-gray regions (the partial hexagons) around the edge of the board. Such groups are known as "stars," owing to their tendency to develop numerous branches. A single piece on one of the six corner spaces touches three dark edge regions, and also counts as a star.

Each star is worth 2 points less than the number of dark regions it touches. (For example, a star touching five dark regions is worth 3 points.) Both players add up the points scored by all their stars, and the player with the most points wins. (As a convenient check on your scoring, note that the two final scores always add up to 31.)

Playing tips, page 185

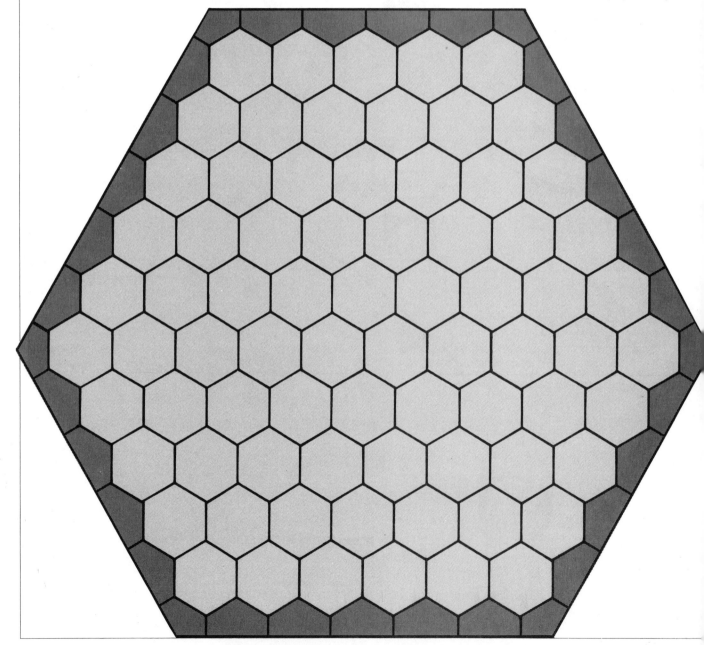

THE ETERNAL TRIANGLE *

BY MICHAEL W. ECKER

There's more than plain geometry to this triangle of triangles. Just play along and you'll observe its mathemagical powers.

To begin, place a whole number in each empty triangle in the top row, so that all six triangles contain a number.

To fill in each triangle in the second row, add the two numbers connected to it from above; find the largest multiple of 5 that is *less* than the sum; subtract the smaller number from the larger one; and finally, enter the result in the triangle. For example, if you have a 31 next to the 6 in the diagram, add the two numbers (6 + 31 = 37), subtract the nearest multiple of 5 that is less than the sum

(37 − 35 = 2), and enter the result (2) in the triangle connected to the 31 and the 6. If your initial sum is 5 or less, enter the result directly, without doing the other calculations.

After filling in all the triangles in the second row, repeat the above procedure to complete the third, fourth, and fifth rows, leaving only the final triangle at the bottom.

Stop! Before you enter that final number, close your eyes and concentrate. Let the final answer come to you across space and time. Here it is . . . that number, the one and only number that will complete this magic triangle is . . . on page 184.

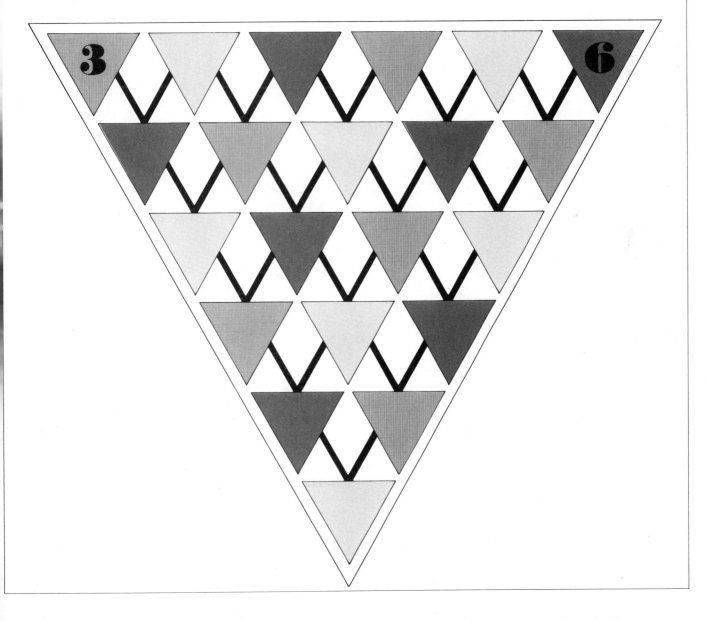

A PERFECT MATCH ★☆

Playing with matches is what we teach children not to do, yet it's a form of recreation with a long tradition. Many of the matchstick puzzles that appear repeatedly in modern puzzle books go back to the volume *Streichholzspiele* ("matchstick games"), by Sophus Tromholt, published in Leipzig in 1889. How much earlier the puzzles were invented is anybody's guess.

Here's a collection of mostly little-known matchstick puzzles selected from many sources, together with one original contribution (puzzle 6), which our test-solvers found either ridiculously easy or ridiculously hard. Some of the other puzzles are like that, too. In all cases, there must be no loose ends or leftover matches in your solutions.

Answers, page 185

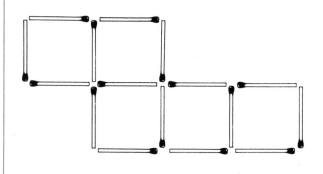

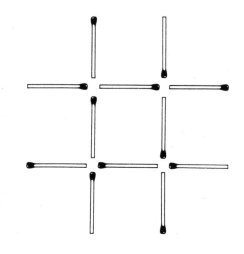

1. ZIGZAG
Move two matches to produce four identical squares. (Interestingly, most people who've solved this puzzle have trouble doing it again when the zigzag is reversed.)

2. TIC-TAC-TOE
This tic-tac-toe grid contains 12 matchsticks. Move three matches to produce three identical squares. (There are several solutions.)

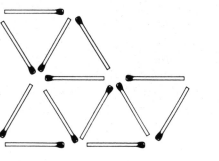

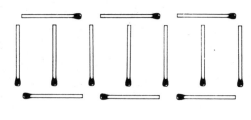

3. AS EASY AS 1-2-3
Remove three matches to leave three triangles.

4. MENTAL HURDLES
Here's a classic teaser from Henry Dudeney, the turn-of-the-century British puzzle genius. The illustration shows 13 matches representing a farmer's hurdles (portable fence pieces), placed so that they form six sheep pens of equal size. After one of these hurdles is stolen, the farmer wants to rearrange the remaining 12 so as still to form six pens of equal size. How can he do it?

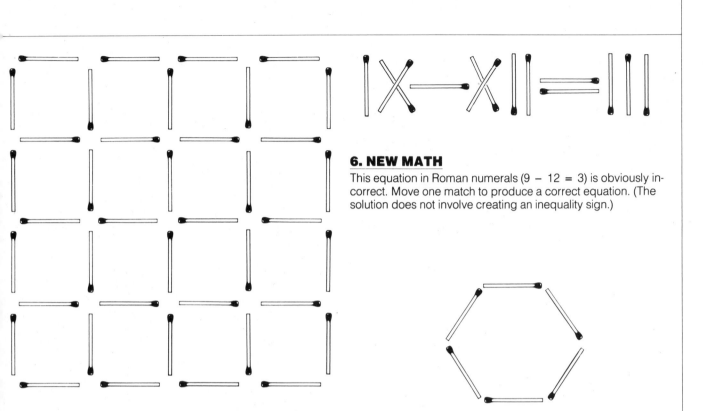

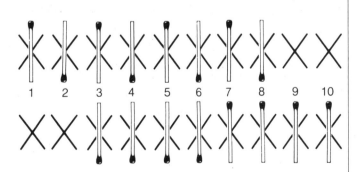

6. NEW MATH

This equation in Roman numerals (9 − 12 = 3) is obviously incorrect. Move one match to produce a correct equation. (The solution does not involve creating an inequality sign.)

5. SQUARING OFF

Counting the sixteen 1x1 squares, the nine 2x2 squares, the four 3x3 squares, and the one 4x4 square, this figure contains 30 squares in all. How many matches must be removed to leave no squares of any size?

7. FACETIOUS?

Here's another tricky Dudeney puzzle. Six matches are arranged to form a regular hexagon. Can you add three more matches and then arrange the nine to show another regular six-sided figure?

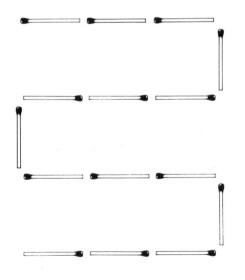

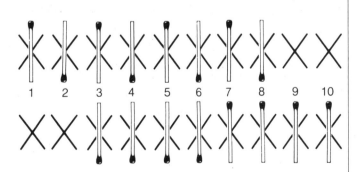

9. HEADS UP (AND DOWN)

Finally, a different sort of match puzzle. Before starting, mark 10 equidistant Xs on a piece of paper and on them place eight matches with heads alternating up and down as shown in the top illustration. The puzzle is to move two adjacent matches at a time to produce the lower arrangement. That is, on each move, take two adjacent matchsticks—without turning them over—and place them on the two empty Xs. The complete switch from the original arrangement to the one below it can be done in four moves.

8. SLITHERING SNAKE

Move four matches to form two squares. (There are several solutions.)

RURAL RHYTHMS LOGIC PUZZLES

MOUNTAIN DO ★

Six grizzled Appalachian mountain men, who were ornery hermits in most ways, enjoyed getting together now and then to play a little old-time music and swig some hooch from a jug. Their names were Lem, Clem, Shem, Flem, Homer, and Billy-Bob, and the instruments in their band were kazoo, banjo, guitar, fiddle, mandolin, and harmonica. Below is a short note sent by one of the hillbillies to another. By reading it, you should be able to determine the instrument played by each band member.

Answer, page 185

Dear Cousin,

You are cordially invited to my cozy cabin tomorrow evening for an invigorating session of music and camaraderie. Alas, our esteemed cousin Clem will be unable to attend, so we shall have to do without one of the nonstringed instruments. (I had hoped we could persuade Homer to stop plucking long enough to fill in for Clem, but as you know Homer has this ludicrous aversion to playing any instrument with as many letters in its name as he has in his own.) At any rate, we shall make do suitably if you bring your fiddle and convince cousin Shem to accompany us upon his guitar. I trust Billy-Bob will provide the customary refreshments. As for me, I'll be happily strumming my instrument with my usual verve.

Your affectionate relative,
Flem

BAR TALK ★★

Out in the west Texas town of El Paso lived five long tall Texas ranchers. Each rancher wore a 10-gallon hat, drank Lone Star beer, and could look a rattlesnake dead in the eye. But what made these ranchers unusual was that each one's last name was the name of a different animal; further, each one drove a car whose name was that of an animal, and each owned a different animal as a pet. The pets, cars, and ranchers' names, in no special order, were Pinto, Cougar, Rabbit, Lynx, Jaguar, Beetle, Eagle, Skylark, Mustang, Llama, Barracuda, Falcon, Spider, Stag, and Impala.

One day the five ranchers got together at a local saloon to have a few beers and listen to the jukebox. From their conversation, you should be able to match up ranchers, cars, and pets.

"You know, Beetle, that pet cat of yours got loose last week and raised one hell of a ruckus in my barnyard."

"Yeah, sorry about that, old buddy. My wildcat's got a mighty willful streak, just like Rabbit's horse. Ain't that right, Rabbit?"

"Aw, heck, that old horse ain't half as ornery as he used to be. Took something out of him when he got bumped by Falcon's car last year. Remember, Falcon?"

"That wasn't *my* car. That was the Stag that knocked your old horse down. My car ain't been in a single accident, and I reckon it takes a mighty careless driver to hit a horse. But hey, leave it to a guy that keeps a six-legged pet!"

"Got more legs than that, pardner. And besides, at least he's *got* legs. Unlike *yours*, Falcon!"

"Now, don't argue, good buddies. Ain't that 'San Antonio Rose' on the jukebox? And I don't guess there's just *one* careless driver among us, with both the Pinto and the Skylark in the shop with bent fenders. You want another beer, Lynx?"

"No, I believe I'll hit the road."

"Say, how about giving me a lift? My brother drove off in my Impala this morning."

"Sure thing. Hey, even if my Jaguar breaks down, you can ride my pet home. He's grazing now over in the cemetery by the courthouse. Well, so long, folks."

"So long."
"So long."
"So long."
"So long."

"Say, I didn't know he let his pet loose in the cemetery. Believe I'll get my Pinto out of the shop and drive over there for a look. So long, Rabbit."

"Take care. Well, buddy, that leaves just the two of us. Have another beer on me. Ain't that 'Faded Love' on the jukebox?"

Answer, page 185

BY EMILY COX AND HENRY RATHVON

SEVEN LITTLE INDIANS ★★

On top of old Smokey all covered with trees,
I met an old geezer whose name was McGeeze.
He told me, "Young feller, I've lived in these pines
For seventy years, taking gold from the mines.

"I'm rich as a king in this tumbledown shack,
And ore that I've dug has filled many a sack.
I've more than I need, and I'm cranky and old,
So I'll give you, young feller, one bagful of gold.

"But first you must answer a riddle I've set.
It's hard, and nobody has answered it yet.
It features some tribesmen, and here is your clue:
Some always speak false and some always speak true.

"The names of these Indians, seven in all,
Are Barjuk, Gooth, Fumfum, Fy, Fo, Fu, and Fol.
Imagine them standing arranged in a row
And making in turn their pronouncements like so:

"The first one says, 'Third in our lineup is Fy,
And fourth is a person who can't tell a lie.'
The second says, 'Let me be honestly heard.
The sixth in our lineup is true to his word.'

"The third one says, "Fumfum will always speak true,
And seventh of all in our lineup is Fu.'
The fourth remarks, 'I have the key that you seek:
You'll find more than half of us lie when we speak.'

"The fifth asserts, 'Fourth in the lineup is Gooth,
And Fu is a tribesman who can't speak the truth.'
The sixth one declares, 'The fifth, second, and I
Cannot be believed, for all three of us lie.'

"The seventh says, 'Barjuk's not sixth in our row.
The man who stands first is the one we call Fo.'
So tell me, young feller," the geezer exclaimed,
"Which tribesmen are honest, and what is each named?"

I pondered the puzzle till round in my head
The pieces all jumbled and tumbled and sped.
On top of old Smokey I sat in a mist,
Alone in the pines with my chin on my fist.

As soon as the moon was alight in the trees
I leaped to my feet and I answered McGeeze.
To gold in a sack I then laid my just claim.
I ask you, dear reader—could you do the same?

Answer, page 185

TOP TEN ★★★

Good afternoon, folks, and welcome to WMOO, the home of country-and-western music. We've got this week's Top Ten Tune Roundup all set to go, so turn your radio up good and loud. I'm looking at the roundup from last week, buckeroos, and I see where this week's Top Ten are the very same foot-stomping tunes—only each song is in a brand-new position now.

I see, too, where there's more songs that went down in the Top Ten than went up. But just to refresh your memories, cowpokes, let me read you the Top Ten from last week. The list goes like this here:

1. "Trailer Courtin' "
2. "Saddle Soap (Will Never Wash Your Lipstick off My Heart)"
3. "Beer Belly Polka"
4. "Tennessee Schmaltz"
5. "Going to Altoona to Get My Alto Tuned"
6. "You Are My Moonshine"
7. "Bumblebee Bop"
8. "Stand on Your Man"
9. "Haystack Hannah
10. "Cole Porter's Daughter"

Well, as I say, this week's roundup is a mite different. "Tennessee Schmaltz" went up the same number of positions as "Saddle Soap" went down. "Bumblebee Bop" went down half as many positions as "Cole Porter's Daughter" went up. "Going to Altoona" gained as many positions as "Tennessee Schmaltz" and one other song combined! I believe that gives you a pretty good picture of this week's Top Ten, so I'll say no more about it, but just get right down to the job of kicking this jamboree off with the number-one hit. And a toe-tapping tune it is, too! Here we go then, with—well, buckeroos, do you know what it is? And can you figure out the order of the rest of the Top Ten?

Answer, page 185

MATH APPEAL

DIGITITIS
BY B. UPTON-ROWLEY

Although Digititis puzzles may look formidable, their solution requires only logic, arithmetic, and perseverance. The object is to replace the numbers, one digit per dash, so that each completed division problem is mathematically correct. Each solution is unique.

You'll learn a lot about these puzzles as you start to solve them, but if you're new to the dividing fever, these hints may help you catch it:

1. When a two-digit number is subtracted from a three-digit number, and the difference is a two-digit number (as in the first subtraction in both of these problems), the hundreds digit of the three-digit number must be 1.

2. It's often useful to work from the bottom up. Since these problems have no remainders, the last two lines of a given problem (not counting the 0) will be identical, and the ones digit in the dividend (that's the number being divided) will be the same as the ones digit on the last two lines.

Now plunge right in, and let your motto be "divide and conquer."

Answers, page 186

PUZZLE 1 ★★

```
              _ _ _ _ _
     _ _  )  _ _ _ _ _ 9
             _ _
          8  _ _
           _ _ _
          0  _ _ _
             _ _
           _ _
             _ _
           _ _
            0
```

PUZZLE 2 ★★★

```
              _ _ _ _ _
     _ _  )  _ 3 _ _ 1
             9 _
             _ _ _
          8  _ _ _
             _ _ _
           _ _
             _ _ _
            0
```

NUMBER SQUARE ★★★
BY BARBARA KING

Turn the filled-in grid upside down for a completed word square.

Answer, page 186

1. Sum of the squares of 3 and 73
2. Number of feet in $^7/_{12}$ of a mile
3. $^1/_{47}$ of this = a perfect square
4. $(x^2 - 1) \div 04$, when $x = 18$

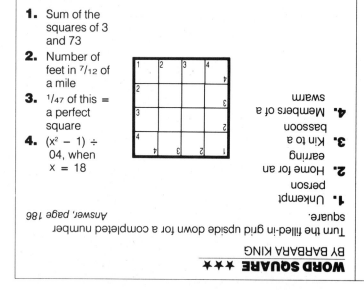

1. Unkempt person
2. Home for an earring
3. Kin to a bassoon
4. Members of a swarm

Answer, page 186

Turn the filled-in grid upside down for a completed number square.

BY BARBARA KING

WORD SQUARE ★★★

MAGIC STAR ★★
BY CAL Q. LEYTOR

Can you place the numbers from 1 to 14 into the circles of this magic star so that each line of four circles totals 30? Five of the numbers have been entered to get you started. *Answer, page 186*

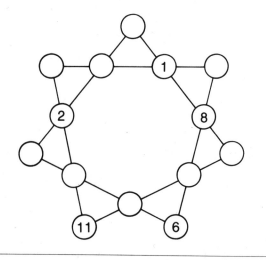

WHEEL OF FORTUNE ★★
BY HENRY HOOK

The lucky wheel at right has 12 sections. Ten of them bear a different number from 1 to 10; the remaining two sections bear stars. From the clues below, determine the layout of the wheel.

Before you start to solve, however, let's see just how lucky you are. Place the number 1 in any section of the wheel (but not the top section with the arrow). After you've solved the puzzle, if a star appears in the arrowed section—it's your lucky day!

Answer, page 186

CLUES

1. The five even numbers appear in order counterclockwise, though not necessarily in consecutive sections.

2. The number 2 is directly across from the section adjacent to the numbers 1 and 3.

3. The number 7 is directly between two sections with numbers totaling seven.

4. Two numbers are one section counterclockwise from their respective square roots.

5. No two adjacent sections have numbers totaling more than twelve.

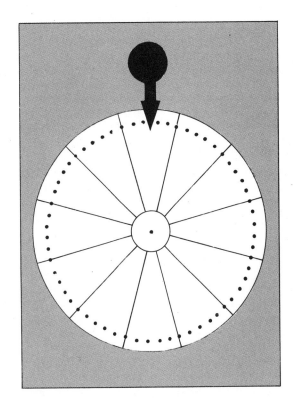

SIX-PACKS ★★
BY A. BRAINE

Insert the arithmetic symbols +, −, ×, and ÷ between the 6s in each line to make the eight different equations true. In each case the arithmetic operations should be performed in order from left to right.

Answers, page 186

5	=	6	6	6	6
8	=	6	6	6	6
13	=	6	6	6	6
42	=	6	6	6	6
48	=	6	6	6	6
66	=	6	6	6	6
108	=	6	6	6	6
180	=	6	6	6	6

BINGO MATH ★★
BY BILL HALLIDAY

There's something unusual about the winning numbers on this bingo card (the top row, left blank here). One of the five numbers was a factor of three of the others, and all the digits 0 to 9 were accounted for somewhere in the row. Can you determine the winner's lucky numbers?

Answer, page 186

CAN YOU THINK LIKE A COMPUTER?

BY R. WAYNE SCHMITTBERGER

It's true that humans need computers—but computers need humans even more. If we don't tell them exactly what steps to perform and in what order to perform them, they are as useless as a dead battery. Confronted with an incomplete or illogical set of instructions, for instance, a computer can't fill in the gaps or make allowances, as humans can, by using reason and common sense, since it has neither. Instead, it simply stops and waits for new orders.

Someday computers may be able to think more like humans, but until they do, computer users will have to get used to thinking like machines. This means being able to describe a task as a series of precisely ordered steps. For example, a human readily understands the simple command "open the door and go in," but a computer might require the following series of instructions to carry out that task:

a. Check to see whether door is locked.
b. If door is unlocked, skip the next two statements.
c. Put key in lock.
d. Unlock door.
e. Open door.
f. If key is in lock, remove key.
g. Go inside.
h. Close door.

If the order of these statements were slightly changed, a human would still know what to do. A computer would be stumped.

The four puzzles that follow are based on the inflexible kind of logic that computers use. Each consists of a mixed-up set of instructions which, when put in proper order, is a literal, step-by-step method of performing a particular task. In all the problems, the first and last instructions are already in their correct positions. Can you put the remaining instructions in the proper order?

Answers, page 185

1. TRAFFIC LIGHTS ★

A procedure is needed to change all the red traffic lights in a small town to green, and vice versa. (Luckily, there are no amber lights in this town, and also no lights that don't work.) Assume that you have a street map that shows the locations of all the lights. (The "skip" statements will help you avoid ending up with all lights the same color.)
a. If all lights on your map are marked "done," skip the next six statements.
b. If the light is red, skip the next two statements.
c. Turn the light red.
d. Turn the light green.
e. On your map, mark the light you just changed as "done" and go back to the first statement.
f. Find a light that is not marked "done" on your map, and check whether it is red or green.
g. Skip the next statement.
h. End.

2. CANDY SALE ★★

Chocolate truffles cost $5 per pound for the first 5 pounds, and only $3 per pound for any amount in excess of 5 pounds. How would you compute the cost of any given amount of truffles?
a. If the amount is over 5 pounds, skip the next two statements.
b. Multiply by 3.
c. Multiply by 5.
d. Add 25.
e. Subtract 5 from the weight in pounds.
f. Skip the next three statements.
g. Write the result, which is the price in dollars.

3. BALANCING BEAMS ★★★

You have three heavy beams marked A, B, and C, and want to find out which one is the heaviest. You also have a scale that tells you which of any two beams is heavier, but it does not give the specific weight of any beam. In what order must you perform the following steps to determine which beam is the heaviest, and to mark it accordingly? Assume that all three have different weights.
a. Weigh A against B.
b. Weigh B against C.
c. Weigh A against C.
d. If A is heavier, skip the next three statements.
e. If A is heavier, skip the next four statements.
f. If B is heavier, skip the next five statements.
g. Mark A "heaviest."
h. Mark B "heaviest."
i. Mark C "heaviest."
j. Skip the next statement.
k. Skip the next two statements.
l. Skip the next three statements.
m. End.

4. LEAP YEAR ★★★

You want to be able to write "leap year" or "not a leap year" for any given year from 1801 to 2101, according to whether or not the given year had or will have 366 days in it. You must remember to take into account that years ending in 00 are leap years only if they are evenly divisible by 400. (Thus, 1900 was not a leap year, but 2000 will be.) Years ending in any other digits, of course, are leap years if and only if they are divisible by 4.
a. Read the year chosen (from 1801 to 2101).
b. Divide the year by 4.
c. Divide the year by 100.
d. Divide the year by 400.
e. Skip the next statement.
f. If there is a remainder, skip the next two statements.
g. If there is a remainder, skip the next two statements.
h. If there is a remainder, skip the next six statements.
i. Write "leap year."
j. Write "not a leap year."
k. End.

A QUIZ FOR ALMOST EVERY OCCASION

1
How many gallons does a ten-gallon hat hold?

2
In what country were Panama hats first made?

3
Where did the game of Chinese checkers originate?

4
Where was the Battle of Bunker Hill fought?

5
The Canary Islands are named for what animal?

6
What kind of musical instrument is the English horn, and where was it invented?

7
Where was the Woodstock Festival held?

8
From what animal does the catgut used to string tennis rackets come?

9
What are camel's hair brushes made of?

10
Where were Venetian blinds invented?

★★

WHO'S BURIED IN GRANT'S TOMB?
BY CHUCK REICHBLUM

Remember the 1950s quiz show *You Bet Your Life?* Whenever a contestant struck out on all the questions, Groucho Marx would then ask—for $50 and a few laughs—a question like "Who's buried in Grant's Tomb?" Questions like this (and the others on this page) seem like money in the bank, but don't bet your life on it.

Answers, page 186

THE PRICE WAS RIGHT ★☆

Step right up, ladies and gentlemen—and step right back in time. You'll travel back to October 28, 1929, the day before the great stock market crash, to guess the advertised retail prices of these 12 common items. So it's up with Prohibition and down with prices—or is it down with Prohibition and up with prices?   *Answers, page 186*

A popular new
STEINWAY
THE INSTRUMENT OF THE IMMORTALS

2. Only five feet seven inches long, the beautiful Steinway Ebonized Baby Grand retains the tone and response of a true grand piano.

5. A one-mile ride in New York City in a brand-new Paramount Taxi Cab is transportation at its most luxurious.

6. For keeping up-to-date on politics, cultural events, and the sporting and fashion scenes, no magazine's more informative than the current issue of *The New Yorker*.

1. Westclox, maker of fine pocket watches and elegant clocks for 40 years, presents the Pocket Ben. It's a nickel-plated timepiece of distinguished reliability.

3. The American Tobacco Company blends fine tobaccos to make every package of Lucky Strike Cigarettes. Their unique toasting process gives that extra-special flavor.

7. What could make a more nutritious lunch than a steaming cup of tomato soup? And nobody makes it better than Campbell's.

4. A one-pound assortment of Whitman's Prestige Chocolates comes packaged in a metal chest. It's a decorative and scrumptious gift!

8. The full-size Plymouth coupe from Chrysler features a "Silver Dome" high-compression engine and hydraulic brakes on all four wheels. It's a dream to drive.

9. Burroughs's 10-digit electric calculator features a new key mechanism that virtually eliminates errors due to incomplete key strokes.

10. This Transcontinental Air Transport round-trip ticket for two between New York and Los Angeles really lets you both relax. Take the TAT air-train service from coast to coast (plane by day, train by night) and cut your travel time in half—to 48 hours.

11. The smart consumer remembers to pick up two rolls of famous ScotTissue, the completely absorbent, chemically pure bathroom tissue from the Scott Paper Company.

12. This standard General Electric vacuum cleaner cleans the entire house thoroughly—all you have to do is push!

LISTOMANIA ★☆

From the Ten Commandments to the Ten Best-Dressed, lists have satisfied a common human trait—the urge to organize. Irving Wallace and family have turned this penchant into a passion, compiling hundreds of lists in their three-volume *Book of Lists*. Here's a sampling of some of their most intriguing efforts—minus the titles. Can you figure out what topic unites each group?   *Answers, page 186*

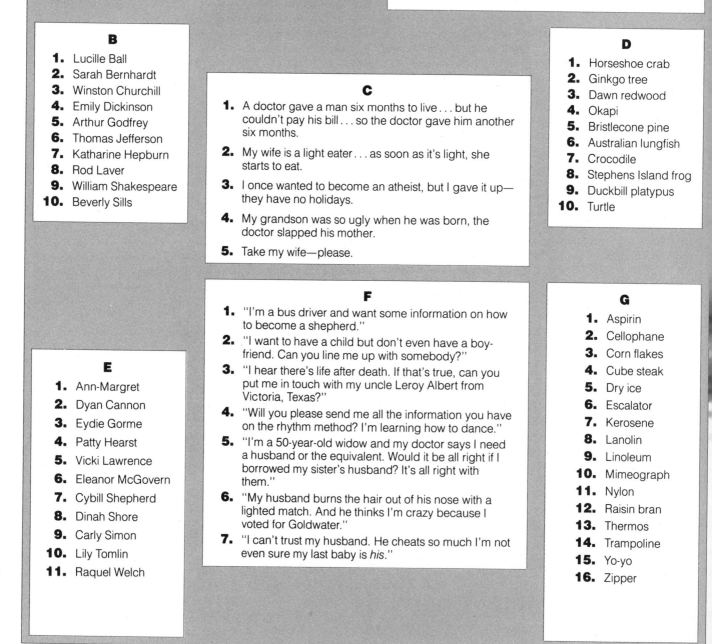

A

1. Eyeglass frame with adjustable rear-view mirror
2. Power-operated pool cue
3. Toilet lid lock
4. Combination deer-carcass sled and chaise longue
5. Carry-all hat with a cavity for cosmetics, jewelry, etc.
6. Fluid-operated zipper
7. Baby-patting machine to put a baby to sleep
8. Electronic snore depressor to shock the snorer

B

1. Lucille Ball
2. Sarah Bernhardt
3. Winston Churchill
4. Emily Dickinson
5. Arthur Godfrey
6. Thomas Jefferson
7. Katharine Hepburn
8. Rod Laver
9. William Shakespeare
10. Beverly Sills

C

1. A doctor gave a man six months to live . . . but he couldn't pay his bill . . . so the doctor gave him another six months.
2. My wife is a light eater . . . as soon as it's light, she starts to eat.
3. I once wanted to become an atheist, but I gave it up—they have no holidays.
4. My grandson was so ugly when he was born, the doctor slapped his mother.
5. Take my wife—please.

D

1. Horseshoe crab
2. Ginkgo tree
3. Dawn redwood
4. Okapi
5. Bristlecone pine
6. Australian lungfish
7. Crocodile
8. Stephens Island frog
9. Duckbill platypus
10. Turtle

E

1. Ann-Margret
2. Dyan Cannon
3. Eydie Gorme
4. Patty Hearst
5. Vicki Lawrence
6. Eleanor McGovern
7. Cybill Shepherd
8. Dinah Shore
9. Carly Simon
10. Lily Tomlin
11. Raquel Welch

F

1. "I'm a bus driver and want some information on how to become a shepherd."
2. "I want to have a child but don't even have a boyfriend. Can you line me up with somebody?"
3. "I hear there's life after death. If that's true, can you put me in touch with my uncle Leroy Albert from Victoria, Texas?"
4. "Will you please send me all the information you have on the rhythm method? I'm learning how to dance."
5. "I'm a 50-year-old widow and my doctor says I need a husband or the equivalent. Would it be all right if I borrowed my sister's husband? It's all right with them."
6. "My husband burns the hair out of his nose with a lighted match. And he thinks I'm crazy because I voted for Goldwater."
7. "I can't trust my husband. He cheats so much I'm not even sure my last baby is *his*."

G

1. Aspirin
2. Cellophane
3. Corn flakes
4. Cube steak
5. Dry ice
6. Escalator
7. Kerosene
8. Lanolin
9. Linoleum
10. Mimeograph
11. Nylon
12. Raisin bran
13. Thermos
14. Trampoline
15. Yo-yo
16. Zipper

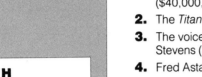

BY IRVING WALLACE, DAVID WALLECHINSKY, AMY WALLACE, AND SYLVIA WALLACE

I

1. The San Francisco–Oakland Bay Bridge ($40,000,000)
2. The *Titanic* ($3,019,400)
3. The voice of New York Metropolitan Opera star Rïse Stevens ($1,000,000)
4. Fred Astaire's legs ($650,000)
5. The crossed eyes of comedian Ben Turpin ($500,000)
6. The comedy team of Bud Abbott and Lou Costello, against disagreement between them ($250,000)
7. The legs of WWII pinup Betty Grable ($250,000)
8. Jimmy Durante's nose ($140,000)
9. Sonja Henie's ice skates ($250,000)
10. Four pairs of special elasticized wool trousers used by flamenco dancer Jose Greco ($3,920)

H

1. Murder of Agamemnon
2. Archimedes' discovery of the Law of Physics
3. Jean-Paul Marat's assassination
4. Richard Wagner's inspiration for his final opera, *Parsifal*
5. Chess player Paul Morphy's death
6. French author Edmond Rostand's writing of *Cyrano de Bergerac*
7. The fall of Norway's King Haakon VII

J

1. Susan B. Anthony
2. Ludwig van Beethoven
3. J. Edgar Hoover
4. Joan of Arc
5. Ralph Nader
6. Florence Nightingale
7. Henry David Thoreau
8. Isaac Newton

L

1. Catherine the Great had her hair brushed.
2. Shirley Chisholm takes a bubble bath.
3. Winston Churchill alternated between twin beds.
4. Alexander Dumas père, at his doctor's suggestion, ate an apple a day at 7 A.M. under the Arc de Triomphe.
5. Cary Grant watches old movies on TV.
6. James Thurber rewrote Poe's "The Raven" from the viewpoint of the bird.

K

1. Philtrum
2. Eponychium
3. Glabella
4. Otoliths
5. Phalanx

O

1. *Casablanca*
2. *King Kong* (1933)
3. *The Magnificent Seven*
4. *The Maltese Falcon*
5. *The Adventures of Robin Hood*
6. *The African Queen*
7. *The Birds*
8. *Citizen Kane*
9. *Miracle on 34th Street*
10. *Girls! Girls! Girls!*

M

1. George Washington's laundry bill ($1,100)
2. Swedish philosopher Emanuel Swedenborg's skull ($2,850)
3. A one-seater 19th-century American oak outhouse ($140)
4. The London Bridge ($2,460,000)
5. One hundred eighty thousand Egyptian mummified cats (3.15 shillings per ton)
6. Coca-Cola gum wrapper, circa 1908 ($90)
7. Shrunken head of a New Zealand Maori ($20,400)
8. Judy Garland's false eyelashes ($125)

N

1. African elephant 640
2. Rhinoceros 560
3. Giraffe 450
4. Cow 280
5. Orangutan 275
6. Human being 267
7. Reindeer 246
8. Panther 93
9. Kangaroo 40
10. Rabbit 31
11. Hamster 16
12. Opossum 13

CAN YOU THINK UNDER PRESSURE? ★☆

BY WILL SHORTZ

This test measures your ability to follow directions and think clearly under pressure. It is said that people who score well make good teachers, computer technicians, and masochists.

You have exactly six minutes to read and answer the following questions. Have a pencil ready, and a clock or stopwatch handy to time yourself. When the six minutes are up, stop working, whether or not you're finished.

On your mark, get set, go!   *Answers and ratings, page 187*

If the letter X appears before the comma in this sentence, cross it out. Otherwise draw a wavy line under the word SEX. Circle the odd one out: *happy, glad, euphoric, gaiety, delighted.* How many cubes are there in the stack below?_____

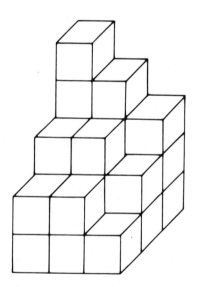

If a horse has five legs, put a dot in this square ☐ , but if it doesn't, leave the square blank, and answer the negative of this question incorrectly: How old are you?_____
What four coins add up to 26¢?_____

_____

If cats and kittens don't bark, write DOG in this space_____, but if Nebraska is larger than Texas, enter BIG here._____ Be sure to write NO here if March is the third month of the year. _____ Read each word

of this sentence in reverse and answer in the space provided: tahW seod ''golf'' lleps drawkcab?_____ Don't write PIG in this blank_____, unless oxygen is a metal or birds can't fly. True or false: All those tested were accepted; Marty was rejected; therefore, Marty was not tested._____
If yesterday was three days before Friday, what will tomorrow be?_____ Name five words that start and end with the letter M._____
What relation is your brother's uncle to you?_____ Don't neglect to put a check mark in this square ☐ , even if Millard Fillmore was once President of the United States. The time

shown by the clock above is 7:12. Approximately what time would it be if the hands were reversed?_____ Write HOT at the bottom of this page—but hold it! If the word COLD doesn't have the same number of letters as HOT, write ICE at the bottom of the page instead, unless a refrigerator is not cooler than a stove, in which case just write BRRRR. Count the number of N's in this sentence and enter your answer, spelled out, in this blank._____ If this quiz was too hard for you, write I QUIT below this sentence. Otherwise just write I QUIT.

COULD YOU GET INTO COLLEGE TODAY? ★☆

One of the most serious games around is the Scholastic Aptitude Test (SAT), used by colleges to help determine which high school seniors to admit. Because of its consequences, most teenagers have trouble seeing the test as a game, and tend to dread it as an unpleasant rite of passage. The College Board, which administers the SAT, perpetuates that dread by laboring under the delusion that the SAT is *not* a game.

Like any game, the SAT has strict rules that you can manipulate to your advantage. One way to approach the SAT is to treat it as a contest, you versus the testmakers. Without the pressures of the real thing, you can take some time to study the questions. See if you can spot the traps the testmakers lay for you. Try to find the "logic" behind the wrong answers—how might you arrive at them by doing the wrong thing? Soon you'll begin to realize that the test is like a jigsaw puzzle: All the elements fit together.

With that approach in mind, we present the following SAT-like test. Of course the GAMES Aptitude Test is *not* an SAT, but we do hope it's an entertaining approximation. Some of the questions are from an actual SAT; others are made up to resemble or parody actual SAT questions.

You may begin.   *Answers and scoring, page 187*

SECTION I: 20 QUESTIONS

Select the lettered word that is the *opposite* of the first word.

1. BOORISH: (A) exciting   (B) refined   (C) distant
(D) brave   (E) tactless

2. ORDAIN: (A) novice   (B) permit   (C) proxy
(D) sustain   (E) proscribe

3. BAFFLING: (A) explicable   (B) culpable
(C) heretical   (D) enigmatic   (E) eventual

4. ASCETIC: (A) basic   (B) sober   (C) solid
(D) prosthetic   (E) libertine

5. INDIGENT: (A) sahib   (B) needy   (C) wealthy
(D) sweet   (E) flotsam

Select the lettered word(s) that best completes each sentence.

6. "Wonder" drugs that have _____ the practice of medicine in the past 40 years have enabled doctors to _____ lives that would have been lost in earlier times.
(A) salvaged . . . alleviate
(B) standardized . . . terminate
(C) socialized . . . regulate
(D) revolutionized . . . rescue
(E) licensed . . . stultify

7. Even if culture is learned rather than inherited, is it possible that what is learned depends upon _____ characteristics?
(A) environmental   (B) interrelated   (C) social
(D) salient   (E) innate

8. The events were timed to _____ with the opening of the hotel.
(A) concur   (B) coincide   (C) contemporaneous
(D) convert   (E) collate

Select the lettered analogy closest to the first one given.

9. BOAR : BORE ::   (A) sleep : tired   (B) sturm : drang
(C) plank : drill   (D) stake : steak   (E) wild : crazy

10. SLOP : HOGS ::   (A) pigs : wings   (B) nest : eggs
(C) grain : silo   (D) mess : troops   (E) pearl : oyster

11. TOWEL : WATER ::   (A) sponge : sea   (B) broom : dust
(C) cloth : sew   (D) stanch : flow   (E) clean : dry

12. CHESS : CHECKERS ::   (A) go : wari   (B) bridge : cribbage   (C) nim : hangman   (D) backgammon : old maid
(E) snooker : pool

If any of the underlined parts of the following sentences contain an error, choose that letter. And if there is no error, choose the letter E.

13. Wayne and Phil <u>decided</u> to be <u>an team</u> in the competition,
              A   B
despite their <u>conflicting</u> <u>modes</u> of play. <u>No Error.</u>
          C   D   E

14. Seismologists <u>have</u> <u>concurred</u> in their evaluation of the
                A   B
dangers <u>from</u> earthquakes and <u>its</u> aftershocks. <u>No Error.</u>
          C   D   E

15. Nobody <u>were</u> able <u>to predict</u> the <u>ultimate</u> consequences of
          A   B   C
<u>too much</u> testing. <u>No Error.</u>
 D   E

16. To prepare for the trial <u>so well</u>, the attorney had to <u>forsee</u>
  A   B   C
all <u>the arguments.</u> <u>No Error.</u>
      D   E

Choose the lettered phrase which best expresses the sense of the underlined portion of the sentence. Do not change the meaning of the original sentence.

17. It is still quite common in rural areas for a person to be born and <u>then you spend your whole life</u> in the same community.
(A) then you spend your whole life
(B) then they spend their whole lives
(C) to spend their whole lifetimes
(D) to spend his whole life
(E) then he would spend his lifetime

18. Because of <u>their obvious inadequacy, the contractor</u> was dropped from the project.
(A) their obvious inadequacy, the contractor
(B) their obvious inadequacies, the contractor
(C) his obvious inadequacy, the contractors
(D) his obvious inadequacies, the contractors
(E) his obvious inadequacy, the contractor

GO ON TO THE NEXT PAGE →

(continued)

COULD YOU GET INTO COLLEGE TODAY?

19. If you do not <u>desist, I shall be forced to resort to physical measures.</u>
(A) desist, I shall be forced to resort to physical measures.
(B) desist, I shan't be forced to resort to physical measures.
(C) stop, I shall be forced to reserve physical measures.
(D) stop, I shall be required to reserve physical measures.
(E) stop, I'll whup you upside the head.

20. If Will had not changed the clue to 20-Across, <u>it was insoluble.</u>
(A) it was insoluble.
(B) it will have been unsoluble.
(C) it would have been insolvable.
(D) it would have been insolvent.
(E) it will be insolvable.

SECTION II: 15 QUESTIONS

21. If x and y are positive integers and $\frac{x}{y} = 3$, then what is the smallest possible value of x + y?
(A) 2   (B) 4   (C) 5   (D) 10   (E) 12

22. What is the next number in this series: 1, 3, 6, 10, . . .?
(A) 11   (B) 13   (C) 15   (D) 16   (E) 20

23. In the figure below, x =
(A) 20   (B) 40   (C) 70   (D) 80   (E) 160

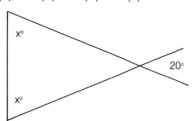

24. If Sharon is twice as old as Dave now, and will be one and one-half times as old as him in four years, how old is she now?
(A) 4   (B) 6   (C) 8   (D) 10   (E) 12

25. A swimming pool is filled in 2 hours by two pipes running simultaneously. If the first pipe is not running, it takes the second pipe 6 hours to fill the pool. How many hours would it take to fill the pool using only the first pipe?
(A) 2   (B) 3   (C) 4   (D) 5   (E) 6

26. Mike and Ron ate in a restaurant. Each left a 15% tip for his part of the meal. If Mike's tip was $1.50, and Ron's tip was $2.25, what percentage of the total bill was Ron's?
(A) 25%   (B) 40%   (C) 50%   (D) 60%   (E) 75%

27. Triangle ABC contains a right angle. If sides AB and BC are both equal to $\sqrt{2}$, what is the length of side AC?
(A) 1   (B) $\sqrt{2}$ (C) 2   (D) $2\sqrt{2}$
(E) It cannot be determined from the information given.

28. Given: ABCD is a quadrilateral
        Angles a and c each measure 60°
        Side AB measures 2 inches

What is the length of diagonal BD?
(A) 1″   (B) 2″   (C) 4″   (D) 8″
(E) It cannot be determined from the information given.

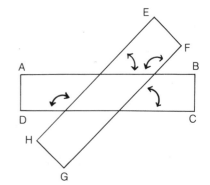

29. In the figure above, if ABCD and EFGH are rectangles, what is the sum of the measures of the marked angles?
(A) 180°
(B) 270°
(C) 360°
(D) 540°
(E) It cannot be determined from the information given.

30. If $\frac{x}{y} = \frac{4}{7}$ and $\frac{y}{z} = \frac{2}{3}$, then $\frac{x}{z}$ =
(A) $\frac{8}{21}$ (B) $\frac{6}{7}$ (C) $\frac{1}{2}$ (D) $\frac{3}{5}$ (E) $\frac{4}{5}$

31. A trucking company imposes a $1 delivery charge, plus $.50 for each mile it carries a package. How many miles was a trip for which the company charged $16?
(A) $7\frac{1}{2}$ (B) 8   (C) 15   (D) 30   (E) 32

32. If 2x + 3x = 15, then 3x − 2 =
(A) 1   (B) 5   (C) 7   (D) 11   (E) 13

33. If 10 scheckels make a lira, and 35 lira make a talent, how many talents do 25 scheckels make?
(A) $\frac{5}{7}$ (B) $\frac{1}{14}$ (C) $\frac{5}{2}$ (D) $\frac{2}{5}$ (E) 14

34. If 3x + 1 is an even number, which of the following is *not* an even number?
(A) x + 2
(B) x − 2
(C) 2x + 1
(D) 2x − 1
(E) All of the above

35. If this were a math problem on an actual SAT, which of the following would be true?
I. The correct answer would not appear on the test
II. The correct answer could not be determined from the information given.
III. A choice of correct answers would be given

(A) Maybe I, never II
(B) Maybe II, never III
(C) I and III always
(D) All of the above
(E) None of the above sometimes

S T O P

IF YOU FINISH BEFORE TIME IS CALLED,
CHECK YOUR WORK ON THIS SECTION ONLY.
DO NOT WORK ON ANY OTHER SECTION IN THE TEST.

AT THE SCENE OF THE CRIME: PART 1**

Study this picture carefully for three minutes . . . then turn the page for questioning by the police. Observe carefully, since you'll be relying solely on your memory.

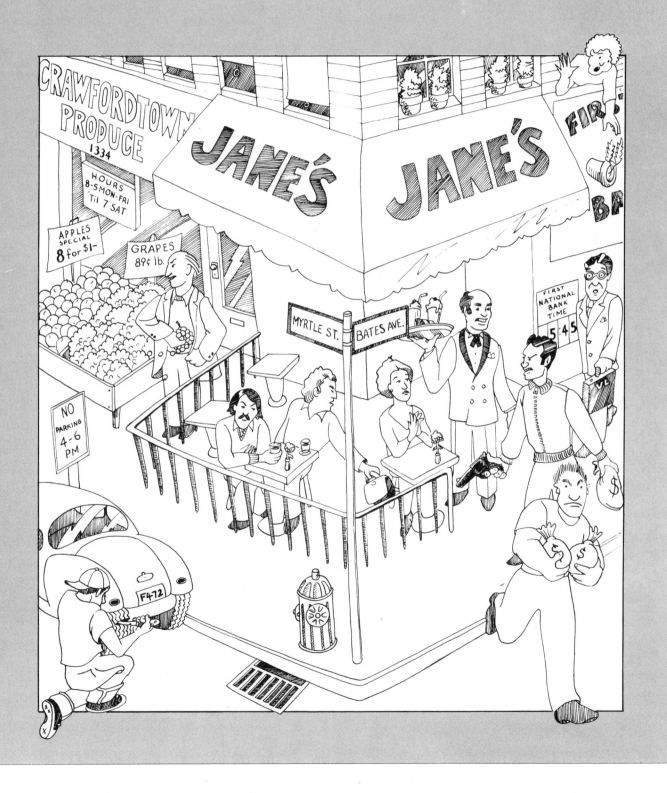

WATCHING TV WATCHING YOU ★☆

BY S. SPADACCINI AND C. SLEPIAN

You're sitting in your living room watching television. Don't look now, but your television is watching you, and it knows plenty about what you watch, and when, and how. Do you know as much about your viewing habits as your TV does?

Answers, page 186

TV OR NOT TV

1. Nothing goes better with beefsteak and cheesecake than Tom Selleck or Victoria Principal. What percentage of people watch TV during dinner?
a. 13%
b. 38%
c. 67%

2. What percentage of viewers talk to other people in the room while gazing into the blue light?
a. 25%
b. 50%
c. 75%

3. The very first Swanson TV dinner rolled off the assembly line in 1952. What were the ingredients of this modern miracle?
a. Fried chicken with mashed potatoes and corn
b. Turkey with stuffing, peas, and sweet potatoes
c. Meat loaf with green beans, potato puffs, and applesauce
d. *Gigot d'agneau avec asperges au beurre et pommes Anna*

PRIME TIME

1. What night of the week do the most people gather around the electronic hearth? What night do the fewest?

2. "All you ever do is sit and watch TV" is most deservedly directed at which of the following groups? And which group is least drawn to the tube?
a. children, aged 2 to 11
b. teenage boys
c. teenage girls
d. women, 18 and up
e. men, 18 and up

3. By the time a person is 18, he is usually more attached to the TV than to his blood relations. How many days of TV has he logged by then?
a. 193   c. 710
b. 459   d. 9,650

STATION BREAKS

1. The first commercial appeared on WNBT in New York City in 1941. How much did it cost the Bulova Watch Company?
a. $9   b. $90   c. $900

2. Forty-three years and countless Pepsi challenges later, the cost of getting a message to the masses has risen steeply. How much did the sponsors of Super Bowl XVIII (January 1984) pay for 30 seconds of air-time?
a. $175,000   b. $310,000
c. $485,000

3. Two people in five leave the room when a commercial comes on. Of the three who remain, how many sit mesmerized by the message?
a. 1   b. 2   c. 3

AT THE SCENE OF THE CRIME: PART 2 ★★

(continued from page 153)

In the rather busy street scene on the previous page, you were witness to one robbery, four misdemeanors, and an approaching calamity. The police would like your firsthand account of what happened, so please answer the following questions as precisely as possible.

Answers and ratings, page 187

1. What time was it by the bank clock?____
2. What day of the week was it?____
3. What was the name of the outdoor café?____
4. On what street was its entrance?____
5. How many thieves were staging the holdup?____
6. Were they armed?____
7. How many bags of loot were they carrying?____
8. Was the thief in the street wearing a hat?____
9. How many people, besides you and the holdup men, were at the scene of the robbery?____
10. What were the initials of the man in the business suit?____
11. What immediate danger was he in?____

12. Was the onlooker from the second floor a man or a woman?____
13. What store was next door to the café?____
14. On what street was its entrance?____
15. What was the shopper stealing?____
16. What was the license number of the car parked in front of the store?____
17. Why was it illegally parked?____
18. What part of the car was being vandalized?____
19. What offense was being committed against the lady diner?____
20. Was there a police phone at the corner?____

BONUS: Please identify the holdup men from this lineup.

A   B   C   D   E

SPELLING BEE ★☆

BY DR. ALLEN SHER

Contrary to popular concensus, misspelling isn't neccesarily a maladiction—for some, it's an art. Anyone can overlook an occassional inacuracy, but a talanted few regard each syllable as a challange. In this spirit, we offer a potpourri of orthagraphic exersizes. Begining with this interduction, which is ridled with errors, can you spell it all out for us—correctly?

Answers, page 187

ONE OUT OF TWO AIN'T BAD

Circle the *correctly* spelled word in each pair.

	A	**B**
1.	decaffinate	decaffeinate
2.	miniscule	minuscule
3.	sincerely	sincerly
4.	mischievous	mischievious
5.	embarassed	embarrassed
6.	possesion	possession
7.	bizzare	bizarre
8.	acquaintance	aquaintance
9.	wierd	weird
10.	carberator	carburetor
11.	innuendo	inuendo
12.	maneuver	manuever
13.	irrelevent	irrelevant
14.	persuade	pursuade
15.	colossal	collossal

GET THE PICTURE?

Can you spell the words these images depict? To get you started, we've provided the first letter for each one.

1. r_____
2. x_____
3. c_____
4. h_____
5. s_____
6. b_____
7. a_____
8. d_____

SAY WHAT?

Can you recognize the familiar words behind these fancy phonetics? Better yet, can you spell each one correctly?

1. 'for-ən-ər
2. sil-ə-'wet
3. 'säf-ə-mōr
4. 'af-'thal-mäl-ə-jəst
5. 'shō-fər
6. dif-'thir-ē-ə
7. 'tȯd-rē
8. bə-'nīn
9. 'sər-fət
10. pə-'rish-ə-nər
11. ə-'shur-əns
12. 'frik-ə-sē

WHAT'S WRONG?

There is one *incorrectly* spelled word in each group of four listed below. Can you find it?

1.
a. lackadaisical
b. hypochondriac
c. philatalist
d. counterfeit

2.
a. superceed
b. vengeance
c. epaulette
d. recognition

3.
a. covenant
b. imminent
c. acoustics
d. paraphenalia

4.
a. profligate
b. sycophant
c. petulant
d. millenium

5.
a. therapeutic
b. occurence
c. intransigent
d. vacillating

6.
a. enforcable
b. sabbatical
c. emphysema
d. interrogative

7.
a. elasticity
b. trousseau
c. petticoat
d. baloon

8.
a. awkward
b. cacophony
c. sacreligious
d. articulate

9.
a. definately
b. forfeit
c. independence
d. ecstasy

10.
a. invidious
b. dilemna
c. conglomerate
d. antibiotic

OUTNUMBERED★★

How many bricks are in the Empire State Building? Would you say about 1,000,000? 10,000,000? Could there be as many as 100,000,000?

If your estimate was 10,000,000, you were right. If it wasn't, you may be suffering from innumeracy, a modern curse whose victims never win Florida vacations by guessing the number of jelly beans in a jar.

This quiz can help. The trick to thinking big—and tiny, too—is to begin with a number you do know, and then to factor in some intuition. Take the Empire State Building, for instance, which you probably knew had about 100 (exactly 102) stories. How many bricks would there be to a floor? Choosing very round numbers, you're likely to realize that 1,000,000 is high, 10,000 is low, and that something like 100,000 ought to do it.

Work your way through the 25 questions on these pages to test, and refine, your numerical common sense.   *Answers, page 187*

WHAT IS...

1. The population of Denver, Colorado?
a. 4,913,960
b. 491,396
c. 49,139

2. The total number of passenger cars sold in the U.S. in 1980?
a. 64,000,300
b. 6,400,030
c. 640,003

3. The estimated number of divorces granted in the U.S. in 1981?
a. 1,193,000
b. 119,300
c. 11,930

4. The elevation of Mt. Everest in feet?
a. 29,000
b. 2,900
c. 290,000

5. The total number of Vietnam war veterans in the U.S.?
a. 9,061,000
b. 906,100
c. 90,610

6. The speed of the world's fastest snail in miles per hour?
a. 0.000313
b. 0.00313
c. 0.0313

7. The number of Valium prescriptions filled in the U.S. in 1981?
a. 310,000
b. 3,100,000
c. 31,000,000

8. The Reagan Administration's 1983 civil defense budget for crisis relocation?
a. $2,520,000
b. $25,200,000
c. $252,000,000

9. The weight of a Boeing 747 Jumbo Jet in pounds?
a. 77,500
b. 775,000
c. 7,750,000

10. The number of U.S. homes with only black-and-white TV sets?
a. 79,900,000
b. 7,990,000
c. 799,000

11. The number of passengers enplaned at Chicago's O'Hare Airport in 1981?
a. 16,380,000
b. 1,638,000
c. 163,800

12. The number of people in the world whose principal language is English (as of mid-1981)?
a. 39,100,000
b. 391,000,000
c. 3,910,000,000

13. The number of acres of forested land in Hawaii?
a. 1,986,000
b. 19,860,000
c. 198,600,000

14. The number of American men registered for the draft as of January 1983?
a. 9,200,000
b. 92,000,000
c. 920,000

BY ROSE RAIDT

15. **The size of an amoeba in millimeters?**
a. 1.0
b. 0.1
c. 0.01

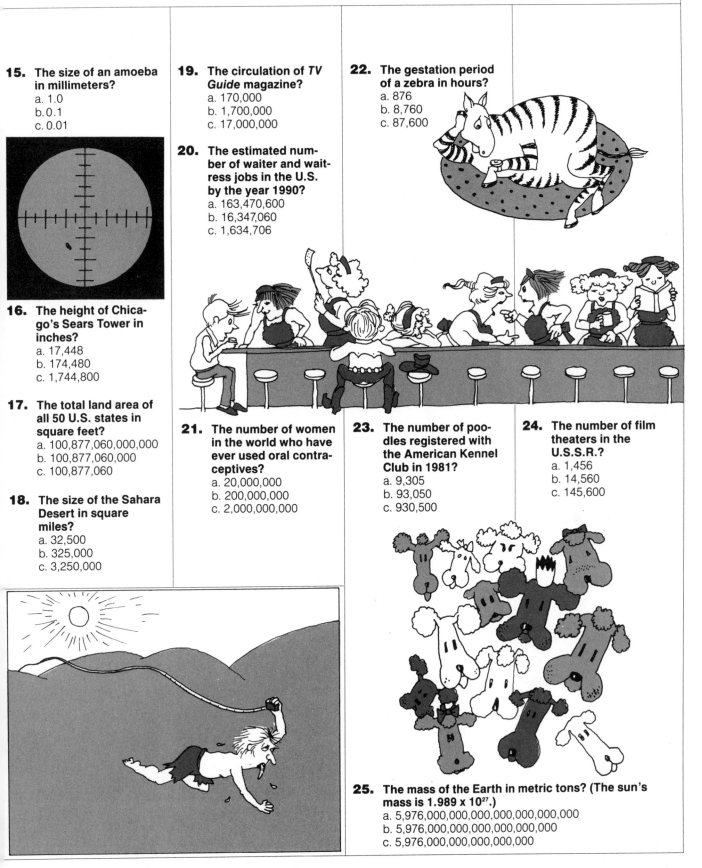

16. **The height of Chicago's Sears Tower in inches?**
a. 17,448
b. 174,480
c. 1,744,800

17. **The total land area of all 50 U.S. states in square feet?**
a. 100,877,060,000,000
b. 100,877,060,000
c. 100,877,060

18. **The size of the Sahara Desert in square miles?**
a. 32,500
b. 325,000
c. 3,250,000

19. **The circulation of *TV Guide* magazine?**
a. 170,000
b. 1,700,000
c. 17,000,000

20. **The estimated number of waiter and waitress jobs in the U.S. by the year 1990?**
a. 163,470,600
b. 16,347,060
c. 1,634,706

21. **The number of women in the world who have ever used oral contraceptives?**
a. 20,000,000
b. 200,000,000
c. 2,000,000,000

22. **The gestation period of a zebra in hours?**
a. 876
b. 8,760
c. 87,600

23. **The number of poodles registered with the American Kennel Club in 1981?**
a. 9,305
b. 93,050
c. 930,500

24. **The number of film theaters in the U.S.S.R.?**
a. 1,456
b. 14,560
c. 145,600

25. **The mass of the Earth in metric tons? (The sun's mass is 1.989×10^{27}.)**
a. 5,976,000,000,000,000,000,000,000
b. 5,976,000,000,000,000,000,000
c. 5,976,000,000,000,000,000

SCIENCE TWISTERS ★☆

Have you ever wondered why elephants have such big ears? Why it's hard to make snowballs on certain winter days? Or why birds fly in V-formation?

These and the other questions posed here are designed to test your intuition, observation, and knowledge of the natural world. Each question is followed by three plausible answers, only one of which is right. You know you can't fool Mother Nature—but can she fool you?

Answers, page 188

1. RAINBOWS
Maybe the reason no one has found the pot of gold at the end of the rainbow is that a rainbow has no end—what we see is only a part of the circumference of a complete circle. Typically, a rainbow can be seen
a. in the morning
b. in the late afternoon
c. either of the above, but not around noon

2. SNOWBALLS
Who can resist a good snowball fight now and then? Snowballs are hardest to make when the temperature is
a. right around freezing (32° F)
b. between 10° and 32° F
c. below 10°F

3. RING AROUND THE MOON
If the weather has been clear, a ring around the moon foretells
a. rain
b. clear weather
c. neither—the presence of the ring has nothing to do with the weather

4. BIRDS AND BATS
Birds and bats fly closer to the ground before a storm. The reason for this is that
a. humid air dampens their wings and makes them heavier
b. they are looking for shelter
c. flying too high in low barometric pressure hurts their ears

5. ECHOES
Since echoes are sound waves reflected off distant objects, it would seem that they'd be heard most often where distant objects are plentiful—in the mountains. But in fact echoes are heard less frequently in mountainous areas than in other places. The reason is that sound waves
a. don't travel as far in thin mountain air
b. are less likely to bounce toward the listener because mountain surfaces are angled upward
c. are absorbed by the foliage that covers the mountains

6. FULL MOON
You may have noticed that the lighted area of the full moon is twice as large as that of the moon in its first or last quarter (i.e., the half moon). But how much *brighter* is the full moon than the half moon?
a. twice as bright
b. five times as bright
c. nine times as bright

7. EARTHRISE
From the earth we can see the moon rise and set. When the day comes that we can live on the moon, will we see the earth rise and set?
a. yes
b. no
c. yes, but only at the summer and winter solstices

8. RAINDROPS
When raindrops keep falling on your head,
a. the large drops fall faster
b. the small drops fall faster
c. the large and small drops fall at the same rate

9. OF MICE AND MEN
Humans consume about $1/50$ their own weight in food daily. But a mouse eats fully half its own weight in a day—or 25 times as much as humans, per pound of body weight. Yet we've never seen an overweight mouse. Why not?
a. Since mice have a more rapid heartbeat and a correspondingly higher metabolic rate than humans, they burn off the calories more rapidly.
b. Mice are more active than humans and need extra food as fuel.
c. In proportion to body weight, mice lose more heat than humans, so they need the extra calories to maintain body temperature.

10. FROGS
Have you ever noticed that the croaking of frogs increases just before a storm? That's because
a. they're warning their mates of the approaching storm
b. falling barometric pressure expands their vocal chambers, which triggers the croaking reflex
c. they feel most comfortable when wet, and the moist air allows them to come out of the water to croak and still feel deliciously damp

BY CHRISTOPHER P. JARGOCKI

11. MUD BATHS

Until somebody invents a bubble bath for our porcine friends, pigs will wallow in mud. Why?
a. It's part of their mating ritual.
b. It's a convenient way to keep cool.
c. The bacteria in mud destroy parasites that can cause disease in pigs.

12. ICE

There's a lot of ice in Antarctica, and in the Arctic too. The amount in Antarctica is
a. about the same as in the Arctic
b. three times greater than in the Arctic
c. eight times greater than in the Arctic

13. FLOATING

It's pretty easy for children of either sex to float on their backs, but adults often have a harder time of it. Which sex finds it easier?
a. Men, because they have larger lungs.
b. Women, because more of their body weight is fat.
c. Both find it equally easy (or difficult).

14. NIGHT LOWS

If the temperature hits 86° F during the day in Miami, it won't get much lower than 68° F at night. But in El Paso, a daytime high of 86° F may dip to 50° F at night. The reason for the difference is that
a. Miami is much closer to the equator
b. Miami is more humid than El Paso
c. Miami is more densely settled, and the resulting pollution creates an artificial "greenhouse effect"

15. JUMPING FLEAS

Some fleas can jump more than a foot—a hundred times their length. If we could jump as far in proportion to our height, we'd be clearing 50-story buildings. Why can't we?
a. A flea's legs, unlike a human's, are well-designed for jumping, since they are anatomically similar to catapults.
b. A human's larger body encounters too much air resistance.
c. With increasing size, the weight of an animal increases much faster than its strength.

16. COLD COAST

People accustomed to swimming in the Atlantic Ocean are often surprised when they visit California and find that Pacific waters are much colder. The temperature difference occurs because
a. on the West Coast the rotation of the earth brings colder water in from the north and from the deeper part of the ocean
b. the water isn't really colder but only seems so because the sun is so much hotter
c. the high concentration of large metropolitan centers on the East Coast warms the water that is nearest the shore

17. ELEPHANT EARS

The enormous ears of the African elephant perform a valuable service. What is it?
a. They add extra surface area to help dispose of body heat.
b. They amplify sound in order to compensate for the elephant's notoriously poor vision.
c. They're useful in brushing away annoying insects.

18. ON THE WING

Migrating birds commonly fly in V-formation. What is the reason for this?
a. That arrangement protects the group from predators.
b. The updraft created by the wings of neighboring birds reduces air resistance and therefore makes flying easier.
c. The lead bird can easily be seen by all members of the group.

WHERENESS AWARENESS ★☆

BY R. WAYNE SCHMITTBERGER

Putting things in their proper perspective is often only of relative importance. Take this quiz, for instance. Most of the places named here are familiar (and we don't mean to trick you—when we say Rome, we don't mean Rome, New York). You've seen them on maps many times—but do you know where they are in relation to other places?

Answers and ratings, page 188

What is the first foreign country you will hit if you travel

1. due east from New York City?

2. due south from eastern Detroit?

3. due west from Seattle?

4. due north from Point Barrow, Alaska?

Which city is farther north,

5. Paris or Montreal?

6. Mexico City or Honolulu?

7. Rome or San Francisco?

8. Moscow or Juneau?

Which has the greater area,

9. California or France?

10. Alaska or the province of Quebec?

11. Maine or the rest of new England?

12. Rank the following in area, from greatest to least: Delaware, the island of Hawaii, Yellowstone National Park.

13. If you travel due east from Tierra del Fuego, at the tip of Argentina, what is the first country you will hit, not counting small islands?

14. Which is farther from Pago Pago—Walla Walla or Wagga Wagga?

Which air distance is greater,

15. London to Berlin, or New York City to Chicago?

16. Rio de Janeiro to Mexico City, or Rome to Montreal?

Which city is farther east,

17. Reno or Los Angeles?

18. Hanoi or Beijing?

19. Warsaw or Johannesburg?

20. If you travel due north from Lima to the North Pole, to which city will you come the closest—Washington, DC, New Orleans, or Phoenix?

21. Which is bigger, one Africa or two Antarcticas?

22. Is Alaska equivalent in size to 2 Californias, 15 Michigans, or 90 Hawaiis?

If you travel around the world on the latitude line that passes through New York City, would you have to travel north or south of your itinerary to visit

23. Paris?

24. Hong Kong?

25. Casablanca?

26. San Francisco?

27. Which is the best approximation of the ratio of the area of Australia to the area of Greenland: 7 to 2, 2 to 1, 5 to 4, or 2 to 3?

28. Which is farther from the equator, Buenos Aires or Lisbon?

29. Which pair of cities out of the following group are the greatest distance apart: Vienna, Melbourne, Caracas, Hong Kong?

30. Where would you rather be: the Bay of Rainbows, the Vinson Massif, or Hell Canyon?

TOUGH
NUTS
FOR
EXPERT SOLVERS

★★★

CHAIN REACTION

BY KEITH RINGKAMP

These five chains are made up of
black, white, and half black, half white links.
Which two of the five chains are identical?

Answer, page 189

CAPITAL IDEAS ★☆

BY MERL REAGLE

If you're wordly wise *and* worldly wise, you'll enjoy answering these questions—each one playfully suggests the name of a different capital city.   *Answers, page 189*

1. Name the European capital that's made up of two men's nicknames.

2. What Middle Eastern capital ends with a U.S. state capital?

3. When each definition is answered correctly, the result will *sound* like a world capital. For example, the first one is ALGIERS ("Al jeers"). How many others can you sound out?
   a. Pacino expresses scorn
   b. Auto graveyard
   c. Shoe size
   d. Taylor hairdo
   e. Fire Yogi
   f. Southern girl got older
   g. Donned a carpenter's tool
   h. Revolution delay

4. A synonym for *continued* followed by a synonym for *continue* yields what seven-letter Asian capital?

5. A certain six-letter word of two syllables could be defined as "health-spa features." When the syllables merely trade places, what well-known island capital is formed?

6. Replace two letters in a European capital and get another European capital.

7. Ignoring for the moment that Cambodia's (or Kampuchea's) capital is two words, pick out four consecutive letters from PHNOMPENH, and then name another well-known (one-word) world capital that contains the same foursome, whole and in order.

8. Name the only six-letter, one-syllable world capital. (It's in Europe.)

9. CZECHOSLOVAKIA contains another country's capital, OSLO, in its exact center. Name the European *capital* that has another *country* in its exact center.

10. When the two syllables of an African country trade places, the result is a capital city in South America. Name both places.

11. A certain South American capital, minus its first and last letters, is an African country spelled backward. Name the capital.

12. A well-known East Asian capital has three syllables. Syllables 2 and 1, when pronounced together (and in that order), become a South American capital. (When you solve this, your reaction might be syllable 3.)

MISSING LINKS ★★★

BY GARY DISCH

The 15 letters below each grid can be inserted to complete a pattern of common words reading across and down. Each of the 15 boxed letters will be used once, and not every square in the grid will be filled in.   *Answers, page 189*

PUZZLE 1

	R	O	A	D		A	S	
R			A			M		
U		T		M	A	P		E
N		O	W		F			O
		P	E	R	T		I	N
			E		U	S		
	A	S	T	E	R		L	
E	L			V		B	E	T
	L		V	E	R	Y		

A	B	C	C	E
H	L	R	S	S
T	T	T	U	X

PUZZLE 2

		P	E	G		A		
C			L		F	I	R	
A	G	R	E	E		L	A	
M			C	H	A	S	M	
	L		T		L		P	
	A		P	A	L			
	I	N	T	O		R		
E		E	N	O	M	A	D	
L	I	S	T			H		

A	C	E	E	E
I	I	L	N	O
O	P	P	S	T

CRYPTIC CONNECTIONS***

BY SCOTT MARLEY

This puzzle is really five games in one. The clues are presented in five sections, each posing a different challenge. We've given an example in each category below to get you started. First answer as many of the clues as you can. Then enter the letters of the answers in the diagram, as indicated by the letter-number pairs. (Thus, A1 represents the square in the upper left corner, R9 the square in the lower right corner.) Many squares are used in more than one answer, so every clue you solve will provide some help with others. When the diagram is filled in, you will find a bit of light verse reading across, line by line, beginning in square A1.

Answers, page 189

	A	B	C	D	E	F	G	H	J	K	L	M	N	P	Q	R
1																
2																
3																
4																
5																
6																
7																
8																
9																

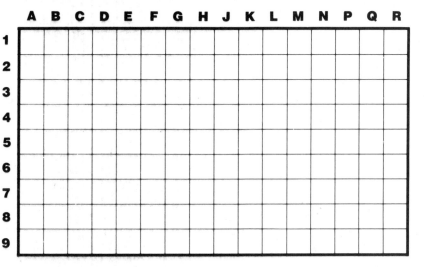

HOOK-UPS

Example tennis ______ grease: ELBOW

1. tail ______ dry: A5 J9 R1 K2
2. sand ______ buggy: L2 F6 C3 L9
3. saw ______ pan: C4 H3 R8 H5
4. soft ______ opera: F2 Q2 R4 F9
5. scenic ______ finder: N5 Q7 G9 Q6
6. ghost ______ house: M2 B9 N7 L5
7. note ______ lock: K7 N9 A2

OPPOSITES

Example white: BLACK

1. out: A5 N3 C9 B2
2. down: F4 H2 E3 R9 J7 C8
3. over: B8 R2 D3 R3 J2 G6 C2 M5 H7 J4 (2 wds.)
4. left: B4 E3 J8 G1 N5 A3 Q9
5. pass: D8 E1 L2
6. square: H6 R1 F9
7. Chance: J3 H9 F1 P8 D9 P2 D2 P3 Q4 N4 E4 G5 C6 A1 (2 wds.)

RATIOS

Example rooster : hen :: ram : EWE

1. daze : knights :: eye : M7 K5 G1 G6 N6
2. boredom : bedroom :: thicken : P4 L1 A1 R7 H6 P5 L3
3. imps : Mississippi :: they : L9 F5 N1 J6 H8 C1 E7 E4
4. 1,501 : dim :: 207 : N4 K3 M1 K6 D6
5. hold : cot :: whack : A7 K9 H4 M3 F7 A9
6. plover : plunder :: shin : C6 P7 N2 D5 K8
7. agent : fee :: J3 C7 F6 Q5 R7 J5 : F8 E1 M6 L8 G2

COMMON FACTORS

Example Chaplin, Groucho, Hitler, Poirot: MUSTACHE

1. The White House, football team, jet, dove: Q6 B3 H1 B5 H7
2. Vine, Wall, Market, State: C8 B7 C2 E8 R6 F8
3. clothesline, hand grenade, boutonniere, sewing kit: D3 M4 L5
4. Gavin, Leigh, Miles, Perkins: Q1 J4 F5 D6 Q3 B9
5. tightrope walking, butterfly collecting, Ping-Pong: L6 A6 K1
6. gas station, hospital, wedding, flight: F4 B6 P3 E5 H1 Q9 D7 L3 G8 E2
7. farm, bridge, clock, audience: F7 E6 P2 D1 P1
8. goatherd, coat hanger, loathsome: Q2 M8 L4 A8

LISTS

Example two, four, six, eight, TEN

1. first, second, third, J5 Q8 F1 A4
2. fingers of a hand, wives of Henry VIII, days of the week, B4 J8 F1 E9 of an R9 M9 L4 N2 K7 J1 E2
3. Ford, Rockefeller, Mondale, A7 D5 K4 L8
4. king, queen, C9 L7 C5 K9, D4 N7 B8 N8
5. Mexico City, Munich, Montreal, Moscow, K9 F3 F2 N9 M7 M3 G7 C5 P6 R8 (2 wds.)
6. hot fudge, blue, Shrove, Ash, Maundy, J6 B1 D7 P9 P4 R5 J2 G3 Q7 G4 P1 (3 wds.)

EUROPEAN TOUR LOGIC PUZZLE****

BY AL PERLMAN

Six couples—the Rosens, the Quinns, the Palmers, the Oglethorpes, the Newkirks, and the Morgans—departed via different flights from New York's Kennedy International Airport one morning not too long ago, each of them bound for a long-anticipated European vacation.

The wives (not respectively) are Lois, Kate, Jessica, Ingrid, Helen, and Glenda. Their husbands are (again not respectively) Fred, Edward, David, Charles, Bertram, and Alan.

These 12 individuals have all achieved a fair measure of success in their respective fields. They are (in no particular order) a photographer, a newspaper columnist, a college professor, a magazine editor, a high school principal, a novelist, a professional golfer, a physician, a television scriptwriter, a public relations director, a fashion designer, and a psychoanalyst.

From among six countries—Denmark, England, France, Italy, Norway, and Spain—each couple elected to visit four, spending exactly one week in each. No two couples visited the same four countries or spent the same week in any given country.

The additional tidbits of information that follow should enable you to (1) match up the first and last names of the six husbands; (2) link up each wife with her husband; (3) name the occupation of each of the 12 individuals; and (4) name the country visited by each couple during each of the four weeks. So tighten your seat belt . . .

Answer, page 189

1. The first week found Edward in Denmark, the high school principal in England, the fashion designer in France, Ingrid in Italy, the Oglethorpes in Norway, and the psychoanalyst in Spain.

2. Alan visited England, France, Italy, and Spain, but not necessarily in that order.

3. Denmark was visited in succession by the photographer, Jessica, Bertram, and the college professor.

4. Charles, Helen, and the college professor are three of the four people who did not visit England.

5. The novelist, the golf pro, and Fred are three of the four people who did not visit Denmark.

6. Fred and his wife limited their picture-taking to black-and-white stills; the Rosens shot color slides exclusively; and the magazine editor and spouse took only movies. Ingrid and her husband were the only couple who didn't bring at least one camera with them.

7. Mr. Palmer, the psychoanalyst, the photographer, and Lois all visited Norway, but not necessarily in that order. No two were there during the same week.

8. Kate and her husband took both still shots and movies in Denmark, France, Italy, and Spain, though they did not necessarily tour the countries in that order.

9. The PR director and spouse got a beautiful color slide of Queen Elizabeth leaving Buckingham Palace to address Parliament. The following week they were so engrossed in further picture-taking that they barely made the flight back to New York.

10. Glenda was in Norway after the magazine editor had been there, but before both the Newkirks and the psychoanalyst.

11. The scriptwriter visited Denmark, England, Italy, and Norway, though not necessarily in that order.

12. Just before they reached the midpoint of their trip, Helen and her husband finished up their last roll of movie film on the top of the Eiffel Tower, and they had to record the rest of their travels via stills.

13. England was the last country visited by the novelist and spouse. It had previously been visited, though in no particular order, by Mr. Rosen, Glenda, and Bertram, all at different times.

14. During the week that the newspaper columnist and spouse were in Norway, Lois was in Denmark, Fred in Italy.

15. Spain was visited, in no particular order, by Charles, Jessica, Mrs. Morgan, and the newspaper columnist, no two of whom were there at the same time.

16. Helen went to Norway the same week that the physician was in France.

17. Mrs. Newkirk and the photographer did not tour Italy.

18. The newspaper columnist, the golf pro, and the magazine editor are the same sex.

19. Alan and the physician are not of the same sex.

20. France was the final country on the golf pro's itinerary.

21. The PR director and the high school principal are the same sex.

COIN TRICK★★★★

BY HOWARD BERGERSON

Ever since the solution to Rubik's Cube was published, some people have complained about a lack of frustration. This puzzle is guaranteed to put the worrying back into their lives. It's an apparently simple challenge that's almost impossible to solve unless you discover the underlying principle.

Alternate four nickels and three pennies in a line, edge to edge, as shown. The object is to change the alignment from N-P-N-P-N-P-N to N-N-N-N-P-P-P by moving two coins—always two adjacent coins of different denominations—at each step. The pair of coins must be moved as a unit, and must always be placed so as to be touching some other coin(s) in the row. Using a trial-and-error approach may keep you busy for eons, but discovering the winning strategy renders the puzzle solvable in a mere 14 moves. *Answer, page 190*

FELLOWSHIP OF THE DIAMOND

BY MIKE SHENK

In order to be accepted into the Fellowship of the Diamond, you must pass three challenges of increasing difficulty. Each involves the nine-hexagon diamond shown here, and the placement of the digits 1 to 9 within the pattern, using each digit exactly once. But be warned: Only the select few ever meet all three challenges successfully. Disregarding reflection and rotation, each solution is unique. *Answers, page 190*

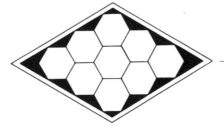

PUZZLE 1★★

Place the digits 1 to 9 in the nine hexagons so that no two adjacent hexagons contain either consecutive numbers or numbers whose names contain the same number of letters.

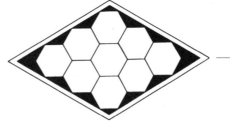

PUZZLE 2★★★

Place the digits 1 to 9 in the nine hexagons so that no two adjacent hexagons contain digits whose sum is a multiple of four or five.

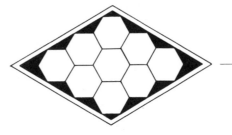

PUZZLE 3★★★★

Place the digits 1 to 9 in the nine hexagons so that the total of the digits in the hexagons adjacent to any given hexagon is a multiple of the digit in the given hexagon.

A SKETCHY MURDER ★★★

olice Inspector Hatch was walking his dog past the Illustrators' Club when he heard a scream. Upon entering the club, he learned that someone had just been found strangled to death. The victim (seen in the inset at lower left) was one of eight artists competing in a self-portraiture show. The suspects were the seven surviving artists, seen here in front of the eight framed self-portraits.

Inspector Hatch questioned the suspects, but since all of them were slightly dotty, they would admit to nothing—not even which self-portrait had been done by which artist.

During his close inspection of the suspects and an equally percipient look at their portraits, Hatch saw a pattern to the way the artists presented themselves and realized that the murderer had left a telling mark on the victim. Hatch then knew who had done the deed and why.

Can you see what Hatch saw?

Clue, page 189   Answer, page 190

BY MARK MAZUT

THE SCARLET LETTER ★★★

BY ANN STONE

In this high-grade cryptogram, each calligraphic variation of A represents a different letter of the alphabet. The answer is an excerpt from—you guessed it—Nathaniel Hawthorne's *The Scarlet Letter*.   *Answer, page 189*

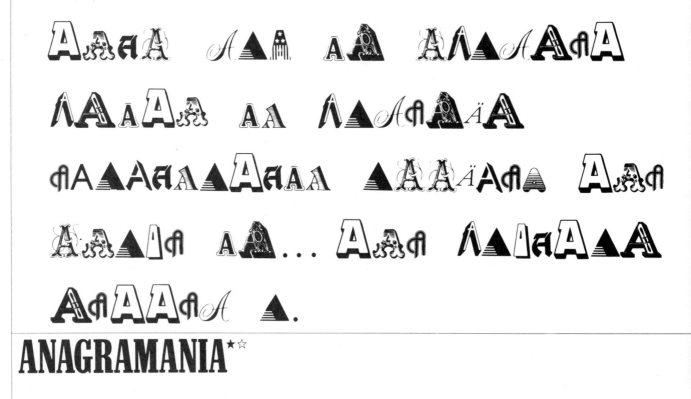

ANAGRAMANIA ★☆

Rearrange all the letters of each phrase to form a new word, name, or phrase of similar meaning. Numbers in parentheses indicate the lengths and the number of the words in each answer; an asterisk denotes a capitalized word. (Thus, the answer to the first clue is two capitalized words, the first one 8 letters long and the second one 10 letters long.)

Some experienced solvers find it helpful to write the letters of the clue, in random order, in a rough diamond shape, because it helps them to see a variety of letter combinations. And if you get mixed up, don't worry— that's the whole idea.   *Answers, page 190*

1. I SET BASIC WORD ENTRY (*8 *10)
2. TSK, I DENY—IT AIN'T ME (8 8)
3. STOP AN INGRESS (2 11)
4. LO! AHA! I PROMOTE PURE NOTES! (*12 *5 *5)
5. SO PAY ME OR NOT, SIR (1 10 4)
6. LARGE INTERMENT LOCATION, NAY? (*9 *8 *8)
7. DOES EASE THIRST (3 6 5)
8. I GO SEARCH A LOT (13)
9. A MORTAL FLEES WAR (*1 *8 2 *4)
10. MUSING LINE TO TOP DISCOVERER (*6 *11 *1 7)
11. AH, ONE TRIED, THE OTHER SAT (3 8 3 3 4)
12. FORD TAKES HERO'S TRAIL (*7 2 3 *4 *3)
13. HEY, METRO NEWS KIT! (*3 *3 *4 *5)
14. MAN'S PASTA TABLE DELIGHT (9 3 9)
15. I PAINT MODERN (*4 *8)
16. CAN'T POOL? BUS, TRAIN TRIP (6 14)

MUSICAL CHAIRS CRYPTIC****

BY EMILY COX AND HENRY RATHVON

A variety cryptic poses a challenge in addition to that of solving the clues. In this case, the answers to the 12 italicized Down clues play musical chairs before being entered in the diagram, i.e., their letters rotate sequentially and drop one member. For example, the word CHAIR as an answer might be entered as HARC with the I dropped, or IRHA, with the C dropped, etc. (It

could not be entered ARIC with the H dropped because the rotation would not be sequential.) The 12 letters discarded in this manner are to be seated at the tops of their respective columns, where they will compose a musical item. Answers include three proper names. Punctuation in the clues may be used deceptively.

Answer, page 190

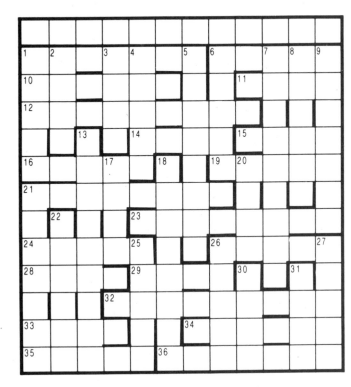

ACROSS

1 Those punk bands are endlessly in hearing range (7)

6 They cover a version of *Tosca* (5)

10 Man is all broken up about the song (6)

11 Alternately sang tunes causing a feverish feeling (4)

12 A composition of Elgar isn't for certain instruments (9)

14 Appealing selection from a record with Elvis' face (4)

15 Gentleman holding center of baton indicates brisk movement (4)

16 Never carelessly pluck (5)

19 Hum ''Over the Rainbow'' starting near the middle (5)

21 Tenor's excited about a number that's rich and loud (8)

23 Let's sing ''Light Shines'' (8)

24 The limitations of brass ensembles (5)

26 ''A Little Bit Me''—tune without an end (5)

28 Polish up the middle of the ditty (4)

29 Dances along with bugle song (4)

32 Wanted: new slide bar on end of trombone (9)

33 Stay for the finale (4)

34 The woman will hold third note, provided it's a little lower! (6)

35 A piano place with entrance at the rear—it's seedy (5)

36 Round thing driven in a wind instrument (7)

DOWN

1 *Dislodge from chair as tune is playing* (6)

2 *An instrument's vital part* (5)

3 *Asians in an opera by Massenet* (5)

4 *When cellist keeps away* (5)

5 *Follower of a Greek or Latin (tops in improvisation)* (9)

6 *Religion makes Indian start to drum* (5)

7 *They're rock standards, musical sounds* (10)

8 *Pipes—a couple heard by Mr. Crosby* (6)

9 *Second part of the scale held by groups to be esoteric knowledge* (7)

13 *Percussion should be beaten out of sound's range* (10)

17 *Half of voices died, making a gap* (4)

18 *Song in last opera transposed* (9)

20 *Bands should keep reeds in the front rows* (5)

21 *An ill way to grate on a jazz singer* (7)

22 *Leaders of music and dance consider all painters crazy* (6)

25 *Motifs from the start of* The Messiah (6)

26 *Soprano, on beat, makes loud vocal sound* (6)

27 *Dancers at middle aren't moving in a waltz step* (6)

30 *Quiet song duet* (4)

31 *Revolutionary Beatle's sound* (5)

Two regular cryptic puzzles, as well as directions for solving cryptic crosswords, appear on pages 124–125.

AT WIT'S END ★★★

And finally, for those of you who still haven't cracked, nine more tough tidbits.   *Answers, page 190*

1. LOGOPHOBIA

Find an animal that many people fear by forming an anagram of a homophone of an antonym of a homophone of an anagram of the word FEAR.

—Henry Hook

2. NUMBER CHAIN

Place the numbers 1 to 9 in the circles such that the arrows will form a path leading from 1 to 2 to 3, and so on up to 9. You will not, of course, use all the arrows in your path.   —Rich Latta

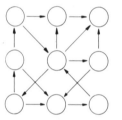

3. BODY TALK

Change the first letter of a four-letter word for a part of the body, and you will have something normally worn on that part of the body. And surprisingly, the second word will not rhyme with the first!

—Doug and Janis Heller

4. CROSSOUT

Cross out 12 of the 36 numbers below so that each row and column is left with exactly four numbers that total 10.

2	1	2	2	5	4
5	1	1	6	2	3
3	3	5	1	3	1
1	7	6	1	1	2
2	5	1	4	1	3
4	1	2	4	2	3

—Henry Hook

5. DEAD LETTER DEPT.

What one letter will complete all four of these common English words?

```
G Y _ E S
L O _ D E D
T I _ N E S S
C A _ Z E
```

—Mike Shenk

6. ELEMENTARY!

Given the equation

$$5 - 4 = IRON$$

what chemical element could replace the question mark in this equation?

$$6 - 9 = ?$$

—Stan Kurzban

7. MAKING THE CUT

The owner of Larry's Luxury Carpet Emporium has a 36-square-yard rug marked in one-yard squares. For advertising, he wants to cut as many L-shaped pieces as possible from this rug. Each piece must consist of four of the one-yard squares (as shown) without requiring any sewing, but since the rug is reversible, backward L's are also allowed. What is the maximum number of L's the owner can get?

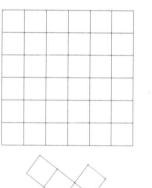

—Cal Q. Leytor

8. TIME TO REFLECT

At right is an ordinary wristwatch seen in a mirror. What time is it?

—Mike Shenk

9. LAST IN LINE

What number belongs under the 9 in the array below?

4	5	6	7	8	9
61	52	63	94	46	?

—Mel Loftus

ALL THE ANSWERS

★
DÉJÀ-VU
BY THE EDITORS

This last puzzle is a Through-the-Book Scavenger Hunt to test your powers of observation just one more time. The 16 swatches of type and bits of illustrations shown above are all taken from the preceding pages of this volume. The images appear exactly as they do earlier in the book, but we've deviously selected and artfully cropped them to increase the challenge of the hunt.

Once you think you've found all 16 images, add up the page numbers on which they appear—if you're correct, they'll total 1,473.

Answers, page 190

1

7 INNER PICK-UP STICKS

The pick-up sticks should be removed as numbered.

8 WHAT'S WRONG?

These are the 12 errors: The ace of spades is printed sideways; the 10 of clubs is played on the jack of spades (black suit on black); three cards shown—the 11 of clubs, the 4 of stars, and the 1 of diamonds—don't exist; the 4 of hearts is shown among the foundation cards, while the 3 of hearts, upon which the 4 must have been played, is still in the tableau; the jack of clubs has a queen's face; one card in the sixth column has the wrong back; the 10 of spades is played on the queen of hearts; the seventh column has too many face-down cards; the 10 of hearts appears twice; the two middle pips of the 7 of clubs are upside-down.

9 COUNTERINTELLIGENCE

The answers begin with the numbers 1 to 14:

1. One for the road
2. Two bits
3. Three Stooges
4. Four-leaf clover
5. Five-o'clock shadow
6. Six-shooter
7. Seven Dwarfs
8. Eight ball
9. Nine lives
10. Ten Commandments
11. Eleventh hour
12. "Twelve Days of Christmas"
13. Thirteen Colonies
14. 14-karat gold

9 WHOSE CLUES?

1. Indira Gandhi
2. Babe Ruth
3. Maria Callas
4. Sigmund Freud
5. Bo Derek
6. Arnold (or Sandra) Palmer
7. Joe Namath
8. Charlie Chaplin
9. Jacques Cousteau
10. John Lennon
11. Chiang Kai-shek
12. William Shakespeare
13. Marco Polo
14. Esther Williams

10 BORDER PATROL

1. OH PA WV
2. NV CA AZ
3. KY VA TN NC GA
4. CO KS OK NM TX
5. NY VT NH MA CT
6. KS MO OK AR TX LA
7. MT WY ID
8. AL GA FL
9. IN IL KY MO TN
10. MN WI IA IL
11. WA OR ID

11 BURMA-SHAVE

1. He played—a sax—had no B.O.—but his whiskers scratched—so she let him go.
2. A peach—looks good—with lots of fuzz—but man's no peach—and never was.
3. The bearded lady—tried a jar—she's now—a famous—movie star.
4. Grandpa's beard—was stiff and coarse—and that's what—caused his—fifth divorce.
5. Riot at—drug store—calling all cars—100 customers—99 jars.
6. Past—schoolhouses—take it slow—let the little—shavers grow.
7. His tenor voice—she thought divine—till whiskers—scratched—Sweet Adeline.
8. Listen, birds—those signs cost—money—so roost a while but—don't get funny.

12 TOM SWIFTIES

1. Triumphantly
2. Mockingly
3. Listlessly
4. Buoyantly
5. Defensively
6. Stuffily
7. Artlessly
8. Testily
9. Sourly
10. Grossly
11. Patronizingly
12. Flatly
13. Candidly
14. Intently
15. Wholeheartedly

12 BUSMAN'S HOLIDAY

The correct route is shown.

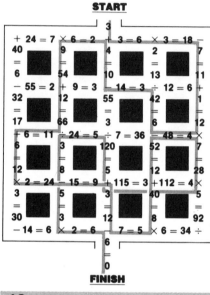

13 ASK A SILLY QUESTION...

First, to make things clear as glass: A fiddle is a pretty sturdy folk instrument. A loon isn't so crazy, though it does have a weird call. And a wink takes .28 to .1 second—pretty quick!

1. (b) A bat is partially blind.
2. (a) According to the Writer's Guild of America, the writer of a prime-time comedy sketch of over five minutes is paid a minimum of $1,239.
3. (d) The moon is on the average 238,857 miles from Earth.
4. (d) At a mannequin supply house, arms go for $18.50, legs for $100.
5. (b) The average adult's belly holds two quarts.
6. (c) Blonds average 140,000 hairs on their heads. (Brunets average about 105,000, redheads about 90,000, and the hairs on an ex-catcher's head vary.)
7. (a) The early bird rises about a half hour before dawn.
8. (a) A duck feather weighs .013 to .063 gram.
9. (b) The skin is $1/16$ to $1/8$ inch deep.
10. (c) Land snails move about two inches a minute.
11. (a) Swallows return to Capistrano annually on March 19 (and leave promptly on October 23).
12. (c) Clonmel, Tipperary, in Southern Ireland, is 3,381 miles from Manhattan.

Adapted from *Easy Answers to Hard Questions* (Fawcett Columbine, New York) © 1979 by Randy Cohen.

14 HOLLYWOOD

1. (G) Charlton Heston as Michelangelo, *The Agony and the Ecstasy*
2. (C) Jane Fonda as Lillian Hellman, *Julia*
3. (E) William Bendix as Babe Ruth, *The Babe Ruth Story*
4. (B) Barbra Streisand as Fanny Brice, *Funny Girl*
5. (A) James Cagney as George M. Cohan, *Yankee Doodle Dandy*
6. (J) Diana Ross as Billie Holiday, *Lady Sings the Blues*
7. (D) Faye Dunaway as Joan Crawford, *Mommie Dearest*
8. (F) Marlene Dietrich as Catherine the Great of Russia, *The Scarlet Empress*
9. (H) Diane Keaton and Warren Beatty as Louise Bryant and John Reed, *Reds*
10. (I) George C. Scott as Gen. George S. Patton, *Patton*

16 CON QUEST

1. Control (con troll)
2. Congesting (con jesting)
3. Contribute (con tribute)
4. Consent (con scent)
5. Conceal (con seal)
6. Conduct (con ducked)
7. Confined (con fined)
8. Condescending (con descending)
9. Contraction (con traction)
10. Concave (con cave)
11. Conceding (con seeding) *or* construing (con strewing)
12. Consensus (con census)
13. Contest (con test) *or* concourse (con course)
14. Conceited (con seated)
15. Conserving (con serving)
16. Contract (con tracked)
17. Contour (con tour)

18 BUBBLE TRUBBLE MAZE

The correct path is shown.

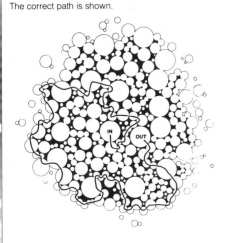

21 FILM-FLAM

1. *Psycho*
   Marion Crane: I've caused you some trouble.
   Norman Bates: No. Mother—my mother—what is the phrase?—she isn't quite herself today.
2. *Duck Soup*
   Mrs. Teasdale: As chairwoman of the reception committee, I welcome you with open arms.
   Rufus T. Firefly: Is that so? How late do you stay open?

19 3-D CROSSWORD

20 DIRTY TRICKS

1. One possible solution:

2. The figure can be divided as shown:

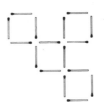

3. The letter S. Each letter in the series is the first letter of its respective word in the question.
4. The missing number is 3. The number in each area denotes the number of bordering areas.
5. The missing numbers, from left to right, are 4, 3, 2, 1. Beginning with the number 1 in the upper left corner, the numbers form counting sequences of increasing length (1; 1, 2; 1, 2, 3; etc.), spiraling into the middle as shown:

1	1	2	1	2	3
5	6	1	2	3	1
4	4	5	6	4	2
3	3	8	7	5	3
2	2	1	7	6	4
1	5	4	3	2	1

22 PATENTLY ABSURD

The phony inventions are (2) the Bravado Rectifier; (3) the Carbonation Resuscitator; (7) the Lipstick Template; and (9) the Swiss Cheese Simulator.

The descriptions of the real inventions are adapted from *Weird & Wacky Inventions* by Jim Murphy. © 1978 by Jim Murphy. Used by permission of Crown Publishers, Inc.

24 PICTURE DOMINOES

The chain proceeds as follows:
A-I-K-H-B-N-F-O-D-G-C-M-E-L-J-A.

26 CAST OF CHARACTERS

Elizabeth Ferret-Frowning
School buses are required by law to stop before crossing a railroad track. When the bus accelerated across the track in order to make the amber light, Lizzie knew it was stolen.

Aunt Hildegarde
At Uncle Toby's, Aunt Hildegarde liked words that can be split in half to make two words; at Aunt Louella's, she favored words that use one letter three times.

Harry Hardway
Harry ordered duck. What he said to the waiter, in simpler form, is: "If Larry ordered the same thing as Gary, I'll have steak." Since Larry ordered steak and Gary ordered fish, Harry does not get steak.

27 EYEBALL BENDERS

1. Strawberry
2. Stick of gum in foil wrapper
3. Cotton swab
4. Record

28 ILLUSIONS & DELUSIONS

The illusion appearing in the introduction was devised in 1889 by German psychiatrist Franz Müller-Lyer.
1. (B) Devised in 1860 by German astrophysicist Johann Zöllner.
2. (A) Published in 1861 by German physiologist Ewals Hering.
3. (C)
4. (B)
5. (C)
6. (A)
7. (B)

Did you notice that there are actually two different kinds of illusions in some sets of figures? One is the classic illusion you were asked to find; the other is its converse—a "delusion," if you will. That is, if the classic illusion has two lines of equal length that appear unequal, then the converse has two lines of unequal length that look equal.

32 KITSCH AND TELL

The pictures should be numbered as follows:

A (14)	F (6)	K (15)
B (3)	G (8)	L (2)
C (12)	H (7)	M (11)
D (10)	I (9)	N (4)
E (1)	J (5)	O (13)

36 EYE EXAM

1. E
2. D
3. C and F
4. The figure can be cut as shown:

5. B
6. D
7. The letters S-T-O-P appear consecutively in the words "lines to produce" in question 4.

30 DUNGEON MAZE

The order in which locked rooms and key rooms must be visited is Start, TC key, SR key, TC key, Storeroom, C key, Storeroom, Crypt, L key, Crypt, Storeroom, Laboratory, A key, Laboratory, Storeroom, Crypt, Archives, Torture Chamber, Finish. The correct path, some sections of which must be retraced several times, is shown.

31 THE HAUNTED HOUSE

From left to right, top to bottom, the errors are as follows:

1. Tree branches both in front of and behind castle tower
2. Bat has frog body
3. Window in bush
4. Left rear castle tower is a pencil
5. Turret roof is concave
6. Stairs lead nowhere
7. Perspective of window in lower right of castle is reversed
8. Right part of castle is a rocket
9. Crescent moon facing wrong way, since light source (the sun) is on the left
10. Darth Vader head on tombstone
11. TV set on tombstone
12. Hitchcock's profile on TV facing wrong way
13. Chain on castle gate doesn't connect
14. Batman mask with Superman sweatshirt
15. Batman's right leg casts shadow in wrong direction
16. No handles on Batman's trick-or-treat bag
17. Watch and tree trunk from Dali painting coming out of tombstone base
18. Floating headstone (in front of fence)
19. Shafts of spears in fence change shape
20. Jack-o'-lantern has floating lid
21. Tombstone next to it loses top right edge
22. Egyptian mummy in open tomb
23. Bush cut in half by tombstone
24. Kid dressed as cowboy wearing Indian headdress
25. Headdress has knife in it
26. Witch with mermaid's tail on trick-or-treat bag
27. Cowboy's right spur is backward
28. Dracula has no gravesite, and his tombstone here shows Bela Lugosi's dates
29. Reflection of tombstone in puddle at incorrect angle
30. Jack-o'-lantern is fishbowl
31. Skeleton forearm should have two bones, upper arm one
32. Base of Weiss tombstone has optical illusion
33. R.I.P. dates reversed on front tombstone
34. Light bulb on left foreground tombstone

And—though it's no error—the truly ghoulish may have noticed the tombstone of a famous person on the picture's far right: Harry Houdini, né Ehrich Weiss, who did die on Halloween of 1926.

34 EYEBALL BENDERS ENCORE

1. Staples
2. Escalator
3. Camera interior
4. Emery boards
5. Toaster
6. Check
7. Razor blade
8. Parking meter
9. Stamps
10. Rubber glove
11. Plastic hairbrush
12. Phone cord
13. Tea kettle whistle
14. Car cigarette lighter
15. Ping-Pong paddle
16. Scrabble tiles
17. Roll of paper towels

38 ARCHITECT'S NIGHTMARE

The seven errors are circled.

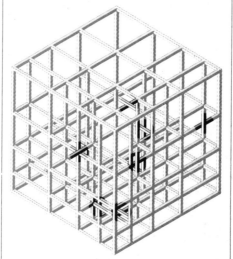

39 THE BONE ZONE

1. Hippopotamus
2. Crocodile (count alligator as correct)
3. Bat
4. Elephant
5. Penguin
6. Reindeer (or deer)
7. Anteater
8. Giraffe
9. Ape
10. Kangaroo
11. Camel
12. Frog (count toad as correct)
13. Lion

40 DECATHLON

Ratings
Gold Medal: 90–100 points
Silver Medal: 70–89 points
Bronze Medal: 50–69 points

Adapted from *The Original Pencil and Paper Sports Game Book* © 1984 by Charles Banasky.

42 GOOD KNIGHT

The 141 homophone pairs are listed alphabetically.

aid—aide	manor—manner
ate—eight	metal—mettle
bald—bawled	mete—meet
baron—barren	mien—mean
bass—base	mind—mined
bee—be	minks—minx
beet—beat	muscles—mussels
bell—belle	nose—knows
blue—blew	nun—none
bomb—balm	oh—owe
bored—board	or—ore
boulder—bolder	paced—paste
brake—break	pale—pail
bred—bread	passed—past
brows—browse	patience—patients
cache—cash	pause—paws
carat—carrot	peace—piece
cause—caws	peek—pique
ceiling—sealing	prince—prints
chased—chaste	raise—rays
choler—collar	real—reel
Claude—clawed	reined—reigned
clothes—close	rode—rowed
coffer—cougher	rood—rude
cowered—coward	Rose—rows
coo—coup	rough—ruff
copse—cops	Russell—rustle
damn—dam	rye—wry
daze—days	seamed—seemed
deer—dear	see—sea
derring—daring	sense—cents
do—dew	sent—scent
doe—dough	serf—surf
ducked—duct	serge—surge
fare—fair	sighed—side
fate—fête	sighs—size
feet—feat	so—sew
flecks—flex	soul—sole
flocks—phlox	steal—steel
flour—flower	straight—strait
four—for	style—stile
frieze—freeze	succor—sucker
furs—furze	sum—some
gait—gate	sun—son
gambling—gamboling	swayed—suede
grays—graze	sword—soared
grille—grill	tacked—tact
grown—groan	tales—tails
guest—guessed	tea—tee
guise—guys	tern—turn
hair—hare	their—there
hansom—handsome	threw—through
hay—hey	tied—tide
hear—here	to—too
heard—herd	tolled—told
heart—hart	use—yews
high—hi	vain—vein
him—hymn	veil—vale
holy—wholly	vile—vial
horse—hoarse	villein—villain
idle—idol	war—wore
instants—instance	wade—weighed
knew—new	waist—waste
knight—night	weak—week
knot—not	wee—we
know—no	wined—whined
lone—loan	wood—would
lute—loot	wrap—rap
lyre—liar	yore—your
magnet—magnate	you—ewe
maid—made	

Based on an idea by J.F. Peirce.

43 3-D WORD HUNT

The 44 relatively common words we found are:

abate	direr	irate	peeve	salve	steep	vivid
above	dirge	lasts	rabid	salvo	stool	voter
areas	diver	loots	rarer	solos	stove	
aster	divot	papal	rater	solve	taboo	
barer	egret	papas	ridge	stare	undid	
barge	grate	pasta	river	state	upend	
boost	green	paste	rivet	steal	verge	

A few of the less common words we found are:

areal	bater	pasts	pupas	soots	stere	toter
arete	easts	pupae	raree	stats	tater	

44 WACKY WORDIES

1. Life of ease
2. Rule of thumb
3. Inverted pyramid
4. "Me and My Shadow"
5. Writer's block
6. Spring fever
7. Sloppy joes
8. Inflated ego
9. Screen test
10. Chief of staff
11. All-star game
12. Old English sheepdog
13. Spinal cord
14. Straw vote
15. Bagpipes
16. Amazing Grace
17. Hollywood and Vine
18. Dead Sea Scrolls
19. Comic strips
20. Dotted swiss
21. Coconuts
22. Holy mackerel!
23. Knotty pine
24. Striped bass
25. Checkered past

46 MENTAL BLOCKS

1. STEWS
   SEETHE
   ESTEEM
   DESSERT
   RESTLESS
   BESTSELLER
   SEAMSTRESS

2. CEASE
   CANCEL
   ACCEDE
   ELEGANCE
   ACADEMIC
   PIECEMEAL
   ACCELERATE

3. BLOOM
   LOBBY
   OBLONG
   BALLOON
   HOBGOBLIN
   BOMBSHELL
   BOONDOGGLE

4. TENSE
   DENOTE
   KITTEN
   DETENTE
   TENEMENT
   INNOCENT
   NINETEENTH

47 RHYME AND REASON

1. Better late than never.
2. Crime doesn't pay.
3. Actions speak louder than words.
4. Beggars can't be choosers.
5. Two heads are better than one.
6. Beauty is only skin deep.
7. Many hands make light work.
8. No news is good news.
9. All roads lead to Rome.
10. Time and tide wait for no man.
11. All good things must come to an end.
12. All's fair in love and war.

47 RARE PAIRS

1. Heart chart
2. Whale tale
3. Bread spread
4. Knight fight
5. Soil toil
6. Four score
7. Finn inn
8. Brain pain
9. Dwelling selling
10. Scratch patch
11. Height fright
12. Skilled guild

48 NOAH'S ARK

1. Caftan
2. Melancholy
3. Investigator
4. Nightmare
5. Rampage
6. Euphonious
7. Cardiac
8. Hypocritic
9. Conceal
10. Bumble
11. Dandelion
12. Tycoon

50 HEART TRANSPLANTS

1. Loner, lover, lower
2. Major, mayor, manor
3. Adept, adapt, adopt
4. Fifth, firth, filth
5. Flesh, flush, flash
6. Laser, later, layer
7. Coups, coops, Corps
8. Flick, flock, fleck
9. Coach, conch, couch
10. Terse, tease, tense
11. Rebel, revel, repel

50 ODD COUPLES

1. Penn
2. Marx
3. Woolf
4. Pyle
5. Welles
6. Wilde
7. Luce
8. Crabbe
9. Baer
10. Hart
11. Caine
12. Lillie
13. Pidgeon
14. Pitts
15. Fischer
16. Dali

Adapted from an idea by Mary Ann Madden in *New York* Magazine.

51 MATCHMAKER

1. Bermuda shorts
2. London broil
3. Grilled sole
4. Roast ham
5. Pool cue
6. Light switch
7. Peanut butter
8. Seat belt
9. Blank check
10. Fall through
11. Legal pad
12. Chafing dish
13. Brussels sprouts
14. Book ends

51 HOW TO HUG

1. (I) *Ragtime*
2. (A) *All the King's Men*
3. (C) *The Day of the Locust*
4. (G) *The Happy Hooker*
5. (J) *Roots*
6. (K) *A Study in Scarlet*
7. (H) *Of Mice and Men*
8. (D) *Deliverance*
9. (B) *The Complete Book of Running*
10. (L) *Watership Down*
11. (E) *For Whom the Bell Tolls*
12. (F) *From Here to Eternity*

52 CHINESE MENU PUZZLE

CAR / PEN / TRY	NEW / SPA / PER
COMB / AT / ANTS	NOR / THE / ASTERN
CON / SIDE / RATE	NIGH / TIN / GALE
DISC / OUR / AGING	PARENT / HE / SIS
END / OR / SING	PROSE / CUT / IONS
FEAT / HERB / RAIN	REIN / FOR / CEMENT
FLU / ORES / CENT	WAR / RAN / TIES
IMP / EACH / ABLE	

52 VOCABULARY

(Additional answers are possible.)

1. Propensity
2. Lifelong
3. Cholesterol
4. Ligament
5. Homeowner
6. Vaudeville
7. Disturbance
8. Unorthodox
9. Propaganda
10. Bathrobe
11. Orthopedic
12. Infrared
13. Exorbitant
14. Ethereal
15. Cobblestone
16. Restaurant

53 PICTURE PALINDROMES

1. Race car
2. Snack cans
3. Navy van
4. Trapeze part
5. Too fat a foot
6. No lemons, no melon
7. Gateman's nametag
8. Space caps
9. Goldenrod-adorned log
10. Party booby trap

Acknowledgments to *Rats Live on No Evil Star: The BackWords Puzzle Book* (Everest House), by Joaquin and Maura Kuhn, for some of the palindromes used in this puzzle.

54 REBUS CARTOONS

ATHLETE: Jimmy Connors (GYM-EEK-HONORS)

FILM ACTRESS: Brooke Shields (BROOK-SHIELDS)

SPORTS EVENT: Super Bowl (SOUP-ER-BOWL)

COMEDIENNE: Lucille Ball (LOU-SEAL-BALL)

FOREIGN CITY: Singapore (SING-UP-OAR)

WORLD CAPITAL: Budapest (BUDDHA-PEST)

FILM CLASSIC: *Citizen Kane* (SIT-IS-IN-CANE)

TV PERSONALITY: Dinah Shore (DINE-ASHORE)

NEWSCASTER: Tom Brokaw (TOM-BROKE-AW)

56 TRANS4MATION: LIST

AF 4 D	GEODE 6	S 10 CIL
ASI 9	GR 8 FUL	STR 8 4 WARD
BE ½	GU 3	S 2 PID
BE 9	HERE 2 4	10 DERLOIN
CA 9	HOLE IN 1	10 NIS
CAR 2 N	100 W 8	3 SOME
CELEBR 8	LEAN 2	2 DLEOO
CLAS 6	OB 2 SE	2 SDAY
CON 4 M	1 CE	2 2
CON 10 T	PE 2 NIA	UN 1
EN 4 CE	PITCH 4 K	UP 2 D 8
EX 10 U 8	PREN 8 AL	VER 1,000,000
5 FOLD	PRE 10 D	W 8 ER
4 EN 6	QUI 9	W 80
4 MUL 8	7 UP	1 DROUS
4 TI 2 DE	6 PENCE	Z 8 A
G 8 WAY	SOME 1	

57 FOLLOW THE CLUES

Counterclockwise from the top, the words are:

Intelligence	Amphitheater	Discourteous
Explain	Impact	Cleanse
Ordinary	Treaty	Incline
Turmoil	Consume	Direction
Petroleum	Entirety	Frightful
Function	Indignation	Honest
Merriment	Burrow	Singleton
Trespass	Brawl	Twitter
Springs	Crude	Intelligence

58 SKELETON: WORD LIST

3-Letter Words: HIT, EON, TWO, DOT

4-Letter Words: GLAD, SAVE, FOWL, WHIZ, REST, PEAK, EAST, TURN, TOTE, NEED, HOSE, ERGO, HELP, WHOA

5-Letter Words: SPICE, SMILE, ZONED, GOWNS

6-Letter Words: RECKON, MAIDEN, PISTOL, MORALS, TAVERN, NATION, NORMAL, GUZZLE

7-Letter Words: STEEPLE, PRESENT

8-Letter Words: FRIGHTEN, DEADLOCK

56 TRANS4MATION

```
K E Y P R E 1 O D L O F 5 O G 1 N D K 1 7
K N U M X 2 A F 5 J E B A F 4 O P L A Z 1 N
D 4 E 4 T C Y P D S H S U G 2 T 8 O W C 2 I
I N O X M N C X E 2 2 V O D C N S V C 9 3 D
S E U E U E H L U B R 9 B M X A 4 E 9 1 S D
O J 6 D A M 8 S K P F G P L A 1 W 1 U G 4 Y
R H I R S T R 4 W A R D C A O N X O O A 4 2
D C S T 1 U C H Y R B X R 1 S 1 2 I I E 3 T
1 O D E R 1 O I N F 1 Z O W T E V 8 E P N
E N 8 A 7 2 Z 2 O O Z R O 1 1 W B 6 Y E N
W 1 H S Q U E 1 N U R O G I A U 2 E Z E
7 Q 6 D 1 P 2 S 1 U O A A P 8 1 R S O E
4 1 2 D E M S 9 E B N O S W L 5 G U 3 H T
```

58 SKELETON CRISSCROSS

```
M A I D E N   F R I G H T E N
O   O   O   O       U   U   E
R E S T   R   W H I Z   R   E
A   A   S M I L E   Z O N E D
L   V   A     L     L   O
S T E E P L E   P R E S E N T
  W   I   A       E   R   A V
G O W N S   S P I C E   G   V
L   H   T O T E   K   H O S E
A   O   O     A     O   I   R
D E A D L O C K   N A T I O N
```

59 SOLITAIRE HANGMAN

I. Mystery
II. Overdue
III. Physics
IV. Minimum
V. Unhappy
VI. Oblique
VII. Chivalry
VIII. Wrought
IX. Communal
X. Heirloom

60 CRYPTOQUIPS

1. I don't want to achieve immortality through my work. I want to achieve it through not dying. (Woody Allen)
2. A man occupied with public or other important business cannot, and need not, attend to spelling. (Napoleon Bonaparte)
3. You know you've reached middle age when your weightlifting consists merely of standing up. (Bob Hope)
4. The fool doth think he is wise, but the wise man knows himself to be a fool. (Touchstone, from Shakespeare's *As You Like It*)
5. I'm a marvelous housekeeper. Every time I leave a man, I keep his house. (Zsa Zsa Gabor)
6. The best minds are not in government. If any were, business would hire them away. (Ronald Reagan)
7. After the fight is over and Frazier don't answer the bell, I'm gonna jump over the ropes and I'm gonna whup Howard Cosell. (Muhammad Ali)

62 BULL'S-EYE

1. Rebelliously
2. Terrific (terrible)
3. Ventriloquism
4. Effete
5. Saturday (sturdy)
6. Overgenerous (verge, onerous)
7. Basic (sick bay)
8. Mute (mate, mete, mite, mote)
9. Go (went)
10. Hijinks
11. Indiscreetly (nicety)
12. Knight (think)
13. Filibuster (fill a bus to)
14. Cablegram (cab, leg, ram)
15. Looped (poodle)
16. Committee
17. Corps
18. Truce (truth)
19. Aspirate (spirate, pirate, irate, rate, ate; "spirate" means "voiceless" or "breathed" according to *Webster's Second*)
20. And
"When in doubt, wear red."—Bill Blass

63 WORD RUMMY

Words							Points
A	C	H	I	E	V	E	
5	5	5	2	3	4	5	29
A	S	P	I	R	I	N	
5	6	7	8	2	2	2	32
B	E	L	I	E	V	E	
A	A	A	2	3	4	5	17
C	H	A	P	T	E	R	
5	5	5	8	9	10	J	52
C	H	E	A	T	E	R	
5	5	5	5	9	10	J	49
C	H	I	M	E	R	A	
4	5	6	7	K	K	K	52
C	L	I	M	B	E	R	
5	6	7	8	A	A	A	29
E	Q	U	A	B	L	E	
10	J	Q	K	A	A	A	43
F	A	C	U	L	T	Y	
3	4	5	Q	Q	Q	Q	52
H	I	M	S	E	L	F	
5	6	7	3	3	3	3	30
I	M	P	E	A	C	H	
6	7	8	5	5	5	5	41
P	R	E	E	M	P	T	
10	10	10	10	7	8	9	64
R	E	L	I	E	V	E	
A	A	A	2	3	4	5	17
R	E	L	I	G	H	T	
A	A	A	6	7	8	9	33
S	L	E	I	G	H	T	
3	3	3	6	7	8	9	39
S	P	I	N	A	C	H	
6	7	8	9	5	5	5	45
T	E	R	R	A	I	N	
9	10	J	2	2	2	2	37
V	A	C	C	I	N	E	
4	4	4	4	8	9	10	43
						TOTAL SCORE	**704**

64 EQUATION ANALYSIS

The Original Test

a. Letters of the Alphabet
b. Wonders of the Ancient World
c. Arabian Nights
d. Signs of the Zodiac
e. Cards in a Deck (with the Jokers)
f. Planets in the Solar System
g. Piano Keys
h. Stripes on the American Flag
i. Degrees Fahrenheit at which Water Freezes
j. Holes on a Golf Course
k. Degrees in a Right Angle
l. Dollars for Passing "Go" in Monopoly
m. Sides on a Stop Sign
n. Blind Mice (See How They Run!)
o. Quarts in a Gallon
p. Hours in a Day
q. Wheel on a Unicycle
r. Digits in a ZIP Code
s. Heinz Varieties
t. Players on a Football Team
u. Words that a Picture is Worth
v. Days in February in a Leap Year
w. Squares on a Chessboard (or Checkerboard)
x. Days and Nights of the Great Flood

In the Last Analysis

Names of contributors appear in italics following their answers.

a. Questions (Animal, Vegetable, or Mineral)
  Gail Rene Katz, Rockville, MD
b. Little Indians
  Gwen Potter, Upper Marlboro, MD
c. Years of Bad Luck for Breaking a Mirror
  Gwen Potter, Upper Marlboro, MD
d. Parts into which All Gaul was Divided
  Eleanor McKinlay, Marathon, FL
e. Pounds in a Ton
  Jim Desmond, Vienna, VA
f. Strings on a Violin
  Katri Rainhold, Milwaukie, OR
g. Trombones that Led the Big Parade
  Karen Graff, St. Louis, MO
h. Gentlemen of Verona
  Dawn Watkins, Silver Spring, MD
i. Little Kittens that Lost Their Mittens
  Gwen Potter, Upper Marlboro, MD
j. Minutes Erased from the Watergate Tapes
  Don Pumsey, Forest Hills, NY
k. Rotten Apple in Every Barrel
  Keith Richards, Holbrook, NY
l. Cigarettes in a Pack
  Thomas M. Moor, Manassas, VA
m. Pockets on a Pool Table
  John E. Guy, Chicago, IL
n. Books of the Bible (in the King James Version)
  Phil Santoro, Pennsauken, NJ
o. Justices of the Supreme Court
  Karen Graff, St. Louis, MO
p. Digits in a Telephone Number (including the Area Code)
  Don Pumsey, Forest Hills, NY
q. Dwarfs with Snow White
  Mrs. Joe Lehman, West Liberty, OH
r. Seconds over Tokyo
  David L. Schneier, Middletown, NY
s. Days a Week (in the Beatles Song)
  Maureen Kennerk, Hicksville, OH
t. Men on a Dead Man's Chest
  David G. Phillips, Silver Spring, MD
u. Blackbirds Baked in a Pie
  Don Pumsey, Forest Hills, NY
v. Spaces (or Squares) in Tic-Tac-Toe
  Gwen Potter, Upper Marlboro, MD
w. Strikes You're Out at the Old Ball Game
  Gail Rene Katz, Rockville, MD
x. Tires on a Car (including the Spare in the Trunk)
  Thomas M. Moore, Manassas, VA

Adapted from an idea by Morgan Worthy in *Aha! A Puzzle Approach to Creative Thinking.*

65 STAR STRUCK

There are 60 sides, or faces, or facets, on the star. The pentagon visible near the center helps identify the figure as a regular dodecahedron (12-sided solid) that has been "stellated" by extending the planes of its pentagonal faces. The lines created from the intersections of these planes join to form the "points" of the large star, as shown in the diagram below. Since the star has 12 such points, each of them made up of five triangles, the total number of faces is 60.

If you interpreted "sides" to mean edges rather than faces, then you'd get a different answer: five edges meet at each of the star's 12 points (a total of 60 edges); add to that the 30 edges of the original dodecahedron that separate the star's points from one another, and you get 90 edges in all. But since all these edges occur in groups of three along the same straight line, it might be more accurate to consider the total number of edges to be one third of 90, or 30.

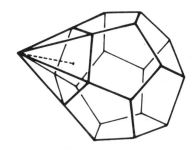

66 A SHORT HISTORY

The correct sequence is F, H, J, B, D, K, I, A, G, C, E.

Copyright © 1979, 1981 by Robert Crumb. Published by Kitchen Sink Press.

70 THE PATCHWORK PUZZLE

The pairs are as follows:

1A and 3D	3B and 5D
1B and 2E	3C and 5E
1C and 2A	4A and 6C
1D and 3E	4B and 6B
1E and 6A	4C and 6D
2B and 3A	4D and 6E
2C and 5B	4E and 5A
2D and 5C	

76 BAR EXAM

The bottles, in order from left to right, are Löwenbräu, Pabst Blue Ribbon, Michelob, Molson, Grolsch, Heineken, Dos Equis, Kirin, Guinness Stout, Beck's, Miller, Budweiser. (Beer aficionados may have noticed a few subtle changes since the puzzle was first printed, in 1981: the shape of the foil on the Löwenbräu and Kirin bottles, the slightly squatter Guinness bottle, the green and white Grolsch label. To those astute few: You have passed the bar exam with flying colors and may now move on to the more intensive case studies.)

68 TRUMP'S GENERAL STORE

The miniature objects masquerading as full-size general store items are listed according to approximate location.

Across ceiling (top third of picture):
playing card ceiling
belt buckle ceiling fixtures with sink stopper hanging lights
lace molding
yardstick molding decorated with pennies
key chain on center ceiling fixture
ball-point pens atop cabinets
padlocks hanging from center ceiling, holding an assemblage made of a nail, safety pin, curtain hook, and nutcracker
tea infuser
scallop shell (below tea infuser)
scissors in ceiling to right of tea infuser
hair clip and tea bags hanging from scissors
key chain with tag near right end of lace molding

Doorway (far left):
pretzels on transom
electric light pull as bell over door
birthday candle as rolled-up window shade
plastic sleeve for 35mm slides as glass panes in door (also used in store window)
peppermint stick outside door
skirt hook door handle
crossword grid entrance tiles
chessboard floor

Christmas tree:
gummed "reward" star set in a birthday candle holder
fruit pastilles, colored popping corn, red hots, and beads as tree ornaments

Store window, top to bottom:
pocket comb
35mm slides as stained glass panels
earring sconces
meat thermometer as bus stop sign outside window
chopsticks and brown cigarettes framing window
Life Saver lime candy as the O in STORE sign
swizzle stick as rod for wooden match curtain
decanter stopper left of curtain
comb chairback with melba toast chair seat and chess piece legs
dice behind chair
cigar holder umbrella stand on top of bottle cap
screw in umbrella stand
lipstick case as ashtray with button top

Behind counter, left cabinet:
pen nibs atop chopsticks separating cabinets
pencils on both sides of cabinets
thermometer across top
lamps: rook chess piece, candy mint, toothpaste caps, pencil sharpeners
ball-point pen refill as shelf molding
next shelf down: sink stopper, thimbles, fuse
whistle (below stopper and thimbles)
35mm film as wrapping paper

Second cabinet from left:
suction-cup shade on cuff link lamp
pin backing under lamp
auto cigarette lighter
cigar ring around salami
next shelf: battery terminal, fruit candy, checker
next shelf: paper caps, screw anchors, tiddlywinks, caramel candy
bottom shelf: salt and pepper shakers as jars

Third cabinet and floor:
top shelf: gum erasers and sugar lumps as cartons
next shelf: stick gum, Bingo counters, and bubble gum as yard goods, ribbons, and notions
crochet hook leaning against cabinet
small hook on crochet hook
leather wallet as cabinet
subway token between shelf sections
fire extinguisher made of a battery, a snap, a hose clamp, and an alligator clip
snail shell vase (with flowers)
crayon box
stamp moistener as pickle barrel
disposable razor and tube of paint as vacuum cleaner on left
nail clipper and bulldog clip as vacuum cleaner on right
three-minute egg timer as table between vacuum cleaners

Right cabinet, table, and floor:
top shelf: film cartridge, jack and pocket screwdriver in front of film, Mary Janes candy as jars
next shelf: bouillon cubes, aspirin tin, toy bullets in tin, spools of thread, mousetrap at right
next shelf: flashlight bulb, Monopoly hotel piece, razor blades, Life Savers, liquor bottle cap
next shelf: Scrabble tile as top of hinged box, wafer cookies as valises
aspirin as soap
postage stamp as comb card
rubber stamps as table
dollar bill as rug
hand grenade as stove with buckle doors; plumbing fittings and Papermate felt tip marker as stovepipe
cinnamon sticks as logs wrapped by rubber band
drawer pull as stove fender
tin can lid under stove
paper grip as ash carrier

Counter front
package carry handle as wrapping paper roll
picture hook at right of wrapping paper
book matches and overalls hook as cash register
leather luggage tags displaying doilies, socks, and gloves
eyes as handles on display cases

Table
drill chuck as coffee grinder
plastic bubble-package material over cheeses
key as foreground cheese board
beer coaster tabletop
champagne bottle wire as breadbasket
pistachio nuts as bread

Meat display case
on top: shelled peanuts, hinge, garter as part of scale
top shelf: fuses as cabinet lights, artists' pastels and crayons as meat
lower shelf: eraser, stone
switchplate as front of case, surrounded by electric cord and watchband bottom

Foreground sacks
paper fasteners as scoops
potting soil as coffee
peanuts in tapioca sack made of sachet bag
clothing label as front coffee sack

In addition, there are many buttons and beads—too many to enumerate—and many items especially made by the artist. Some items not listed are toys made for dollhouses.

72 THE PARTY THAT TIME FORGOT

	Arrived with	Played ...	with	Drank ...	with	Left with
Crawford	Murphy	Tennis	Fields	Lemonade	Presley	Gable
Keaton	Fields	Golf	Murphy	Bloody Marys	Gable	Presley
Monroe	Presley	Croquet	Gable	Martinis	Fields	Murphy
West	Gable	Horseback riding	Presley	Champagne	Murphy	Fields

74 REMEMBER WHEN?

The chronological order of the *Newsweek* covers is:

S. (1950) U.N. Headquarters opens. (Cover date, 9/18/50)

J. (1954) Supreme Court orders end to public school segregation. Washington, DC, is first major system to comply. (9/13/54)

F. (1957) Russians launch Sputnik. (10/14/57)

Q. (1959) Castro ousts Batista in popular revolution, proclaims democratic state. (1/19/59)

M. (1960) Nixon and Kennedy debate on television (10/10/60)

B. (1961) Nazi war criminal Adolf Eichmann is tried and executed in Israel. (4/17/61)

K. (1962) John Glenn is first U.S. astronaut to orbit earth. (3/5/62)

E. (1964) Ford Mustang is introduced. Lee Iacocca's small car is an immediate success. (4/20/64)

G. (1966) "Pop" art bursts on scene. (4/25/66)

H. (1968) Riots at Chicago convention hurt Humphrey's presidential bid. (9/9/68)

U. (1969) Man walks on moon. (7/28/69)

C. (1970) National Guardsmen kill four antiwar demonstrators at Kent State University. (5/18/70)

I. (1972) President Nixon visits Communist China, opening way for relations. (3/6/72)

P. (1973) Hank Aaron approaches Babe Ruth's home run record (breaks it in April 1974). (8/13/73)

O. (1974) President Ford's "Whip Inflation Now" campaign is a dismal failure. Republicans lose elected offices nationwide in wake of Watergate. (11/18/74)

T. (1975) Ex-Manson follower attempts assassination of President Ford. (9/15/75)

R. (1976) Outbreak of "Legionnaires' Disease" at Philadelphia convention baffles medical science. (8/16/76) .

N. (1978) Louise Brown, first "test tube baby," is born (8/7/78)

L. (1979) Three Mile Island accident focuses public attention on nuclear safety. (4/9/79)

D. (1980) Volcano at Mt. St. Helens erupts. (6/2/80)

A. (1981) John McEnroe wins U.S. Open tennis championship, and Voyager 2 sends pictures of Saturn at same time. (McEnroe also won in 1980, and Voyager 1 passed Saturn in 1980, but the events were far apart.) (9/7/81)

82 BIG CITY SHADOWS

1. Person in a car
2. Police barricade
3. Fire hydrant spouting water
4. Motorcycle
5. Padlock
6. Awning
7. Traffic light
8. Handles of a glass door
9. Salt, pepper, and ketchup on a wire table
10. Traffic cone
11. Outdoor faucet
12. Parking meter
13. Trash poker
14. Trash basket
15. Bicycle pedal
16. Horse

84 9 COUPLES

The reunited couples are

1–17	4–10	8–12
2–14	5–7	9–16
3–18	6–13	11–15

88 ALL EYES ON INDY

The close-up scenes were viewed by the various cameras as follows: A–7, B–10, C–5, D–3, E–1, F–6, G–4, H–8, I–9, J–2.

78 BEGUILERS

Diamond Cutting
The lines are drawn as shown.

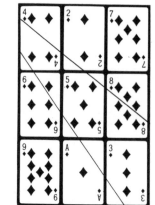

Join the Club
The 5 is complete.

Call a Spade a Spade
The face-down card is the 10. The cards are arranged as shown below.

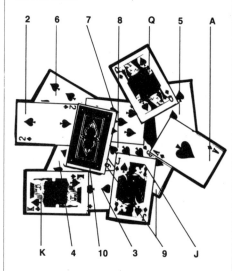

Change of Heart
Invert the 7 and the 8.

96 EYEBALL BENDERS IN ORBIT

The images on page 96 are satellite photographs of various regions of the United States. The Landsat spacecrafts that took the pictures use "remote sensing" photography, in which colors do not appear as they would to the eye: vegetation shows up red; water, blue or black; soil, either blue, yellow, or brown; and cities, blue or black, typically with crisscrossing lines. The tops of all the photos are oriented north, or slightly east of north.

Clockwise from upper left:

Los Angeles. The metropolitan area is at the lower right. Numerous fault lines appear as grooves in the surrounding mountains and valleys; the famous San Andreas fault is the line running left-right just above the brown area in the center.

The U.S.–Soviet border. The land mass on the left is Siberia; on the right, Alaska. The large Soviet island in the center, Big Diomede, is only three miles from Little Diomede, the small U.S. island next to it. The irregular arc of blue-white in the Bering Strait is probably a line of sea ice.

The island of Hawaii. The most outstanding features are the volcanoes Mauna Loa, in the center of the dark blue area in the middle of the island, and Mauna Kea, further north. Through the cloud cover, part of Hilo Bay can be seen on the northeast shore.

Boston and Cape Cod. The light blue region in the upper left is Boston. Beneath the Cape are the islands of Martha's Vineyard (left) and Nantucket (right). Halfway up the left edge is Providence, Rhode Island.

New York City and Long Island. The Hudson River prominently marks the west side of Manhattan; Staten Island is seen to the southwest. On the left of the photo (below the middle) is Trenton, New Jersey, on the Delaware River. The white lines along the Jersey and Long Island coasts are various barrier islands and peninsulas.

94 LOST IN THE OZONE

As you've probably figured out, all these images end in O.

Left-hand third of the page, roughly left to right, top to bottom:
Franco Harris
Piano
Al Pacino (extra credit if you also named *Serpico*)
"Hi-yo Silver!"
Tonto
Pogo
Art Deco (rug)
Crisco
Han Solo (*Star Wars*)
Pablo Picasso
Tuxedo
Placido Domingo
Dumbo
Sluggo
Captain Furillo (*Hill Street Blues*)
Mr. Potato Head and Mrs. Potato Head (extra credit if you knew they're produced by Hasbro)
Lego block
Go (Monopoly)
Silo
Lasso (extra credit for rodeo and bronco)
Volcano
Pinocchio
Pluto
Domino

Center third:
Marlon Brando
Texaco
Phil Esposito
Jell-o
Apollo 15 (moon mission)
Tabasco sauce

Joe DiMaggio
Harpo, Chico, and Groucho Marx
Buffalo Bill Cody
Elvis Costello
Ringo Starr
Oreo cookie
Zippo lighter (or so we thought. Actually, this is a non-Zippo lighter, which still ends in O.)
Photo of Rudolph Valentino
Devo
Greta Garbo
Marlboro cigarettes
Ohio (postcard)
Flamingo

Right-hand third:
Radio
Norelco shaver
Tomato
Bluto
Lucy and Ricky Ricardo
Bingo
Uno
Cadillac Eldorado
Fats Domino
Go (the game)
Palomino
Rocky Marciano
Zorro
Alamo
C-3PO
Mexico (flag)
Brillo
Mario Lanza
Go-Go's
Cameo
Louis "Satchmo" Armstrong

90 WILL IT FLY?

The phony fliers are the Phipps Skybus, the Agricycler, the DC-3 Thermoking, the Grumman Inverted-Flight Special, and the Pitts Pathfinder.

86 TIME PIECE

The order of the photographs following photo 1 (which is inside photo E) is E, H, A, G (inside photo F), I, D, B, C, F, J.

The large overall photo had to have been taken last, since it includes all the other pictures, so the watch at the lower left (J) must read 11:00.

The first shot, taken at 10:10 and labeled #1, was rephotographed several times during the sequence, both before and after being cut apart. The "real" watch in photo H reads 10:20, so the original 10:10 photo was cut apart by that time. Hence E, which is a photo of the 10:10 picture *before* it was cut apart, must have been taken at 10:15.

Photo G, which appears within photo F, reads 10:30. Since photo I was taken at 10:35, after photo A (which is included in I), photo A must have been taken at 10:25, the only 5-minute increment before 10:35 not yet accounted for.

Photo B shows the 10:10 watch in two pieces, so B had to have been taken after photo D, which shows the same watch before it was cut in half (the inner pushpin in photo D, and the fact that the chain doesn't go all the way to the edge, show that it was cut out of the photo labeled #1). Since photo B was taken at 10:45 (reading the "real" watch directly), D must have been shot at 10:40, the only increment before 10:45 not accounted for.

Photo C is obviously 10:50, and F must be 10:55, the only remaining increment.

Lying on the table, both next to the real watch at left and under the scissors at right, are the remains of the original 10:10 photo, which appeared first in photo E, then was cut up for photo H, pinned up for photo D, and finally cut in half for photo B. The original 10:30 photo (G), which appears in photo F, is lying to the left of the scissors.

92 INTERGALACTIC TACTICS

Our scores were achieved as shown:

80 DAY FOR NIGHT

Beginning at the building with the awning (upper left) and proceeding roughly clockwise, by quadrants, we found that the night scene differs from the day scene in the following 61 ways:

Upper Left
The poles supporting the awning have been replaced by supports from above; the door under the awning has disappeared; the building has gained a story and the terrace has moved up.

The cobblestones in the alley have been replaced by stone squares.

"Miller's" department store has become "Muller's"; the "Open 9–6 Daily" sign has become "Open 365 Days"; the store is still open (though a clock elsewhere shows it's past 6 P.M.); the Christmas display in the window has become a New Year's display; the chimney has been replaced by a water tank.

The one-way sign in front of the store is missing; the arrow on the monument sign is reversed.

The angled curb corners have become rounded.

The theater marquee advertising the "third smash week" for *Day of the Locust* is now touting *Night of the Iguana;* the theater's drama mask, frowning in the day scene, is now smiling; the theater's seat prices are less expensive at night.

The "Civic Barber Shop" has become the civic opera house (showing *The Barber of Seville*); a large window has displaced the barbershop's door; the stripes on the barbershop pole are reversed; and lines have been added to the roof of the barbershop.

McDonald's has switched to Burger King.

The trees have lost their leaves.

"Roy's Disco Dancing" has become "Roy's Disco Skating," and the building's mural has changed from dancers to skaters.

The football field in the background has become a soccer field.

The pond is larger and the dock is missing.

The moon, as reflected in the pond, is due north (as indicated by the way the shadows are pointing at noon in the day scene), an astronomically impossible situation.

Upper Right
The street lights are different.

The digital clock has become an old-fashioned clock.

The circus poster is missing (though it's clear the circus has arrived in town from the runaway elephant being chased down the street by the clown).

The street names Main and Elm are reversed.

The "Salon" has become a "Saloon"; the "Happy Hair" sign in the window is now "Happy Hour" (and the newly coiffed woman in the day scene has met her beau; they are heading for the saloon); the salon's revolving door has become saloon swinging doors.

Lower Right
A crosswalk has been added to the street; the sewer grate is missing; the stop sign has become a traffic light; the newspaper box has become a mailbox; the bus stop has been replaced by a taxi stand.

The right-turn lane is gone, replaced by a "No Right Turn" sign; the open trash basket has become a closed can.

The mustachioed candidate "Blutz" on the campaign poster has become the clean-shaven "Blitz."

The painted bowling sign has become neon; the bowling alley seen through the windows has become an exercise class.

The flat roof has become sloped; the clothes-drying rack has become a TV antenna.

Lower Left
The hydrant is missing one nozzle; the neat lawn has become a weed patch; the wooden fence is now cast-iron; the normal bike has turned into a bicycle built for two; cracks are missing from the sidewalk; and sidewalk sections are different.

"Ye Olde Hearth," advertising chili burgers, has become "To Your Health," advertising tofu burgers.

The curtains in the restaurant are replaced by venetian blinds; the air conditioner has become a flower box; the solar panels on the roof have become a skylight; the brick facade is replaced by cinder blocks; the number of panes in the upstairs window is different.

The steps on the telephone pole are missing; and the number of telephone wires has changed.

97 HOLLYWOOD BAD GUYS

Clockwise from top: Lon Chaney, Jr. *(The Wolf Man)*; Bela Lugosi *(Dracula)*; Boris Karloff *(Frankenstein)*; James Cagney *(Man of a Thousand Faces)*

98 WHOSE ZOO

1. Greyhound
2. Trix cereal
3. Playboy
4. John Deere
5. Pocket Books
6. Mustang
7. Hush Puppies
8. RCA Victor
9. Hartford Life Insurance
10. Kiwi shoe polish
11. Jordache
12. Volkswagen Rabbit
13. Merrill Lynch
14. Schlitz Malt Liquor
15. U.S. Postal Service
16. Kellogg's Sugar Frosted Flakes
17. Camel Cigarettes
18. Borden
19. Bantam
20. Cougar
21. Exxon

102 ON BROADWAY

1. *Sophisticated Ladies*
2. *My Fair Lady*
3. *Mame*
4. *A Funny Thing Happened on the Way to the Forum*
5. *Evita*
6. *Stop the World, I Want to Get Off*
7. *A Chorus Line*
8. *Hair*
9. *Grease*
10. *How to Succeed in Business Without Really Trying*
11. *Sweeney Todd*
12. *The Best Little Whorehouse in Texas*
13. *Cats*

105 STAR CROSSED: LIST

Diane Keaton
Sally Field
Sissy Spacek
Robert Redford

Robert De Niro
Dustin Hoffman
Jon Voight
Meryl Streep

104 PENCIL IN-TERTAINMENT

Movie Shorts
1. *Casablanca*
2. *Earthquake*
3. *Cabaret*
4. *It Happened One Night*
5. *Animal House*
6. *Annie Hall*
7. *The Odd Couple*
8. *Last Tango in Paris*
9. *Superman*
10. *Lawrence of Arabia*
11. *Notorious*
12. *Interiors*
13. *Dial M for Murder*
14. *All About Eve*
15. *Bonnie and Clyde*
16. *Deep Throat*
17. *Jaws*
18. *Airport*
19. *Diner*
20. *Dr. No*
21. *Alfie*
22. *Body Heat*

The Idiot Box

Across	Down
1. *Kung Fu*	1. *Quincy*
2. *Batman*	2. *Benson*
3. *Harry-O*	3. *Mannix*
4. *Family*	4. *Lassie*
5. *Dallas*	5. *Topper*
6. *Cannon*	6. *F Troop*

"Television is like chewing gum for the mind."
—Frank Lloyd Wright

On a First-Name Basis
1. Country singers (Cash, Williams, Rogers, Parton)
2. Tennis stars (Ashe, McEnroe, Connors, Wade)
3. Film directors (Hitchcock, Brooks, Preminger, Polanski)
4. Cartoonists (Schulz, Kelly, Trudeau, Young)
5. *M*A*S*H* stars (Alda, Swit, Farr, Farrell)
6. Astronauts (Shepard, Glenn, Borman, Armstrong)
7. TV game show hosts (Barker, Cullen, Rayburn, Dawson)
8. Quarterbacks (Staubach, Bradshaw, Namath, Tarkenton)
9. Olympic figure skaters (Fleming, Fratianne, Hamill, Hamilton)
10. Chess players (Fischer, Evans, Capablanca, Spassky)

110 HAIR APPARENT

1. Ronald Reagan
2. Bob Marley
3. Princess Diana
4. Albert Einstein
5. Captain Kangaroo
6. George Washington
7. Elvis Presley
8. Bo Derek
9. William Shakespeare
10. Groucho Marx
11. Yul Brynner (or Telly Savalas, Daddy Warbucks, etc.)

100 THE SOUND OF MUSIC

Ladies' Aid
1. "Second Hand Rose," Barbra Streisand
2. "Bette Davis Eyes," Kim Carnes
3. "Georgia on My Mind," Ray Charles (also "Linda on My Mind," Conway Twitty)
4. "Long Tall Sally," Little Richard
5. "Maggie May," Rod Stewart
6. "Runaround Sue," Dion
7. "Honeysuckle Rose," Fats Waller
8. "Good Golly Miss Molly," Little Richard
9. "Eleanor Rigby," The Beatles
10. "Proud Mary," Creedence Clearwater Revival
11. "Alice's Restaurant," Arlo Guthrie
12. "Ruby Tuesday," The Rolling Stones
13. "Judy's Turn to Cry," Lesley Gore
14. "Help Me, Rhonda," The Beach Boys
15. "Wake Up Little Susie," The Everly Brothers

Horray for Hollywood
1. *Midnight Cowboy*
2. *The Graduate*
3. *Deliverance*
4. *Butch Cassidy and the Sundance Kid*
5. *A Star Is Born*
6. *Saturday Night Fever*
7. *The Spy Who Loved Me*
8. *Nashville*
9. *Casablanca*
10. *Rocky III*

Where or When?
1. "Downtown" (Tony Hatch)
2. A banker with a motor car, a fireman with an hourglass, a pretty nurse selling poppies from a tray ("Penny Lane," Lennon/McCartney)
3. Watch me wallabies feed, keep me cockatoo coo, take me koala back, mind me platypus duck. ("Tie Me Kangaroo Down," Rolf Harris)
4. About half-past eight; "Darktown Strutters' Ball" (S. Brooks)
5. Slip out the back Jack, make a new plan Stan, hop on the bus Gus, drop off your key Lee ("50 Ways to Leave Your Lover," Paul Simon)
6. The salt in my stew, the starch in my collar, the lace in my shoe, the sail of my loveboat, the captain and crew ("You're the Cream in My Coffee," De Sylva/Brown/Henderson)
7. "Up on the Roof" (Gerry Goffin/Carole King)
8. The Louvre Museum, a melody from a symphony by Strauss, a Bendel bonnet, a Shakespeare sonnet, and Mickey Mouse are possible answers from the first verse. ("You're the Top," Cole Porter)
9. "Strumming on the old banjo" and, in a later verse, "makin' love" ("I've Been Working on the Railroad," Traditional)

Where Credit Is Due
1. Pat Boone
2. Mick Jagger
3. Joni Mitchell
4. Carole King
5. Cher

Spliced Tapes
1. "True Love" (Cole Porter)/"Wouldn't It Be Loverly" (Lerner and Loewe)
2. "Sympathy for the Devil" (The Rolling Stones)/"Misty" (Errol Garner/Johnny Burke)
3. "The Animal Fair" (Traditional)/"Someone to Watch Over Me" (George and Ira Gershwin)
4. "Still Crazy After All These Years" (Paul Simon)/"A Good Man Is Hard to Find" (E. Green)
5. "Get Back" (Lennon/McCartney)/"Bad, Bad Leroy Brown" (Jim Croce)
6. "Dedicated to the One I Love" (Ralph Bass/Lowman Pauling)/"Mrs. Robinson" (Paul Simon)
7. "On the Street Where You Live" (Lerner and Loewe)/"I'm Gonna Wash That Man Right Outa My Hair" (Rodgers and Hammerstein)
8. "Where Have All the Flowers Gone?" (Pete Seeger)/"Send in the Clowns" (Stephen Sondheim)
9. "Hungry Heart" (Bruce Springsteen)/"Truckin'" (The Grateful Dead)

The Party's (Over)
1. Dolly
2. weather
3. Raindrops
4. overcoat
5. cold
6. wave
7. sunny
8. roses
9. Tonight
10. tonight
11. Billy
12. Joe
13. Joe
14. head
15. hand
16. cheek
17. cheek
18. skin
19. Tom
20. Dooley
21. April
22. autumn
23. time
24. Bill
25. feets
26. Irene
27. rain
28. shine

Famous Last Words
1. "London Bridge," Traditional
2. "Blue Suede Shoes," Carl Perkins
3. "Aquarius," James Rado/Gerome Ragni/Galt McDermot
4. "Get Me to the Church on Time," Lerner and Loewe
5. "Home Sweet Home," John Howard Payne/Sir Henry Bishop
6. "Bring Back My Bonnie to Me," Charles E. Pratt/H.J. Fuller

I Got Rhythm
1. "The Birth of the Blues" (Henderson/De Sylva/Brown)
2. "Mr. Tambourine Man" (Bob Dylan) (also "Mr. Bass Man," Johnny Cymbal)
3. "Boogie Woogie Bugle Boy" (Don Raye and Hughie Prince)
4. "Band on the Run" (Paul McCartney)
5. "Jailhouse Rock" (Elvis Presley)
6. "Alexander's Ragtime Band" (Irving Berlin)
7. "It's Only Rock 'n' Roll" (Mick Jagger/Keith Richards)
8. "The Beat Goes On" (Sonny Bono)
9. "American Tune" (Paul Simon)
10. "Boogie On Reggae Woman" (Stevie Wonder)

With thanks to Billy Mernit, to Raymond D. Love, and to Jack Lechner's *Ivy League Rock & Roll Quiz Book* (Delilah).

106 HERE'S JOHNNY!

Monologue
1. Downtown Burbank
2. Joan Rivers
3. Fred de Cordova
4. Tommy Newsom
5. Mandrake Curvy
6. Commissary
7. Goodshaft
8. Jim Fowler
9. Joan Embery
10. Rodney Dangerfield
11. Bob Hope
12. Carl Sagan
13. Stump the Band
14. Blends

Segue: After the monologue, Johnny (d) swings an imaginary golf club.

The King of Comedy
1. (b) *Who Do You Trust?*
2. (c) Vinnie Abruzzi's Little Touch of Newark
3. (a) They have erasers on both ends.
4. (a) Steve Allen and (d) Jack Paar
5. (a) On the plains of Nebraska
6. (d) The fear of walking backward into a cold doorknob
7. (b) 15.5 million
8. (d) Clipping his fingernails

Time Flies
Johnny's been hosting *The Tonight Show* for 22 years as of October 1, 1984. The correct order of pictures is (D) 1963; (B) 1967; (A) 1970; and (C) 1980.

Second Bananas
1. (c) Carl; trumpet
2. (a) Socks with the toes cut off
3. (b) A pig and a horse (Ed takes the side of the horse.)
4. (d) Alpo and Budweiser

Johnny's Jests
1. (e) Ronald Reagan
2. (g) Don Rickles
3. (h) John Glenn
4. (b) Prince Charles
5. (d) Richard Nixon
6. (a) Ed McMahon
7. (c) Billy Martin
8. (f) Gerald Ford

In Character
1. Picture A, G. Walter Schneer; B, Aunt Blabby; C, Floyd R. Turbo, American; D, Carnac the Magnificent; E, Art Fern.
2. (c) Carol Wayne
3. (d) Cut off your slauson.
4. (a) "What's the bra size of a flat-chested shark?" (b) "What does it say on St. Peter's answering machine?" (c) "How does a congressman keep track of who he's dating?"
5. (d) Hermetically sealed in a mayonnaise jar on Funk & Wagnalls' porch since noon

105 STAR CROSSED

The faces are composed of the following actors and actresses (top to bottom):

1. Robert Redford
   Robert De Niro
   Diane Keaton
2. Sissy Spacek
   Dustin Hoffman
   Meryl Streep
3. Diane Keaton
   Sally Field
   Sissy Spacek
4. Dustin Hoffman
   Sissy Spacek
   Jon Voight
5. Jon Voight
   Meryl Streep
   Robert Redford
6. Sally Field
   Diane Keaton
   Robert De Niro
7. Meryl Streep
   Jon Voight
   Sally Field
8. Robert De Niro
   Robert Redford
   Dustin Hoffman

108 COMIC STRIP STRIP

1. (H) Flash Gordon, *Flash Gordon*, by Alex Raymond
2. (K) Annie, *Little Orphan Annie*, by Harold Gray
3. (L) Pogo Possum, *Pogo*, by Walt Kelly
4. (M) Hans and Fritz Katzenjammer, *The Katzenjammer Kids*, by Rudolph Dirks
5. (F) Snuffy Smith, *Barney Google and Snuffy Smith*, by Fred Lasswell
6. (I) Sergeant Snorkel, *Beetle Bailey*, by Mort Walker
7. (B) Betty Boop, *Betty Boop*, by Max Fleischer
8. (G) Prince Valiant, *Prince Valiant*, by Hal Foster
9. (N) Charlie Brown, *Peanuts*, by Charles Schulz
10. (A) Mike Doonesbury, *Doonesbury*, by G.B. Trudeau
11. (C) Dennis, *Dennis the Menace*, by Hank Ketcham
12. (J) Hägar, *Hägar the Horrible*, by Dik Browne
13. (E) Olive Oyl, *Popeye*, by Elzie Segar
14. (D) Henry, *Henry*, by Carl Anderson

111 NUMBER PLEASE!

The key number is 65.

A. 9 + 8 = 17	N. 80 ÷ 4 = 20
B. 12 × 2 = 24	O. 32 − 10 = 22
C. 5 − 4 = 1	P. 5 + 5 = 10
D. 8 + 0 = 8	Q. 12 + 0 = 12
E. 13 + 2 = 15	R. 13 + 6 = 19
F. 39 − 16 = 23	S. 7 × 3 = 21
G. 4 + 1 = 5	T. 9 ÷ 3 = 3
H. 16 − 9 = 7	U. 8 + 3 = 11
I. 7 + 7 = 14	V. 14 + 4 = 18
J. 66 − 50 = 16	W. 5 × 5 = 25
K. 360 ÷ 90 = 4	X. 17 − 15 = 2
L. 18 − 12 = 6	Y. 10 − 1 = 9
M. 10 + 3 = 13	

A	B	C	D	E
17	24	1	8	15
F 23	**G** 5	**H** 7	**I** 14	**J** 16
K 4	**L** 6	**M** 13	**N** 20	**O** 22
P 10	**Q** 12	**R** 19	**S** 21	**T** 3
U 11	**V** 18	**W** 25	**X** 2	**Y** 9

112 CAN YOU ANSWER?

1. *The Guinness Book of World Records*
2. The mosquito wins, 47 to 32.
3. Bowling.
4. On a standard Snellen eye chart.
5. The strawberry.
6. Clark Gable, when he went undershirtless in the movie *It Happened One Night*.
7. 86
8. All three.
9. The choice was decided by a coin toss. (History does not record who won the toss, however.)
10. Zero. Local gambling is illegal.
11. Typewriter (1829), can opener (1858), ice cream freezer (1864), carpet sweeper (1876).
12. Their respective hit recordings of ''O Sole Mio,'' ''There's No Tomorrow,'' and ''It's Now or Never'' all use the same melody.
13. Red. *Colorado* comes from the Spanish for ''color red''; *Oklahoma* is Choctaw for ''red people''; and *Rhode Island* is derived from the Dutch words for ''red island.''
14. Hockey.
15. Seeing, hearing, and speaking out loud—they're the see-no-evil, hear-no-evil, speak-no-evil monkeys.
16. Ten cents.
17. Rin Tin Tin.
18. *American Gothic*, by Grant Wood.
19. 10
20. A red-and-green traffic light.
21. Greece's, with 158 verses. Japan's has only four lines, and the anthem of Qatar (a small Arab country on the Persian Gulf) has no lyrics at all.
22. It indicates how the rider died: four hooves on the ground, died naturally; one hoof raised, died of battle wounds; two hooves raised, died in battle.
23. A bag.
24. To throw at weddings.
25. *Moby Dick*, by Herman Melville.
26. To prevent food from freezing—the refrigerator was warmer than the outside temperatures.
27. The money, $105, came from Sanders's first Social Security check, when he was 65.
28. Alaska, at 2¢ per acre; Louisiana cost 3¢ per acre.
29. The echo of blood pulsing in your ear.
30. Mattel, which sells over 20 million outfits for Barbie dolls annually.

113 BEEHIVE

Based on a puzzle in *Facili Cruciverba* (Florence, Italy).

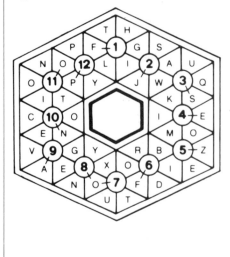

114 RIGHT ANGLES

Puzzle 1

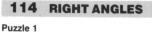

Puzzle 2

115 MISSING IN ACTION

STAR	SILO	CANE
NINO	PROVE	ORAL
ALTO	HOTEL	NEIL
GLISTEN	RASCALS	
TARS	TIE	
SCHEME	AGITATE	
LIARS	CIAO	LURK
ALI	RADON	TAN
BIRD	OPAL	GOOSE
AYEAYES	DECREE	
BIB	FIAT	
VACATES	ENRAGED	
ALIT	ALIVE	GAVE
NOTE	NADER	OMEN
SEED	MARS	NEST

116 SPELL WEAVING

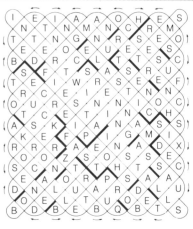

117 PETAL PUSHERS

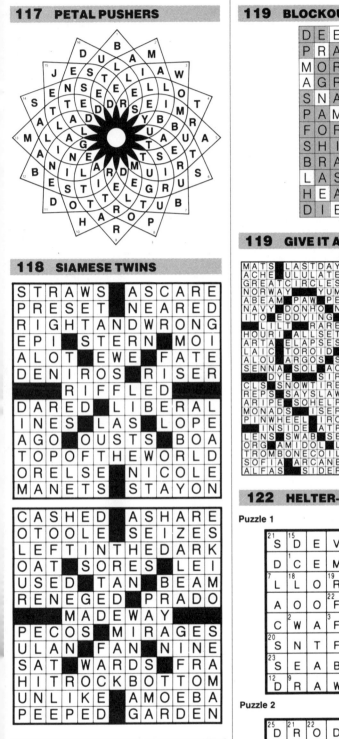

118 SIAMESE TWINS

S	T	R	A	W	S			A	S	C	A	R	E
P	R	E	S	E	T			N	E	A	R	E	D
R	I	G	H	T	A	N	D	W	R	O	N	G	
E	P	I			S	T	E	R	N			M	O	I
A	L	O	T			E	W	E			F	A	T	E
D	E	N	I	R	O	S			R	I	S	E	R
			R	I	F	F	L	E	D			
D	A	R	E	D			L	I	B	E	R	A	L
I	N	E	S			L	A	S			L	O	P	E
A	G	O			O	U	S	T	S			B	O	A
T	O	P	O	F	T	H	E	W	O	R	L	D	
O	R	E	L	S	E			N	I	C	O	L	E
M	A	N	E	T	S			S	T	A	Y	O	N

C	A	S	H	E	D			A	S	H	A	R	E
O	T	O	O	L	E			S	E	I	Z	E	S
L	E	F	T	I	N	T	H	E	D	A	R	K	
O	A	T			S	O	R	E	S			L	E	I
U	S	E	D			T	A	N			B	E	A	M
R	E	N	E	G	E	D			P	R	A	D	O
			M	A	D	E	W	A	Y			
P	E	C	O	S			M	I	R	A	G	E	S
U	L	A	N			F	A	N			N	I	N	E
S	A	T			W	A	R	D	S			F	R	A
H	I	T	R	O	C	K	B	O	T	T	O	M	
U	N	L	I	K	E			A	M	O	E	B	A
P	E	E	P	E	D			G	A	R	D	E	N

123 CONNECT-A-WORD

1 HIGH	2 FLYING	3 FISH	4 BONE	5 HEAD
6 SIGN	7 IN	LINE	9 DRY	10 LAND
11 UP	12 COMING		13 COUNTY	
14 TURN	15 OUT	16 PLAY	17 FAIR	18 TRADE
19 OVER	20 LOOK	21 BACK	22 GROUND	23 DOWN
	24 SEE		25 FLOOR	26 PILLOW
27 BIG	28 RED	29 DOG	30 SHOW	31 CASE
32 FOOT	33 LIGHT	34 HOUSE	35 BOAT	36 LOAD

119 BLOCKOUT

D	E	E	P	E	R
P	R	A	G	U	E
M	O	R	A	L	S
A	G	R	E	E	D
S	N	A	C	K	S
P	A	M	P	E	R
F	O	R	A	G	E
S	H	I	N	N	Y
B	R	A	N	D	O
L	A	S	T	O	F
H	E	A	R	S	E
D	I	E	T	E	D

119 GIVE IT A WHIRL

M	A	T	S		L	A	S	T	D	A	Y		L	U	G	E	R		C	A	D	I	S
A	C	H	E		U	L	U	L	A	T	E		E	L	I	N	O	R		A	G	O	N	Y
G	R	E	A	T	C	I	R	C	L	E	S		T	U	R	N	T	U	R	N	T	U	R	N
N	O	R	W	A	Y		Y	U	M	A	S		D	I	A	N	A	S		B	E	G	
A	B	E	A	M		P	A	W		P	E	R	T	H		S	T	O	M		O	L	D	E
N	A	V	Y		D	O	N	H	O		N	O	W	O	R		E	U	R	O	P	E
I	T	O		E	D	D	Y	I	N	G		W	I	N	E		S	T	O	N	E	H	A	M
	L	I	L	T		R	A	R	E		S	O	D	A		D	I	N	E	R	O
H	O	U	R	I		A	L	L	S	E	T		T	R	E	N	C	H		T	U	L	I	P
A	R	T	A		E	L	A	P	S	E	S		A	C	E	T	O	U	S		P	I	S	E
L	A	I	C		T	O	R	O	I	D		A	G	A	M	E	M	N	O	N		X	E	D
A	L	O	U		A	R	G	O	S		S	P	A	R	S		X	I	I
S	E	N	N	A		S	O	L		A	C	R	I	D		M	O	D		M	C	R	A	E
	D	Y	E		S	I	R	E	N		C	A	L	I	F		H	O	W	L
C	L	S		S	N	O	W	T	I	R	E	S		S	H	E	L	V	E		D	U	A	L
R	E	P	S		S	A	Y	S	L	A	W		I	T	A	L	I	A	N		I	N	K	A
A	R	I	P	E		S	O	H	E	L	P		N	U	R	S	E	S		C	E	D	E	S
M	O	N	A	D	S		I	S	E	R		K	N	I	T		I	O	N	A
P	I	N	W	H	E	E	L		I	R	O	N		T	O	R	N	A	D	O		N	F	C
	I	N	S	I	D	E		A	T	P	A	R		T	O	A	D	Y		O	D	E	R
L	E	N	S		S	W	A	B		S	E	N	O	R		M	E	D		M	U	R	R	E
O	R	G		A	M	I	D	O	L		L	O	U	I	S		G	O	T	O	U	T
T	R	O	M	B	O	N	E	C	O	I	L		S	P	I	R	A	L	N	E	B	U	L	A
S	O	F	I	A		A	R	C	A	N	E		T	U	N	I	S	I	A		I	N	A	N
A	L	F	A	S		S	I	D	E	R		S	P	E	A	K	E	R		D	D	S	S

122 HELTER-SKELTER

Puzzle 1

21 S	15 D	E	V	O	16 T	E	E
D	C	E	M	E	11 H	10 C	S
7 L	18 L	O	19 R	D	R	A	6 H
A	O	O	22 F	4 A	I	R	S
C	2 W	3 A	F	F	L	E	A
20 S	N	T	F	N	L	14 G	B
23 S	E	A	B	E	17 E	A	A
12 D	9 R	A	W	E	8 R	13 S	W

Puzzle 2

25 D	21 R	22 O	D	E	N	T	6 S
E	I	E	23 R	13 A	19 C	N	P
9 T	T	A	H	15 C	14 O	18 I	I
O	I	I	G	C	R	12 T	T
24 N	16 P	A	P	O	20 O	17 S	E
I	T	U	8 G	S	N	U	F
10 C	O	U	S	T	E	11 A	U
5 S	3 E	X	I	S	T	D	L

126 DOUBLE PARKING

Puzzle 1

1 M	2 S		3 M	4 L	
A	K		A	E	
5 K	E	S	D	6 R	I	F	T
		7 C	I	O	Y
A	R	M	N
8 F	A	S	9 E	10 C	T	H
L	P	T	E
11 O	W	R	12 T	E	R

Puzzle 2

1 G	2 A		3 C	4 A	
A	A		H	N	
5 S	R	Y	R	N	E
P	Y		R	N	E
7 N	E	D	E	R
E	G	N	E
8 Q	U	I	9 T	O	L	10 I	R
		A	L	S		E	R	G	O

Based on a puzzle in *Krzyżówka* Magazine (Warsaw).

127 MARCHING BANDS

D	I	S	C	O	V	E	R	M	O	U	T	H
S	L	E	D	G	E	R	A	T	T	R	A	P
L	E	M	O	N	A	D	E	M	E	R	C	I
I	D	A	H	O	O	V	E	R	B	I	T	E
A	I	R	S	H	I	P	P	O	E	T	I	C
S	H	A	D	E	D	E	N	C	L	A	V	E
S	E	R	E	N	E		T	R	I	B	E	S
A	S	T	R	O	S	O	N	A	T	I	N	A
W	R	E	S	T	S	S	E	T	T	L	E	S
N	O	B	E	L	B	A	S	E	L	E	S	S
W	H	I	T	E	C	A	P	S	E	N	S	E
O	D	E	S	S	A	M	A	N	I	A	C	S
D	E	M	O	C	R	A	T	L	A	D	E	S

Based on a puzzle in *La Settimana Enigmistica* (Milan).

128 THE SPIRAL

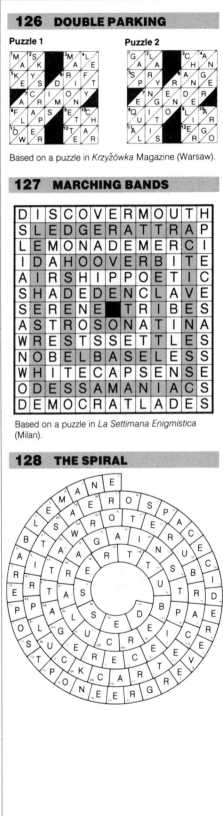

124 SOLVING CRYPTICS

Warm-Up 1
ACROSS
1. ARSON. The word ARSON ("setting fire to a building") is PARSON ("preacher") beheaded, or missing its first letter.
4. ROOST. The word ROOST ("nest," as a verb) is literally found among the letters of "kangaROOS Temporarily."
5. DREAD. If you rearrange the letters of ADDER, you get the answer DREAD ("fear"). The word "coiling" suggests the mixing of letters.

DOWN
1. AIRED. The word AIRED ("televised") is IRE ("anger") inside AD ("commercial").
2. SCORE. The word SCORE means both "twenty" and "songs in a musical."
3. NOTED. The words NO (given directly in the clue) and TED ("member of the Kennedy family") make NOTED ("famous").

Warm-Up 2
ACROSS
1. USHER. The word USHER (meaning "seat," as a verb) combines US ("you and me") and HER ("the woman over there").
4. ICING. If you take the phrase "look into exotic ingredients" literally, you'll find the consecutive letters of the answer, ICING ("cake topping").
5. EASEL. The word EEL ("fish") placed around AS ("while") forms EASEL ("art equipment").

DOWN
1. UNITE. The letters of UTE IN "dancing"—i.e., in rearranged form—spell the answer, UNITE ("join").
2. HAIRS. The word HAIRS ("fur") sounds the same as the word HARE'S ("rabbit's"). The homophone is indicated by the word "say."
3. REGAL. The word REGAL ("fit for a king") is the word LAGER ("beer") "served up"—i.e., spelled from bottom to top in the puzzle grid.

125 CRACKERJACK CRYPTICS

Puzzle 1
ACROSS
1. Topical (tropical − r)
5. Parapet (part + ape)
9. Minaret (are + mint)
10. Remorse (re + Morse)
11. Loose (WaterLOO'S Environs)
12. Restraint (train + rest)
13. Start (two meanings)
14. Laplander (pun)
17. Portrayal (ray + portal)
19. Caper (AmeriCA PERhaps)
22. Spaghetti (at the pigs)
25. Rites (tries)
26. Kittens (Kit's + ten)
27. Trivial (trial + VI)
28. Narrate (near art)
29. Yangtze (get zany)

DOWN
1. Tamales (tales + Ma)
2. Pandora (pa + and/or)
3. Carpenter (Carter + pen)
4. Laterally (late + rally)
5. Parts (strap)
6. Rumor (roomer)
7. Partied (I depart)
8. Theater (th + eater)
15. Palmistry (m + is + paltry)
16. Accordion (a + C + cord + I + on)
17. Pushkin (push + kin)
18. Reactor (creator)
20. Patriot (Pat + riot)
21. Resolve (two meanings)
23. Hyena (yen + ha)
24. Taste (a test)

Puzzle 2
ACROSS
1. Microwave (MI + crow + Ave)
6. Brain (Britain − it)
9. Scant (can + St.)
10. Starlight (That Girl's)
11. Option (potion)
12. Givers (GI + verse − e)
15. Tip O'Neill (tip + one + ill)
17. Roach (Charo)
18. Norse (nose + r)
20. Test cases (cassettes)
22. Phobia (hop + bias − s)
23. Abacus (grAB A CUStomer)
27. Windswept (winds + wept)
28. Rabbi (rabbit − t)
29. Seedy (see + D.Y.)
30. Egyptians (I Spy agent)

DOWN
1. Misfortune (M + is + for + tune)
2. Coast (tacos)
3. Outworn (Our Town)
4. Also (radicAL SOcialist)
5. Evangelist (gets an evil)
6. Bolivar (boar + LIV)
7. Algerians (grain sale)
8. Nuts (stun)
13. Vietnamese (navies meet)
14. Ghost ships (high spots + s)
16. Perchance (perch + cane)
19. Embassy (mess by a)
21. Cabaret (bare + cat)
24. Cobra (Cora + b)
25. Ewes (use)
26. Stay (JameS TAYlor)

129 BREAKING THE CODE

The answer is P. The numbers have been assigned according to the number of unattached end points of strokes used to make up the letters. Accordingly, M = 2, N = 2, O = 0, P = 1, etc.

132 TRAVEL FEVER LOGIC

Three Vacations
The third statement, "Miss English did not go to France," is the only one that can be true and satisfy the conditions of the puzzle. Therefore, Ms. Lapp went to France, Miss English went to Lapland, and Mrs. French went to England.

July 4 Homecoming
Keith and Linda, from Utah, arrived at 8 A.M. with three children.
Ron and Eileen arrived from Texas at 10 A.M. with two children.
George and Jill arrived from Japan at noon with one child.
Frank and Carol arrived from Germany at 2 P.M. with one child.
Bob and Pat arrived from Wyoming at 3 P.M. with three children.
Bert and Wendy arrived from Arizona at 5 P.M. with two children.

Will the Real John Smith Stand Up?
Order of flights from first to last:
John S. Smith, accountant, New York, chess tournament
John F. Smith, surgeon, Paris, vacation
John M. Smith, editor, Washington, convention
John H. Smith, steelworker, Los Angeles, wedding
John A. Smith, actor, Houston, job interview

On the Road to Canterbury
Order of tales from first to last:
Lewis, the clerk, told the tale of Narcissus.
Thomas, the miller, told the tale of Esther.
Derek, the franklin, told the tale of Orlando.
Hugh, the summoner, told the tale of Robin Hood.
Piers, the knight, told the tale of St. George.

135 FAMILY PICTURES

The families are as follows:
Colors Green (golf), violet (flower), orange (fruit)
Units of length Foot, rod (fishing), meter (parking)
Words ending in X Sphinx, fox, jukebox
NFL teams Jets, Bills, Vikings
Metallic elements Nickel, silver (the Lone Ranger's horse), iron
Homophones of letters Bee, tea, eye

Adapted from an idea by Nancy Schuster.

137 ETERNAL TRIANGLE

No matter what numbers you place in the triangles in the top row, the final triangle will always contain a 4.

130 10 BRAINTEASERS

1. The arrows indicate which two matches move, and where.

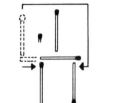

2. It is only necessary to cut the three links of one piece. They can then be used to join the remaining three pieces into the circular bracelet.

3. Simply divide the square as shown.

4. Continue the deal by taking cards from the *bottom* of the packet of undealt cards, dealing first to yourself, then counter-clockwise around the table.

5. Sal wins again. In the first race she ran 100 yards in the time it took Saul to run 90. Therefore, in the second race, after Saul has gone 90 yards, Sal will have gone 100, so she will be alongside him. Both will have 10 more yards to go. Since Sal is the faster runner, she will finish before Saul.

6. The symbols are the numerals 1, 2, 3, 4, 5, 6, 7 shown alongside their mirror reflections. The next symbol, therefore, is the double 8, as shown at the far right, below.

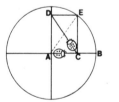

7. You need only shake one coin from the box incorrectly labeled 15 cents. Suppose it is a dime. The coin still in that box cannot be a nickel, because the box would then be *correctly* labeled. Therefore it is a dime. The box labeled 10 cents cannot contain two nickels (or it would be labeled correctly), nor can it contain two dimes because two of the three dimes are in the box labeled 15 cents. Therefore it must contain a dime and a nickel. This leaves two nickels for the box labeled 20 cents.

But if the coin shaken from the box labeled 15 cents is a nickel, similar reasoning will identify the contents of all boxes.

8. The dotted line (AE) in the illustration below shows the other diagonal of the rectangle. The diagonals of a rectangle are equal, therefore CD = AE. And since AE is a radius of the circle, CD also has the length of a radius. But AB is a radius, too. Consequently AB = CD, and the race will be a tie.

9. The trick is to move the queen beyond the borders of the nine squares through which it *must* pass.

10. Miss Gray's dress cannot match her name, so it must be white or black. Since the lady in black replies to Miss Gray's remark, Miss Gray's dress cannot be black. Therefore it is white. Now consider Miss Black. Her dress cannot be black (or it would match her name), and it cannot be white because Miss Gray is wearing white. Therefore it is gray. This leaves the black dress for Miss White.

136 STAR: PLAYING TIPS

When playing Star, it's important to realize that when you connect two of your stars, you gain 2 points. That's because when you tally your points at the end of the game, you will have to subtract two points from only one star, instead of from each of two stars.

Plays near the middle of the board usually give a player more "influence," that is, greater potential to connect stars. But plays at the edge of the board are needed to create stars in the first place, and are probably the best choices early in the game. If you play in the center too early, you may later find that some of the moves you have made there were unnecessary, or that they would have accomplished more had they been placed a little differently.

To offset the advantage of going first, players of equal ability may wish to use the following rule: To begin the game, one player places the first piece, and the other player then has the option of either responding as usual or of switching colors instead. If he chooses to switch colors, he must accept the first piece as his own move. Players of greatly different strengths and experience can use a simple handicap system: The weaker player makes more than one move at the start of the game, after which play alternates as usual. The number of extra first moves can be increased or decreased until each player wins about half the time.

Many new games are billed as being "as easy to learn as tic-tac-toe, but as challenging to master as chess." Star is the rare game that lives up to that description. The history of the game, along with strategy tips, problems, and a sample game, appeared in the September 1983 issue of GAMES.

140 RURAL RHYTHMS LOGIC

Mountain Do
Lem, fiddle; Clem, kazoo; Shem, guitar; Flem, banjo; Homer, mandolin; Billy-Bob, harmonica

Bar Talk
Beetle drives a Pinto and has a pet cougar; Rabbit drives a Skylark and has a pet mustang; Falcon drives an Impala and has a pet barracuda; Lynx drives a Jaguar and has a pet llama; Eagle drives a Stag and has a pet spider.

Seven Little Indians
Begin with the statement of the sixth speaker. If it is true, then the sixth speaker would be a liar, which is contradictory; therefore he must be a liar, and either the fifth or second speaker, or both, must be truthtellers. But since the second speaker says that the sixth is a truthteller, and we know that the sixth speaker is a liar, the second speaker is a liar; therefore, the fifth speaker must be a truthteller. (Since the fifth speaker is telling the truth, the fourth speaker is Gooth and Fu is a liar.)

Now suppose that the first speaker is a liar. Then the fourth speaker is also a liar (and we already know that the second and sixth speakers are liars) That means that more than half the Indians are liars, and that the fourth speaker is telling the truth, which is a contradiction. Therefore the first speaker must be a truthteller. From here the complete answer is easily deduced: First in line is Fol, a truthteller; second is Fu, a liar; third is Fy, a liar; fourth is Gooth, a truthteller; fifth is Fo, a truthteller; sixth is Barjuk, a liar; and seventh is Fumfum, a liar.

Top Ten
1. "Going to Altoona to Get My Alto Tuned"
2. "Tennessee Schmaltz"
3. "Trailer Courtin' "
4. "Saddle Soap (Will Never Wash Your Lipstick off My Heart)"
5. "Beer Belly Polka"
6. "Cole Porter's Daughter"
7. "Haystack Hannah"
8. "You Are My Moonshine"
9. "Bumblebee Bop"
10. "Stand on Your Man"

138 A PERFECT MATCH

1.

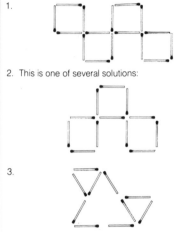

2. This is one of several solutions:

3.

4. Place the 12 hurdles in a hexagonal "pie":

5. Nine is the least number that must be removed to leave no squares of any size. This figure shows one possible arrangement. For a proof that nine is the minimum number, see Chapter 9 of Martin Gardner's *Mathematical Carnival* (Knopf, 1975).

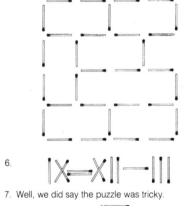

6.

7. Well, we did say the puzzle was tricky.

8. This is one of several solutions:

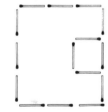

9. Move 2–3 to 9–10; 5–6 to 2–3; 8–9 to 5–6; and 1–2 to 8–9.

144 COMPUTER

1. a, f, b, c, g, d, e, h
2. a, c, f, e, b, d, g
3. a, d, b, f, k, c, e, i, l, h, j, g, m
4. a, b, h, c, f, d, g, i, e, j, k (f and g are interchangeable)

142 MATH APPEAL

Digititis

Puzzle 1

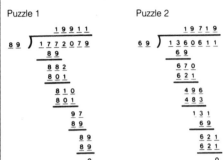

Puzzle 2

Number Square

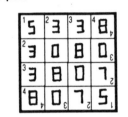

Magic Star

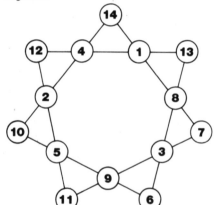

Based on a puzzle by Kenneth Kelsey.

Wheel of Fortune

Clockwise from 1:
1, 9, 3, 8, *, 6, 4, 2, 7, 5, *, 10

Six-Packs

5 = 6 × 6 − 6 ÷ 6	48 = 6 × 6 + 6 + 6
8 = 6 + 6 ÷ 6 + 6	66 = 6 + 6 × 6 − 6
13 = 6 ÷ 6 + 6 + 6	108 = 6 + 6 + 6 × 6
42 = 6 ÷ 6 + 6 × 6	180 = 6 × 6 − 6 × 6

Based on a puzzle by Pierre Berloquin.

Bingo Math

The winning numbers were B–14, I–28, N–39, G–56, and O–70.

145 GRANT'S TOMB

1. A ten-gallon hat holds only about ¾ gallon. The "gallon" is derived from the Spanish *galón*, a braid used to decorate hats.
2. Panama hats were originally made in Ecuador. Panama was the distribution center for the hats.
3. Chinese checkers, derived from an English game called Halma, was invented in Sweden and was marketed under the name Chinese Checkers in the U.S.
4. The Battle of Bunker Hill, a pyrrhic British victory in the Revolutionary War, was fought at neighboring Breed's Hill.
5. The Canary Islands were named after the Latin *Insulas Canarias* ("Island of the Dogs"), a reference to the wild dogs the Romans found there.
6. The English horn is an oboe, probably first developed by the Viennese and later refined by the French.
7. The Woodstock Festival was held in Bethel, New York, 45 miles from Woodstock.
8. Catgut used in tennis rackets and many stringed musical instruments comes from the intestines of sheep.
9. Camel's hair brushes are made from the tails of squirrels.
10. Venetian blinds were invented in Japan.

And who's buried in Grant's Tomb? If you said Ulysses S. Grant, you're only half right. His wife, Julia, is there too—and technically speaking, they're entombed, not buried.

146 THE PRICE WAS RIGHT

1. Pocket watch: $1.50
2. Piano: $1,425
3. Lucky Strikes: 15¢
4. Chocolates: $2
5. Taxi ride: 30¢
6. *The New Yorker:* 15¢
7. Tomato soup: 12¢
8. Plymouth Coupe: $685
9. Calculator: $300
10. TAT ticket: $1,408
11. ScotTissue: 25¢
12. Vacuum cleaner: $35

148 LISTOMANIA

A. Recently patented inventions whose time has not yet come
B. Renowned redheads
C. Henny Youngman's favorite one-liners
D. Prehistoric things alive today
E. Women who were cheerleaders in high school
F. "Dear Abby" Van Buren's readers' most unusual problems (Give yourself half-credit if you guessed Ann Landers.)
G. Brand names that have become generic words
H. Famous events that happened in the bathtub
I. The most memorable things ever insured (and the value for which each was insured)
J. Noted people who never married
K. Body parts you didn't know had names. (The *philtrum* is the vertical groove in the middle portion of the upper lip; *eponychium* is another word for the fingernail cuticle; the *glabella* is the part of the forehead just above the nose, and between the eyebrows; *otoliths* are the particles of calcium carbonate in the inner ear that regulate equilibrium; and a *phalanx* is one of the bones in the fingers or toes—there are 14 in each hand or foot.)
L. Famous insomniacs, and how they induced sleep (Dumas père's doctor hoped an early morning apple would force his patient into a regular schedule of rising and retiring.)
M. Unusual objects offered at auction (and their selling prices)
N. The gestation period (in days) of 12 animals
O. Movies most often shown on television

List E is reprinted from *Is There Life After High School?* © 1976 by Ralph Keyes, published by Little, Brown Company. G is reprinted from *Stylebook for Writers and Editors* © 1977 by U.S. News and World Report. O is reprinted from *TV Guide* magazine, © 1977 by Triangle Publications, Inc. All others, excerpts from *The Book of Lists* © 1977 by David Wallechinsky, Irving Wallace, and Amy Wallace (pages 299, 272, 278, 474, 16, 132, 100) and from *The Book of Lists #2* © 1980 by Irving Wallace, David Wallechinsky, Amy Wallace, and Sylvia Wallace (pages 370, 276, 231, 484). By permission of William Morrow & Co.

154 WATCHING TV

TV or Not TV

1. (b) 38% (Roper survey, 1982)
2. (c) 75% (TV Audience Assessment Study, 1981)
3. (b) Turkey, etc. (*The Official Couch Potato Handbook*)

Prime Time

1. Sunday is the favorite night for TV; Friday is the least favorite (Nielsen Report on Television, 1983).
2. (d) Women, 18 and up watch the most; (c) teenage girls watch the least (Nielsen).
3. (c) 710, or 17,040 hours; that's more than 10% of each little life (*Guinness Book of World Records*).

Station Breaks

1. (a) $9 (*The Official Couch Potato Handbook*)
2. (c) $485,000 (Young and Rubicam, Inc.)
3. (a) 1 (*Newsweek* "Eyes on Television" survey, 1980)

150 UNDER PRESSURE

Score one point for each correct answer.
1. The letter X should be crossed out in the first sentence.
2. The word *gaiety* should be circled.
3. The stack contains 25 cubes.
4. The square should be left empty.
5. The blank should contain your correct age.
6. 10¢, 10¢, 5¢, 1¢.
7. The space should contain the word DOG.
8. The next space should be empty.
9. The next space should contain the word NO.
10. The word GOLF should appear in the next space.
11. The next blank should be empty.
12. True.
13. Thursday.
14. MADAM, MEDIUM, MOM, MUM, MUSEUM. Many other answers are possible.
15. Uncle.
16. The square should contain a check.
17. 2:36.
18. The word ICE should be written at the bottom of the page.
19. Eleven.
20. The words I QUIT should appear at the end of the sentence.

Ratings:
18–20 points—Ace. You work exceptionally well in situations requiring rapid and tricky brainwork. Unfortunately, this skill has no positive correlation with income.
14–17 points—Very good. You can fill out an IRS 1040 on time without the help of H & R Block.
10–13 points—Fair. But sometimes you are confused by tricky instructions and sometimes even by not so tricky instructions.
Under 10 points—Try another quiz.

151 COLLEGE EXAM

Section I

1. B	10. D	19. E (or maybe
2. E	11. B	A, if you live
3. A	12. E	north of the
4. E	13. B	Mason-Dixon
5. C	14. D	and get beat
6. D	15. A	up a lot)
7. E	16. C	20. C
8. B	17. D	
9. D	18. E	

Section II

21. B	26. D	31. D
22. C	27. C	32. C
23. D	28. E	33. B
24. C	29. C	34. E
25. B	30. A	35. E (we think)

Scoring Guide
To obtain your verbal score on the GAMES Aptitude Test, count the number of correct answers you had in Section I, subtract ¼ point for each incorrect answer, and multiply the result by 30. Then add 200, and round to the nearest 10. To obtain your math score, count the number of correct answers you had in Section II, subtract ¼ point for each incorrect answer, and multiply the result by 40. Add 200, and round to the nearest 10.

Where does that leave you? Well, the average SAT-taker scores about 450 on each part, and gets into college.

153 SCENE OF THE CRIME

Score one point for each correct answer to questions 1 to 20, and two points for each correct identification in the final bonus question.
1. 5:45
2. Saturday, the only day the produce store was open after 5:00
3. Jane's
4. Bates Ave.
5. Two
6. Yes
7. Three
8. No
9. Eight
10. V.L.
11. A falling potted plant
12. Woman
13. Crawfordtown Produce
14. Myrtle St.
15. Grapes
16. F472
17. It was parked in a 4–6 P.M. No Parking zone.
18. Left rear tire
19. Her purse was being picked.
20. No
Bonus: B and E

Ratings
20–24: Lieutenant Columbo
16–19: Old Hawk Eyes
10–15: Sharp Observer
5–9: Inspector Clouseau
1–4: Amnesiac

156 OUTNUMBERED

1. (b) 491,396
2. (b) 6,400,030
3. (a) 1,193,000
4. (a) 29,000
5. (a) 9,061,000
6. (c) .0313
7. (c) 31,000,000
8. (c) $252,000,000
9. (b) 775,000
10. (b) 7,990,000
11. (a) 16,380,000
12. (b) 391,000,000
13. (a) 1,986,000
14. (a) 9,200,000
15. (b) .1
16. (a) 17,448
17. (a) 100,877,060,000,000
18. (c) 3,250,000
19. (c) 17,000,000
20. (c) 1,634,706
21. (b) 200,000,000
22. (b) 8,760
23. (b) 93,050
24. (c) 145,600
25. (b) 5,976,000,000,000,000,000,000

Adapted from an idea by Douglas R. Hofstadter, in a *Scientific American* column.

155 SPELLING BEE

The misspelled words in the introduction are listed here in italics, followed by the correct spelling, in parentheses.
concensus (consensus)
neccesarily (necessarily)
maladiction (malediction)
occasional (occasional)
inacuracy (inaccuracy)
talanted (talented)
challange (challenge)
orthagraphic (orthographic)
exersizes (exercises)
begining (beginning)
interduction (introduction)
ridled (riddled)

One Out of Two Ain't Bad
1. (B) decaffeinate
2. (B) minuscule
3. (A) sincerely
4. (A) mischievous
5. (A) embarrassed
6. (B) possession
7. (B) bizarre
8. (A) acquaintance
9. (B) weird
10. (B) carburetor
11. (A) innuendo
12. (A) maneuver
13. (B) irrelevant
14. (A) persuade
15. (A) colossal

Get the Picture?
1. referee
2. xylophone
3. chandelier
4. hippopotamus
5. scissors
6. beetle
7. ambulance
8. dachshund

Say What?
1. foreigner
2. silhouette
3. sophomore
4. ophthalmologist
5. chauffeur
6. diphtheria
7. tawdry
8. benign
9. surfeit
10. parishioner
11. assurance
12. fricassee

What's Wrong?
Correct spellings are given in parentheses.
1. (c) *philatalist* (philatelist)
2. (a) *superceed* (supersede)
3. (d) *paraphenalia* (paraphernalia)
4. (d) *millenium* (millennium)
5. (b) *occurence* (occurrence)
6. (a) *enforcable* (enforceable)
7. (d) *baloon* (balloon)
8. (c) *sacreligious* (sacrilegious)
9. (a) *definately* (definitely)
10. (b) *dilemna* (dilemma)

158 SCIENCE TWISTERS

1. RAINBOWS. (c) The center of the circle formed by a rainbow lies below the horizon along a straight line passing from the sun through the viewer's head. As the sun goes down, the center of the circle goes up. When the sun is nearest the horizon, in the morning and afternoon, the rainbow is at its greatest height and appears to be a semicircle; but when the sun is high, as at noon, the rainbow vanishes below the horizon.

2. SNOWBALLS. (c) To make a snowball you apply pressure with your hands, which melts enough ice to produce a layer of water between the snowflakes. With the pressure removed, the flakes stick together because the water forms a cohesive bond that is reinforced by the refreezing water. When the temperature is very low, the pressure required to melt the ice is too great to be exerted with the hands.

3. RING AROUND THE MOON. (a) Ice crystals form in high-altitude cirrus clouds that precede a rain front. These crystals refract light from the moon and give the appearance of a ring.

4. BIRDS AND BATS. (c) The ears of birds and bats are very sensitive to the lower air pressure that occurs when a storm front is approaching. They fly lower at such times to avoid the ear pain they would suffer at higher altitudes, where the air pressure is even lower.

5. ECHOES. (b) To be audible, sound waves must be reflected in the listener's direction. If you stand at the foot of a hill and shout or clap your hands, the sound waves will bounce off the hill at an upward angle—that is, away from you (like light off a mirror, or a pool ball off a cushion)—because the angle of reflection is always equal to the angle of incidence. In mountainous regions, all the reflecting areas are angled away from you (unless you happen to be atop one of the mountains)—so the sound waves never reach you.

6. FULL MOON. (c) The lunar surface is full of craters, mountains, and other irregularities. When lit obliquely by the sun, as during the first and last quarters, these features cast long shadows, increasing the dark areas of the moon. But when the sun illuminates most of the lunar surface from directly above, there are fewer such shadows, and the brightness increases by a factor of nine.

7. EARTHRISE. (b) The moon's rotation is synchronized with its revolution about the earth, which is why we always see the same hemisphere of the moon. Therefore, to an observer on the moon, the earth will always appear to be at the same point in the sky, although it will appear to rotate—both hemispheres of the earth will be visible (at different times).

8. RAINDROPS. (a) A falling drop is subject to two opposing forces: gravity and air resistance. The constant force of gravity pulls the drop at increasing speed, but as the drop falls faster it is acted upon more strongly by air resistance—until finally air resistance and gravity equal a net force of zero. At this point the drop falls at a uniform rate, its "terminal speed." If the size of the drop is increased, the force of gravity increases proportionally to the drop's volume, that is, to its radius cubed. Air resistance increases too, but proportionally to the cross-sectional area of the drop; that is, to its radius squared. This means that a larger drop can reach a greater terminal speed before air resistance catches up with it.

9. OF MICE AND MEN. (c) The heat loss in animals is mainly through their surface, and so varies in proportion to an animal's surface area. Heat production, however, occurs in all cells, and varies in proportion to an animal's volume. Since volume (proportional to the cube of an animal's average length) increases faster than surface area (proportional to the square of an animal's average length) as the size of an animal increases, small animals have a much greater surface-to-volume ratio than people do, and lose a great deal more heat in proportion to their body weight. To maintain their correct body temperatures, therefore, mice must consume proportionally more calories (which are a measure of heat energy).

10. FROGS. (c) To be comfortable, frogs have to keep their skin wet, which is why they live around ponds and dive underwater every so often. But frogs can't croak underwater. Since storms are often preceded by humid air, a frog's skin can remain moist even while the frog stays out of the water.

11. MUD BATHS. (b) Pigs, having no sweat glands, are not cooled by the evaporation of perspiration. Immersion in mud keeps them cool.

12. ICE. (c) Antarctica is a land mass, and land is a poor conserver of heat (which is why winters are harsher deep inland). But Arctic ice lies over an ocean, and water conserves heat well. As a result, much less ice is formed in the Arctic.

13. FLOATING. (b) The body weight of women is about 25 percent fat on average, that of men only 15 percent. Since fat is lighter than water, the overall density of the female body is less than that of the male body—which means women can float more easily. Also, since men have more volume around their shoulders than anywhere else, their center of buoyancy is in their upper body, far from their center of gravity. A woman's center of buoyancy is in the large pelvic area, closer to her center of gravity, which gives her more stability while afloat.

14. NIGHT LOWS. (b) The earth radiates most of its energy in infrared wavelengths, and water vapor is an excellent absorber of infrared radiation. Miami's more humid atmosphere absorbs and therefore retains heat, whereas in El Paso's drier air the heat of the day dissipates much more rapidly when the sun goes down.

15. JUMPING FLEAS. (c) An animal's weight varies according to the cube of its volume, its strength according to the square of its muscle-and-bone cross-section. A human's strength relative to his size and weight therefore keeps him earthbound. If a flea's size were increased a thousandfold, its weight would be a billion times greater but its strength only a million times greater. The poor thing would be crushed by its own weight.

16. COLD COAST. (a) The Coriolis force, caused by the rotation of the earth, forces water away from the California shore toward the southwest. The departing water is replaced by colder water rising from depths of several hundred feet and by cold currents of water flowing down from the north.

17. ELEPHANT EARS. (a) As the largest land mammal on earth, the elephant has less surface area compared to its weight than smaller animals. Living in a hot climate, it needs the larger surface area provided by its ears to dispose of extra body heat through radiation and evaporation.

18. ON THE WING. (b) A bird flies by pushing down on the air below it, which creates an updraft that helps nearby birds stay aloft. Calculations prove 25 birds in formation can fly 70% farther than one bird flying solo.

160 WHERENESS AWARENESS

Distances and areas are given in miles and square miles, respectively.

1. Portugal
2. Canada
3. Soviet Union
4. None, while traveling north, since it is not possible to travel north beyond the North Pole. If you continue in the same line of movement, however, you will hit Norway first.
5. Paris
6. Honolulu
7. Rome
8. Juneau (but only by about 2° of latitude)
9. France (210,038 to 158,693)
10. Quebec (594,860 to 586,412)
11. The rest of New England (but only by 33,393 to 33,215!)
12. The island of Hawaii is largest (4,021), then Yellowstone National Park (3,468), and last Delaware (2,057).
13. Chile (after traveling all the way around the world). If you left from the southern part of Tierra del Fuego, you would hit an island that is part of Chile; if you left from the northern part, you would hit the Chilean mainland.
14. Walla Walla (Washington) is much farther from Pago Pago (American Samoa) than is Wagga Wagga (in southeastern Australia).
15. New York to Chicago (714 compared to 580 for London to Berlin).
16. Rio de Janeiro to Mexico City (4,769, compared to 4,102 for Rome to Montreal).
17. Los Angeles (!)
18. Beijing (by a long shot).
19. Johannesburg
20. Washington, D.C.
21. One Africa (11,682,000 as compared to about 11,000,000 for two Antarcticas).
22. 90 Hawaiis
23. North
24. South
25. South
26. South
27. Seven to two (If you thought Greenland was larger, you may have been thinking of the flat Mercator projections in many atlases, where areas in polar regions look disproportionately large.)
28. Lisbon
29. Hong Kong to Caracas is the greatest distance (10,171). Next are Vienna to Melbourne (9,802) and Caracas to Melbourne (9,703).
30. Probably Hell Canyon (a creek in southwest South Dakota). If you said the Bay of Rainbows, you will coincidentally find yourself right next to the Sea of Rains; unfortunately, both places are on the moon. We also doubt you would want to visit the Vinson Massif—the highest peak in Antarctica. But there's no accounting for one's sense of adventure, so score a point regardless of your answer.

Ratings
28–30 Lake Superior
22–27 Goodnews, Alaska
15–21 Fair Play, Missouri
1–14 Disappointment Island
0 Goose Egg, Wyoming

161 CHAIN REACTION

The second and fifth chains match. The second will have the same pattern visible as the fifth, if you turn it upside down and rotate it 180°.

162 CAPITAL IDEAS

1. London
2. Jerusalem (Salem, Oregon)
3. a. Algiers
   b. Khartoum
   c. Tripoli
   d. Lisbon
   e. Canberra
   f. Belgrade
   g. Warsaw
   h. Kuwait
4. Rangoon (ran + go on)
5. Nassau (saunas)
6. Bonn (Germany), Bern (Switzerland)
7. Copenhagen (PENH)
8. Prague
9. Tirana (Albania), Iran
10. Mali, Lima (Peru)
11. Bogota (Colombia), Togo
12. Tokyo, Quito (Oh!)

166 MURDER: CLUE

Hatch saw various graphic patterns in the self-portraits. As sometimes happens, it was the exception to the rule that solved the crime.

168 THE SCARLET LETTER

"This rag of scarlet cloth on careful examination assumed the shape of the capital letter A."
—Nathaniel Hawthorne, *The Scarlet Letter*.

162 MISSING LINKS

Puzzle 1

Puzzle 2

163 CRYPTIC CONNECTIONS

Hook-Ups
1. spin
2. dune
3. dust
4. soap
5. view
6. town
7. pad

Opposites
1. safe
2. across
3. in progress
4. arrived
5. bid
6. hip
7. Community Chest

Ratios
1. neigh (homophones of opposites)
2. kitchen (anagrams)
3. eyeteeth (same letters, used repeatedly)
4. civic (Roman numerals)
5. blight (spoonerisms: cold : hot :: black : white)
6. shout (same beginning letters, opposite endings)
7. church: tithe

Common Factors
1. wings
2. street
3. pin
4. *Psycho*
5. net
6. attendants
7. hands
8. oath

Lists
1. home (bases)
2. arms of an octopus
3. Bush (Vice-Presidents)
4. full, twin (bed sizes)
5. Los Angeles (Summer Olympics sites)
6. Thank God it's (days of the week)

The Verse
The diminutive spider is second to none
In producing a thread that is sticky as glue;
Yet he never gets caught in the web that he's spun,
Which is better than most of us people can do.

164 EUROPEAN TOUR LOGIC PUZZLE

Last Name	Husband's First Name	Wife's First Name	Husband's Occupation	Wife's Occupation	Week 1	Week 2	Week 3	Week 4
Rosen	David	Jessica	PR director	Psychoanalyst	Spain	Denmark	England	Norway
Quinn	Charles	Kate	Fashion designer	College professor	France	Italy	Spain	Denmark
Palmer	Fred	Glenda	High school principal	Professional golfer	England	Norway	Italy	France
Oglethorpe	Bertram	Lois	Television scriptwriter	Magazine editor	Norway	England	Denmark	Italy
Newkirk	Edward	Helen	Photographer	Newspaper columnist	Denmark	France	Norway	Spain
Morgan	Alan	Ingrid	Novelist	Physician	Italy	Spain	France	England

165   COIN TRICK

The coins can be aligned in the following 14 moves:

```
0.  N P N P N P N
1.      N P N P N N P
2.        N P N N P N P
3.          N N P N P N P
4.      N     N P N P N P
5.    N P N P N P       P
6.        N N P N N P P
7.      N     N N P P N P
8.      N P N N N P       P
9.          N N N P N P P
10.       N N     N P P N P
11.         N N P N N P     P
12.       N     N N P N P P
13.     N P N N N       P P
14.         N N N N P P P
```

165   THE DIAMOND

Puzzle 1

Puzzle 2

Puzzle 3

166   A SKETCHY MURDER

Each of the eight artists embodies a different line style: The woman on the far right displays a brickwork pattern, the man next to her shows a grid pattern, the man third from right (seen from behind) shows solid horizontal lines, and so on.

Inspector Hatch noticed that there was a framed picture to match the line style favored by each artist (e.g., the Queen of Hearts self-portrait matches the brickwork pattern of the artist at far right), but no picture to match the victim's zigzag pattern. In addition, there were *two* pictures using short vertical lines, the style of the artist with the beret (fourth from right). One of these two pictures, that of the dragon, suggested the victim's tattoo and was also framed in the victim's zigzag line style.

Hatch reasoned that the victim must have copied the other artist's style, and then gone on to win the prize at the show (note the first-place ribbon on this picture). Furious, the artist in the beret killed the winner, and literally left his "mark"—short vertical lines—on his victim's neck.

168   ANAGRAMANIA

1. Webster's Dictionary
2. mistaken identity
3. no trespassing
4. Metropolitan Opera House
5. a promissory note
6. Arlington National Cemetery
7. the desert oasis
8. archaeologist
9. A Farewell to Arms
10. "Doctor Livingstone, I presume."
11. the tortoise and the hare
12. Raiders of the Lost Ark
13. The New York Times
14. spaghetti and meatballs
15. Piet Mondrian
16. public transportation

Anagrams 1 through 8 are by David Shulman; 9 through 11, Janet Cohen; 12, Mike Ventrella; 13, Joseph J. Demma; 14, Marilyn Malpass; 15, Barry L. Cohen; and 16, Helen Bernhardt.

169   MUSICAL CHAIRS

ACROSS
1. Earshot (those + are − e)
6. Coats (*Tosca*)
10. Anthem (man + the)
11. Ague (sAnGtUnEs)
12. Triangles (Elgar isn't)
14. Cute (cut + e)
15. Stir (sir + t)
16. Nerve (never)
19. Drone (done + r)
21. Resonant (tenor's + a + n)
23. Glistens (let's sing)
24. Bands (b and s)
26. Meson (me + song − g)
28. Edit (thE DITty)
29. Taps (two meanings)
32. Desirable (slide bar + e)
33. Last (two meanings)
34. Heifer (her + E + if)
35. Apple (a. + p + pl + e)
36. Ocarina (o + car + in a)

DOWN
1. Unseat (as tune)
2. Organ (two meanings)
3. Thais (two meanings)
4. Hence (wHEN CEllist)
5. Platonist (Latin, tops)
6. Creed (Cree + d)
7. Flagstones (flags + tones)
8. Tubing (two + Bing)
9. Secrets (sects + re)
13. Supersonic (percussion)
17. Void (voices − ces + d)
18. Pastorale (last opera)
20. Tiers (ties + r)
21. Rubella (rub + Ella)
22. Madcap (Music And Dance Consider All Painters)
25. Themes (THE MESsiah)
26. Scream (s + cream)
27. Canter (c + aren't)
30. Pair (p + air)
31. Lenin (Lennon)

Discarded letters spell SOUTH PACIFIC.

```
S O U T H P A C I F I C
E A R S H O T C O A T S
A N T H E M P R A G U E
T R I A N G L E S S B C
U G E I C U T E S T I R
N E R V E R O D R O N E
R E S O N A N T S N G T
U M O I G L I S T E N S
B A N D S E S M E S O N
E D I T T A P S P L N T
L C C D E S I R A B L E
L A S T M T H E I F E R
A P P L E O C A R I N A
```

170   AT WIT'S END

1. Logophobia
WOLF. The chain is FEAR, FARE, FAIR, FOUL (as in baseball), FOWL, WOLF.

2. Number Chain

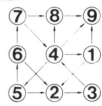

3. Body Talk
FOOT/BOOT

4. Crossout
The following digits should be crossed out: column 1—3 and 4; column 2—3 and 5; column 3—6 and the 1 beneath it; column 4—2 and 6; column 5—both 2s; column 6—4 and 2.

5. Dead Letter Department
The letter is the Greek psi, completing the words GYPSIES, LOPSIDED, TIPSINESS, and CAPSIZE.

6. Elementary!
Sulfur. In both cases, the Roman numeral for the subtracted number is deleted from the word for the first number; i.e., FIVE − IV = FE, the chemical symbol for iron. Similarly, SIX − IX = S = sulfur.

7. Making the Cut
One solution is shown. It is impossible to get nine complete pieces.

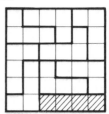

8. Time to Reflect
The time is 8:20. The watch is inverted as well as reflected, as indicated by the position of the stem.

9. Last in Line
The number is 18. Each number in the lower row is the square of the number above it, with the digits reversed.

171   SCAVENGER HUNT

The order of the page numbers corresponds to the order of the pictures in each row, from left to right.

Row 1: page 110
Row 2: pages 53 and 7
Row 3: pages 14, 115, and 143
Row 4: pages 70, 163, 167, and 45
Row 5: pages 150, 83, and 61
Row 6: pages 99 and 155
Row 7: page 38

Having had the good fortune to be part of the life of GAMES Magazine, and to select the puzzles for this volume, also gives me the opportunity to thank and toot the horns of the following: the group that came to be called the Book Team at GAMES, for the tremendous effort in producing the book quickly, carefully, and with extraordinary good humor; our colleagues at Workman Publishing, for sharing our enthusiasm, and helping us do it our way; the editors and art directors of GAMES, for sustaining a remarkable level of creativity and quality over the years, and the staff without whom that creativity would never find its way to the printed page; the puzzle constructors for chasing the cobwebs from our brains; and the many GAMES readers for the support and scrutiny that keeps us on our toes.—Ronnie Shushan

BIG BOOK OF GAMES

Editor Ronnie Shushan
Associate Editor Lori Philipson
Permissions Georgiana Dwight
Proofreader Toni Green
Designer Don Wright
Art Production Kathy Kesting
Production Martha Weber
Assistant Jane Greenberg
Layout Artists Marybeth Farrell,
Joe Diamond

WORKMAN PUBLISHING

Publisher Peter Workman
Production Wayne Kirn
Editor Suzanne Rafer
Layout Artist Gabrielle Maubrie

GAMES MAGAZINE

Editor Jacqueline Damian; *Senior Editors* R. Wayne Schmittberger, Will Shortz; *Associate Editor* Curtis Slepian; *Editorial Administrator* Georgianna Dwight; *Assistant Editors* Robert Leighton, Lori Philipson, Mike Shenk, Stephanie A. Spadaccini; *Assistant to the Editor* Patricia McCabe; *Editorial Assistants* Suzanne Gardner, Toni Green; *Copy Editor* Burt Hochberg; *Design Director* Don Wright; *Associate Art Directors* David Herbick, Barry Simon; *Art Associate* Kathy Kesting; *Picture Researcher* Debra Kagan-Chevat; *Layout Artists* Todd Betterley, Carole Popolo, Laura Walworth; *Production Director* Martha Weber; *Editorial Production Manager* Sarah Scrymser; *Advertising Production Manager* Michael Arpino; *Typesetter* Kathy Lum; *Production Assistant* Jane Greenberg; *Contributing Editors* Jamie Adams, Emily Cox, Bernie De Koven, Roger Dionne, Henry Hook, Andy Meisler, Marvin Miller, Henry Rathvon, Merl Reagle, Gloria Rosenthal, Sid Sackson, Joe Schick, Mary Ellen Slate; *Contributing Artists and Photographers* Stan Fellerman, Mark Mazut, Ken Robbins, Walter Wick

Publisher Jerry Calabrese; *Business Manager* Ben Wolman; *Operations Manager* Sam Ananian; *Assistant to the Publisher* Jan Elstun; *Office Services Assistant* Joseph J. McCabe; *Receptionist* Cheryl Page; *Advertising Director* Paula Fierman; *Account Executives* Joe Failla, Marilyn Matty, Sheila Phillips, Tracey Wilen; *Promotion Manager* A. Mimi Anderson; *Administrative Assistant* Linda Verdun; *Advertising Assistant* Francine Malara; *Marketing Director* Alan Inglis; *Subscription Manager* Cathy Woll; *Fulfillment Coordinator* Yvette Watts; *Subscription Promotion Assistant* Will Marks

October 1984

ART CREDITS

Page
- 1: Illustration by Tom Bloom.
- 3: Illustration by Rick Tulka.
- 9: Illustration by Bob Neubecker.
- 14: All photos, Movie Still Archives.
- 15: Photos A, C, and J, Wide World Photos; B, D, and I, Movie Still Archives; photo E and illustrations F and G, The Bettmann Archive; photo H, Houghton Library, Harvard University.
- 21: *Psycho* photo, Movie Still Archives; *Duck Soup*, The Bettmann Archive.
- 22-3: Illustrations by Isadore Seltzer.
- 28-9: Illustrations by Joe Lertola.
- 30: Illustration by Joe Lertola.
- 32-3: Illustrations by Lisa Pomeroy.
- 34-5: Photographs 1, 3, and 5, Kimberly Butler; 2 and 6, Suely Sinto; all others, Jane L. DiMenna.
- 36-7: Illustrations by Robert Leighton.
- 40: Illustration by Carole Popolo.
- 44-5: Illustrations by Joe Lertola.
- 47: Illustration by Mark Mazut.
- 50: Illustration by Leo Pando.
- 52: Illustration by Tom Bloom.
- 53: Illustrations by Michael Witte.
- 54-5: Illustrations by Kimble Mead.
- 60-1: Jester illustration by David Klein; photo 1, Movie Still Archives; 3, 6, and 7, UPI; 5, Movie Star News; illustration 2, The Bettmann Archive.
- 68-9: Photograph by Walter Wick.
- 70-1: Quilt designed by Margit Echols; sewn by Margit Echols and Emiko Loeb. Photograph by Aaron Rezny.
- 78-9: Photograph by Kimberly Butler.
- 88-9: Illustrations by Jon Friedman. Photo courtesy of Indianapolis Motor Speedway.
- 90: Illustration by Wayne McLoughlin.
- 92-3: Computer graphics by National Image Makers.
- 96: Photographs from NASA's Landsat Program, courtesy of General Electric Photographic Lab.
- 97: Dracula photo, The Bettmann Archive; all others, Movie Still Archives.
- 100-1: Illustration by Larry Ross.
- 105: Photos of Sally Field, Diane Keaton, and Sissy Spacek, UPI; all others, Globe Photos.
- 106: Photo A, courtesy of NBC; B, Wide World Photos; C, The Bettmann Archive; D, Wide World Photos.
- 107: Photos A and E, Photoreporters; B, C, and D, courtesy of NBC.
- 110: Illustrations by Rick Tulka.
- 111: Illustration by Leo Pando.
- 115: Illustration by David Suter.
- 127: Illustration by Gabriel Giurgea.
- 132-3: Illustration by Elwood Smith.
- 135: Illustration by Philip Anderson.
- 153: Illustration by Steve Parton.
- 155: Illustration by Enno Peorsch.
- 156-7: Illustrations by Sandy Forrest.
- 158-9: Illustrations by Scott Reynolds.
- 168: Illustration by Tom Bloom.
- 191-2: Illustrations by Rick Tulka.